AntiPatterns

Refactoring Software, Architectures, and Projects in Crisis

WILLIAM J. BROWN
RAPHAEL C. MALVEAU
HAYS W. McCORMICK III
THOMAS J. MOWBRAY

WILEY COMPUTER PUBLISHING

John Wiley & Sons, Inc.
New York • Chichester • Weinheim • Brisbane • Singapore • Toronto

Publisher: Robert Ipsen
Editor: Theresa Hudson
Managing Editor: Micheline Frederick
Text Design & Composition: North Market Street Graphics

This book is printed on acid-free paper. ∞

Published by John Wiley & Sons, Inc.

Published simultaneously in Canada.

Library of Congress Cataloging-in-Publication Data:
AntiPatterns / William J. Brown . . . [et al.].
     p.   cm.
   Includes bibliographical references and index.
   ISBN 0-471-19713-0 (cloth : alk. paper)
    1. Computer software—Development.   2. Computer software—Reliability.   I. Brown, William J., 1954– .
   QA76.76.D47A54   1998
   005.1—dc21   97–39023
                                           CIP

Printed in the United States of America.

10 9 8 7 6 5 4 3 2 1

This book is dedicated to our families:
Kate Brown,
Carrie Malveau,
Kim McCormick,
and
Kate Mowbray, CPA

"And ye shall know the truth and the truth shall set you free"
—John 8:32

C O N T E N T S

F O R E W O R D

We're very honored to have been asked to write the introduction to this book on AntiPatterns. When we heard this term mentioned for the first time, we were more than a little puzzled and, unless you already know what an AntiPattern is, the chances are that you'll be puzzled, too. But after looking into this in some detail, we've found that this is a very interesting topic indeed, and of great practical value.

Most of us are reasonably familiar with (or at least have heard of) the concept of design patterns, whether in a software development context or otherwise. The term design patterns is pretty much self-explanatory: Designs that have been proved to have been successful (in practice) in the past and can therefore be reused again successfully.

But what is an AntiPattern? Is it something that isn't a design pattern? Is it something that hasn't been done before and lacks robust design; or is it something that just doesn't work? Just as the use of design patterns can save time, money, and effort by reusing tried and tested designs, the inadvertent application of AntiPatterns leads to the completely opposite situation.

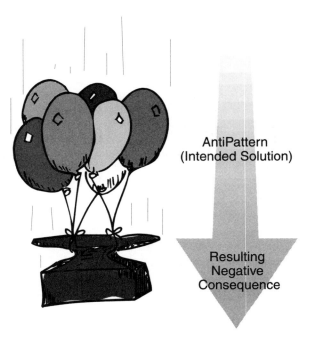

AntiPattern
(Intended Solution)

Resulting
Negative
Consequence

Sometimes the consequences of patterns outweigh the advantages.

By definition a pattern is: an arrangement of repeated parts; a design
or shape to direct the cutting of cloth; a model or specimen. But a pattern
can also be one of behavior. Negative patterns of behavior in all walks of
life (especially software development) have been witnessed worldwide by
the authors of this book; and perhaps more interestingly, at all scales and
all levels of experience.

AntiPatterns tell you what to avoid, and the identification of what to
avoid is a critical factor in successful software development. This book
details software-related AntiPatterns in many categories and identifies (in
a humorous and lighthearted way) various AntiPatterns of software design,
architecture, and management behavior that should be avoided at all
costs.

Jack Hassall/John Eaton
Object Management Group
Co-Chairs, Financial Domain Task Force
(aka: "The Crazies" from Manchester)

P R E F A C E

AntiPatterns are fun to read and discuss with friends. But get serious! This book is about the truth of software technology and development. In it, we define what's really happening in technology and on software projects, and what you can do about it. AntiPatterns identify those bad design concepts, technical approaches, and development practices that lead to poor-quality software and project failure. This book also explains how projects identified and avoided these problems to improve their designs and practices for software success.

Can you handle the truth? The truth is surprisingly hard to communicate, and often regarded as politically incorrect and undiplomatic. The truth does not make everybody happy. In order to make this exposition of our industry palatable, we resort to comedy wherever feasible; and it has been said that comedy is the most serious tragedy. The truth is that the state of software engineering today is a tragedy: Five out of six corporate development projects are considered unsuccessful. [Johnson 95]. Most software systems that are delivered fall far short of the desired features, and virtually every system is a stovepipe, unable to accommodate changing business needs.

In trying to explain this universal lack of software success, we came to the conclusion that there are many more AntiPatterns in practice than design patterns. In Internet time, technology is changing so fast that the design patterns of yesterday are quickly becoming the AntiPatterns of today. This book explains the most common AntiPatterns we have seen recurring in practice, products, and software literature. Then, for each, we include a refactored solution that shows the way toward resolution, based on solutions that we have used or seen work in the real world.

Contents Overview

In the first part of this book (Chapters 1–4), we introduce design patterns and AntiPatterns. Next, we provide an AntiPatterns reference model to establish the common definitions that we use in the AntiPattern descriptions. Experienced readers should begin with the reference model description in Chapter 2. The second part (Chapters 5–7) contains the AntiPatterns descriptions, which begins with a discussion of development AntiPatterns. Then we cover the architecture AntiPatterns, followed by the managerial AntiPatterns. Lastly, the third part of this book provides resources for further study and application of the AntiPatterns.

Relation of AntiPatterns to Design Patterns

AntiPatterns are the next generation of design patterns research. They cover a much wider range of challenges by addressing existing practices, legacy designs, and forward engineering solutions.

Supplemental Materials

The AntiPatterns home page is located at: www.serve.com/hibc/Anti-Patterns/index.htm. The authors will post any updates to the material at this site.

A C K N O W L E D G M E N T S

Although we wish to thank all of the people who made this book possible, we cannot enumerate everyone who gave us ideas, help, and encouragement; but, in particular, we wish to recognize:

Rohit Agarwal
Don Awalt
Tom Beadle
Pier-Yves Bertholet
Irv Boeskool
John Brant
Frank Buschmann
Bruce Caldwell
Ian Chai
Hugh Chau
Vic DeMarines
David Dikel
John Eaton
Karen Eaton

Dennis Egan
Marty Faga
Jack Flannagan
Brian Foote
Alejandra Garrido
Tom Gleeson
Julie Gravallese
Steve Gulick
Dr. Patrick Harrison
Dan Harter
Jack Hassall
The Hebden brothers
Christy Hermansen
Ruth Hilderberger

Roy Hiler
Steve Hirsch
Michael Hoagland
Bill Hoffman
Jon Hopkins
Dr. Barry Horowitz
Bill Ide
Tom Jenkins
Ralph Johnson
Pat Jones
Michael Josephs
David Kane
David Kekumano
Ajay Khater

Ken Kinman
John Kogut
Gary Larson
Steve Latchem
Eric Leach
Dave Lehman
Dr. Barry Leng
David Lines
Dr. Pat Mallett
Dr. Mark Maybury
Dave Mayo
Kate Mowbray
Lewis Muir
Diane Mularz
Eiji Nabika
Jason Novak
Jeanne O'Kelley
Ed Peters

John Polger
Don Roberts
Darrel Rochette
Mark Rosenthal
Henry Rothkopf
Bill Ruh
David Samuels
Thad Scheer
Dr. Robert Silvetz
Bruce Simpson
Theresa Smith
Dr. Richard Soley
Ed Stewart
Shel Sutton
Fred Thompson
Dr. Bhavani
  Thuraisingham
Pat Townes

Kurt Tran
Kevin Tyson
Doug Vandermade
James Van Guilder
Robert Wainwright
Kim Warren
The Washington DC
  Software Book Study
  Club
John Weiler
Diane Weiss
Anthony Whitson
Jerry Wile
Deborah Wittreich
Joe Yoder
Ron Zahavi
Tony Zawilski

AUTHOR BIOGRAPHIES

William Brown holds the post of Process Director for Product Development at Concept Five Technologies, Inc. His background is one of project management and the development of business and technical architectures and supporting object-oriented development processes. Bill's expertise is primarily in large scale object-oriented project developments. He has a proven track record in delivering new technology systems due to his strong leadership and technical knowledge. He has worked on projects in military, health, real-time control systems and financial domains. His object-oriented financial project deliveries include insurance, investment banking and retail banking. Prior to joining Concept Five he specialized in financial systems migration to object-oriented technology.

Raphael Malveaux is the chief scientist at Eidea Labs (www.eidea.com) which develops enterprise business object frameworks for engineering domains. He is also co-author of *CORBA Design Patterns*.

Hays "Skip" McCormick is a lead engineer in the Emerging Technology Engineering Department at MITRE-Washington. Skip is currently MITRE's project lead for the National Imagery and Mapping Agency (NIMA) Interoperable Technology Reification with Objects (NITRO) which

is the 1997 implementor follow-on from the Data Integration and
Synergistic Collateral Usage Study (DISCUS). Having a wide range of
experience in distributed systems both from a security and a software
engineering perspective, and a background in artificial intelligence and
expert systems development, he has published and presented several arti-
cles for various ADPA and AFCEA conferences and symposia.

Mr. McCormick holds the B.S. degree in Computer Science from the
United States Naval Academy at Annapolis, Maryland.

Tom Mowbray, Ph.D. is Chief Scientist at Blueprint Technologies,
Inc. (www.blueprint-technologies.com), a company developing design
patterns tools, architecture consulting, and training. Dr. Mowbray is an
Honorary Fellow of the Object Management Group, and co-authors the
AntiPatterns column with William Brown in *Distributed Computing*
Magazine. He co-authored three books on distributed object architec-
tures: *The Essential CORBA*, *CORBA Design Patterns*, and *Inside CORBA*.
Dr. Mowbray writes the Software Architectures column for *OBJECT*
Magazine.

Dr. Mowbray holds the B.S. degree in Electrical Engineering from the
University of Illinois, Champaign-Urbana, the M.S. degree in Computer
Engineering from Stanford University, and the Ph.D. in Computer Science
from the University of Southern California.

EXECUTIVE SUMMARY

This book will help you identify and overcome prevalent, recurring road-blocks to successful software development. AntiPatterns clearly define software mistakes that most of us make frequently. In fact, most of us could achieve ISO 9001 with our consistency! AntiPatterns also provide solutions: How to fix existing problems and how to avoid repeated mishaps in the future. In short, AntiPatterns describe and solve real-world problems. The following questions are a sample of what Anti-Patterns have to offer:

1. *What are the two most common software design mistakes? How can I recognize them?* See the AntiPatterns the Blob and Poltergeists in Chapter 5.
2. *What can we do to fix (or refactor) bad software?* See the AntiPatterns Spaghetti Code in Chapter 5, and Stovepipe Systems in Chapter 6.
3. *Our design project is going around in circles; how can we get it back on track?* See the AntiPatterns Analysis Paralysis in Chapter 7 and Design by Committee in Chapter 6.

4. *How do I know when I'm being misled by a software vendor?* See the AntiPatterns Vendor Lock-in in Chapter 6, and Smoke and Mirrors in Chapter 7.

5. *Is the latest standard or technology breakthrough going to solve my problems?* See the AntiPatterns Wolf Ticket in Chapter 6 and Continuous Obsolescence in Chapter 5.

6. *Is our software project headed for disaster?* See the AntiPatterns Death by Planning in Chapter 7, and Mushroom Management in Chapter 5.

7. *What are the "gotchas" of software reuse?* See the AntiPatterns Cut-and-Paste Programming and Golden Hammer in Chapter 5.

AntiPatterns clarify the negative patterns that cause development roadblocks, and include proven solutions for transforming software development problems into opportunities. AntiPatterns serve two important purposes: to help identify problems and to help implement solutions. Understanding the problem is the first step to recovery. Solutions are of little use without a state problem to solve. AntiPatterns have a variety of causes, with associated symptoms and consequences. We convey these aspects of each AntiPattern to clarify the motivation for change. We then offer proven, recurring solutions for the AntiPattern.

AntiPatterns are closely related to another important software concept: *design patterns*, which document recurring solutions. A design pattern becomes an AntiPattern when it causes more problems than it solves.

FIGURE E.1 Build your own nightmare.

All patterns have consequences. There are situations when a pattern is a good solution to a problem and other situations when it becomes an AntiPattern. The context-dependent consequences are important to understand in order to make an informed decision inclusive of side effects. We examine this viewpoint for each pattern and describe when an AntiPattern can actually provide benefit:

- Managerial (managing processes and people)
- Architectural (defining a technical strategy)
- Developmental (coding practices)

Managerial, architectural, and developmental AntiPatterns are defined in Chapters 5 through 7. If you are new to design patterns or AntiPatterns, we provide introductory material in Chapters 1 through 3. For design patterns practitioners, the AntiPatterns reference model is explained in Chapter 2; the template is explained in Chapter 3. These introductory chapters are instrumental for getting the most out the AntiPattern descriptions.

Why You Should Read This Book

An understanding of AntiPatterns is essential to your software success, for these key reasons:

- *AntiPatterns are all around you.* Many more software projects fail than succeed. Bad software designs, decisions, and projects are much more prevalent than good ones. The real world of software is full of AntiPatterns, as well as highly effective solutions. As you read this book, this will become clear.
- *AntiPatterns clarify the most common software design mistakes.* Bad designs and bad software are the result of consistent causes, common misunderstandings, and classic mistakes. AntiPatterns explain why bad software happens, how to refactor bad designs and bad software, and how to avoid repeating mistakes. Through AntiPatterns, you can learn to identify and fix mistakes in time to prevent serious consequences.
- *AntiPatterns expose the truth about the software industry.* Commercial software technology is plagued by defects, contradictions, false promises, and AntiPatterns. This book reveals the truth about software technologies from an insider's perspective. AntiPatterns docu-

ment the essential information about commercial technology that
you need to survive the emerging paradigm of commercial off-the-
shelf (COTS)-driven development.

■ *AntiPatterns explain the reality of software projects.* Most software
projects are chaotic, unpredictable, and hazardous to careers.
AntiPatterns explain how software projects really work and how to
manage their avoidable consequences.

■ *AntiPatterns are necessary for change management.* AntiPatterns establish a clear definition of negative software practices. They are useful
descriptions of practices that your organization wants to change. This
book provides a comprehensive catalog of AntiPatterns that facilitate
change management.

■ *AntiPatterns define an important terminology.* Each AntiPattern
defines popular terminology for common software practices. There
are many AntiPattern terms used to describe why things go wrong.
Like design patterns, AntiPatterns reference complex concepts
through the use of a key phrase. It is no longer necessary to reinvent
these concepts. Organizations and individuals that utilize this terminology can increase their effectiveness.

■ *AntiPatterns are a more effective form of design patterns.* We are true
believers in the design patterns movement. In *CORBA Design Patterns*,
some of the shortcomings of patterns as a literary form were
addressed. [Malveau 97] In this book, we go much further: We re-
define and extend the pattern paradigm into a totally new form, the
AntiPattern.

The AntiPattern form has appeared sporadically on the Internet, with
informal AntiPatterns written by authors from the design patterns community. Based on the Internet forums, there is strong consensus in the patterns community that AntiPatterns are a worthwhile research area. This
book fully develops the AntiPatterns concept; and our conclusion is that
AntiPatterns are a highly effective form for problem solving.

Here are some of the key reasons why we believe that AntiPatterns
are effective. Ordinary design patterns start with a prolonged discussion of
the context and forces that logically lead to a unique solution. And though
the design pattern solution may seem simple and obvious compared to the
literary overhead required to introduce it, many readers find this style
tedious. In contrast, AntiPatterns start with real-world situations leading
to dramatic consequences. By highlighting the potential catastrophe,
AntiPatterns describe intriguing situations instead of abstract forces. A
constructive solution follows the AntiPattern description. Through the

elaboration of symptoms and consequences, AntiPatterns define a compelling rationale for change that no ordinary design pattern can match. Furthermore, AntiPatterns capture your interest and imagination unlike any design pattern ever encountered.

Read this book with an open mind, and you will find that AntiPatterns are fun to learn and discuss with colleagues. AntiPatterns are based upon real-world comedies and tragedies in software development. We hope you have as much fun reading this book as we have had writing and sharing AntiPatterns.

DILBERT reprinted by permission of United Feature Syndicate, Inc.

FIGURE E.2 Executive decision making AntiPattern.

AntiPatterns

C H A P T E R   1

Introduction to Patterns and AntiPatterns

AntiPatterns represent the latest concept in a series of revolutionary changes in computer science and software engineering thinking. As the software field approaches the 50-year mark of developing programmable, digital systems, we have yet to resolve some fundamental problems that arise when humans translate business concepts into software applications. Many of the most significant problems are generated from the human processes that require shared vision, cooperation, and collaboration to realize systems. The majority of the published works in software sciences have focused on positive, constructive solutions. This book is different; we start by looking at the negative solutions.

Academic researchers and practitioners have developed thousands of innovative approaches to building software, from exciting new technologies to progressive processes. Even with all these great ideas, the likelihood of success for practicing managers and developers is grim. A survey of hundreds of corporate software development projects indicated that five out of six software projects are considered unsuccessful [Johnson 95], and approximately a third of software projects are canceled. The remaining projects delivered software at almost double the expected budget and time to develop as originally planned.

"Fasten your seat-belts, it's going to be a bumpy night."

—Joseph L. Mankiewicz

Virtually all systems delivered are *stovepipe systems*, systems that cannot accommodate change. Adaptability is perhaps the most important quality of software. More than half of all software cost is due to changes in requirements or the need for system extensions [Horowitz 93]. Some 30 percent of the development cost is due to changes in requirements during system construction.

AntiPatterns: AntiHype

Software was supposed to make digital hardware much more flexible. Instead, software technology has promulgated a series of failed promises. The promise that software would make hardware flexible was only the first. What went wrong? Within our careers, we have seen any number of software fads come and go that were successful in a limited way for specific aspects of software development, but did not deliver the promised "silver bullet" (see Figure 1.1). Remember some of these major trends?

- *Structured programming* was supposed to improve software productivity and remove most software defects.
- *Artificial intelligence* was supposed to make computers much more capable.
- *Networking* technologies were supposed to make all systems and software interoperable.
- *Open systems* and standards were supposed to make application software portable and interoperable.
- *Parallel processing* was supposed to make computers much more powerful and scaleable.
- *Object orientation* was supposed to solve the problems of software productivity and adaptability, and make software highly reusable.
- *Frameworks* were supposed to make software highly reusable and software development much more productive.

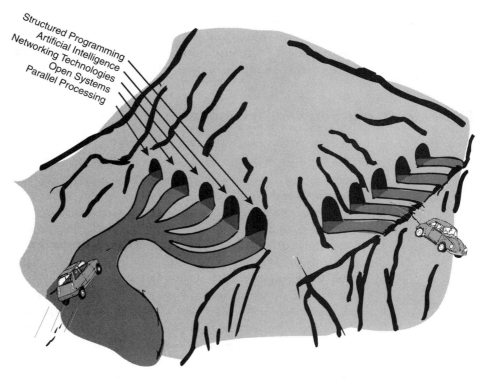

Structured Programming
Artificial Intelligence
Networking Technologies
Open Systems
Parallel Processing

FIGURE 1.1 There are many paths to disaster.

These claims sound like a broken record; every new software fad makes similar promises. History has not been written on many of today's software buzzwords, but their claims sound very similar to what we have heard before. Current examples include:

The Internet
Component software
Distributed objects
Business objects
Software reuse
Scripting languages
Software agents

We promised to tell the truth about software, and it should be clear by now that we really mean it. A goal for this book is to end the perpetual cycle of hype and disillusionment that characterizes software technology.

And let us quickly point out, it's not just the vendors who are at fault. There are several things that we (application developers and managers) can do to mitigate software problems. Regardless of the vendor hype, it's really how you use the technology that determines your success.

The Truth about Software Technology

Eighty-four percent of software projects are unsuccessful, and virtually all deliver stovepipe systems. Why?

Vendors will tell you:

- Our new technology changes the whole paradigm.
- Business objects will make your ordinary developers productive (substitute any buzzword for "business objects").
- We'll have all the features you need in six months.
- We make no warranty express or implied regarding our software, its *merchantability,* or its fitness for any particular purpose. Vendors rarely guarantee that their software does anything useful at all. And if it does something bad; it's not their fault. Proprietary technologies change every 4 to 18 months. Rapid technology changes can dominate software maintenance costs and impact software development. After purchasing a software license, vendors expect to make four times as much money from the same customer for training, consulting, support, and maintenance. Is it possible that the more difficulties application developers have, the more money vendors make?

Software gurus will tell you:

- Their new method improves upon anything they said in the past.
- Their tools fully support software development, including code generation.
- You need more tools!
- You need more training!
- You need more consultancy!

We gurus disagree with each other, and we change our minds—frequently. Gurus also sell new ideas that contradict those they sold people in the past. Gurus' methodologies are too generic for any real project. The important details of their methods are hidden in their expensive products;

for example, production-quality code generation from modeling tools is still years away. More often, they never state the important details at all.

The bottom line is, regardless of the excitement and hype, software technology is in the Stone Age (see Figure 1.2). Application developers, managers, and end users are paying the price.

What Is an AntiPattern?

An AntiPattern is a literary form that describes a commonly occurring solution to a problem that generates decidedly negative consequences. The AntiPattern may be the result of a manager or developer not knowing any better, not having sufficient knowledge or experience in solving a particular type of problem, or having applied a perfectly good pattern in the wrong context. When properly documented, an AntiPattern describes a general form, the primary causes which led to the general form; symptoms describing how to recognize the general form; the consequences of the general form; and a refactored solution describing how to change the AntiPattern into a healthier situation.

FIGURE 1.2 Software technology is in the Stone Age.

AntiPatterns are a method for efficiently mapping a general situation to a specific class of solutions. The general form of the AntiPattern provides an easily identifiable template for the class of problems addressed by the AntiPattern. In addition, the symptoms associated with the problem are clearly stated, along with the typical underlying causes of the problem. Together, these template elements comprise a comprehensive case for the existence of a particular AntiPattern. This form reduces the most common mistake in using design patterns: applying a particular design pattern in the improper context.

AntiPatterns provide real-world experience in recognizing recurring problems in the software industry and provide a detailed remedy for the most common predicaments. AntiPatterns highlight the most common problems that face the software industry and provide the tools to enable you to recognize these problems and to determine their underlying causes. Furthermore, AntiPatterns present a detailed plan for reversing these underlying causes and implementing productive solutions. AntiPatterns effectively describe the measures that can be taken at several levels to improve the developing of applications, the designing of software systems, and the effective management of software projects.

AntiPatterns provide a common vocabulary for identifying problems and discussing solutions. AntiPatterns, like their design pattern counterparts, define an industry vocabulary for the common defective processes and implementations within organizations. A higher-level vocabulary simplifies communication between software practitioners and enables concise description of higher-level concepts.

AntiPatterns support the holistic resolution of conflicts, utilizing organizational resources at several levels, where possible. AntiPatterns clearly articulate the collaboration between forces at several levels of management and development. Many problems in software are rooted in managerial and organizational levels, so attempts to discuss developmental and architectural patterns without taking into account forces at other levels would be incomplete. For this reason, we have gone to great lengths in this book to bring together all relevant forces at many levels to both describe and address core problem areas.

AntiPatterns provide stress release in the form of shared misery for the most common pitfalls in the software industry. Often, in software development, it is much easier to recognize a defective situation than to implement a solution. In these cases, where the power to implement an AntiPattern solution is lacking, an individual subjected to the consequences of the AntiPattern forces can find solace in knowing that his or her dilemma is, in whole or part, shared by many others throughout the industry. In some such cases where the AntiPattern has severe consequences, the AntiPattern can also serve as a wake-up call for a victim to set his or her sights on other employment opportunities in the industry and to start preparing his or her resume.

Where Did AntiPatterns Come From?

Design pattern languages have taken the programming community by storm, and reflect an intense desire from software professionals to improve the quality and standards of the industry. It's not possible to dispute the intrinsic value of design patterns, given the growing number of projects, which attribute the use and creation of reusable design patterns for their success. However, the current paradigm falls short of fully expressing the intended range and scope of the intended use of design patterns, giving rise to a new literary form that flies directly in the face of existing definitions of patterns. This new literary form is the AntiPattern. In order to fully grasp its significance in software development, it's important to understand its origins and how the current design pattern phenomenom has given rise to the AntiPattern.

The idea of a design pattern originated with Christopher Alexander, an architect who documented a pattern language for the planning of towns and the construction of buildings within towns [Alexander 77]. His pattern language clearly articulated his vision for how architecture should be modeled, and explained why some towns and buildings provided a better environment than others. His method of capturing expertise was innovative, as it made explicit many of the "soft" attributes that were previously attainable only through years of experience in planning and building towns.

Portland Pattern Repository

The Portland Pattern Repository (http://c2.com/ppr/) publishes an evolving collection of design patterns and pattern languages. Currently sponsored by Ward and Karen Cunningham (Cunningham and Cunningham, Inc.), it is a fun and exciting place to collaborate on design patterns with other design pattern aficionados throughout the Internet community. The AntiPatterns reference material is available from this site.

In 1987, several leading-edge software developers rediscovered Alexander's work and applied it to documenting design decisions in developing software. Specifically, Ward Cunningham and Kent Beck developed a design pattern language for developing user interfaces in the Smalltalk programming language. In the years that followed, they attracted several people who shared similar ideas about using design patterns to aid in reusing software designs and were able to grow fledging interest in an early design pattern movement.

What was the attraction in applying Christopher Alexander's work to software development? The answer must be addressed in the context of the contemporary crisis in software development. Even in the '80s, it was readily apparent that the number of talented architects in object-oriented software development were far too few to support the industry. Furthermore, the academic community failed in providing the detailed knowledge in problem solving and in engineering dynamic software solutions that could cope with the changing requirements, which were commonplace in the industry. Such knowledge took years of industry experience to gain, and the immediate demands of the industry limited the ability of many architects to spend time mentoring less experienced colleagues. Also, rapid industry turnover left many employers reluctant to invest large amounts of their senior personnel's time in mentoring others, rather than solving their own mission-critical software problems. This created an urgent and compelling need for a reusable form of capturing the expertise of experienced developers to be used repeatedly to train the less experienced. In addition, the design patterns could be used at the industry level to open dialog for creating industrywide design solutions to enable domain frameworks to interoperate at the industry and even global level.

Christopher Alexander believed that while most processes involved in designing physical structures were variable, there was always a single common invariant process underlying all other processes, which precisely defined the principles of the structure's design and construction. Such invariant processes are the holy grail of software development, as they provide a common framework of knowledge, and expert software solutions can be built upon—rather than contributing to—the current morass of custom, noninteroperable stovepipe solutions.

It wasn't until 1994 that design patterns entered the mainstream of the object-oriented software development community. In mid-1994, the Hillside Group hosted the first, and now historic, industry conference on software design patterns, Pattern Languages of Program Design (PLoP), which featured several patterns and pattern languages for developing software applications. Of special note was Jim Coplien's paper titled "A

Development Process Generative Pattern Language" which was the first example of design patterns applied to organizational analysis [Coplien 94]. Coplien's paper immediately helped to set the stage for the patterns movement to incorporate not just software design patterns, but analysis, organizational, instructional, and other issues as well.

This preceded the launching of the now-classic text on software design patterns, *Design Patterns: Elements of Reusable Object-Oriented Software* [Gamma 94]. Object-oriented software architects rallied behind the book because it presented several common, practical software design constructs that could be easily applied to most software projects. Of greater note, the patterns it contained were recognized by many as describing constructs that they had already applied in previous software projects.

Initial industry reaction was universally positive, as the vocabulary and design focus was elevated from the level of data structures and programming idioms to the architecture level, and *facades, adapters,* and *visitors* became well-known terms in the design discussions. Software developers frequently organized grassroots groups that applied design patterns in their software development projects and championed their use by others. Design pattern study groups were organized around the world to discuss using software design patterns as the basis for improving software quality. Consultants arose to aid organizations in mining design patterns within their own organizations to aid less experienced developers in adopting the techniques of their more experienced counterparts. For a brief shining moment, it appeared that design patterns were a step toward revolutionizing the entire software industry to focus on design reuse and engineering software for more effectively dealing with changing requirements.

How to Kill a Software Project

- Show the same demo twice to the same audience.
- Focus on the technologies, not the problems and scenarios.
- Fail to maximize return on investments; for example, developing proof-of-concept prototypes is more effective than adding additional content to an existing prototype.
- Change project focus from the larger scale to the smaller scale.
- Don't maintain consistency between releases.
- Isolate team efforts from other groups within an organization.
- Rewrite existing clients, servers, and applications.
- Change the purpose of the system, so that the models describe the wrong focus and objects.

Since 1994, there has been exponential growth in the publication of design pattern literature. This growth has both a bright and a dark side. To the skilled object-oriented architect, there is now a large and growing base of reusable designs that can be evaluated and applied to a software development effort. Furthermore, there is a wealth of papers and seminars to assist an architect in documenting his or her own domain knowledge into design patterns so they can be more readily used by other professionals in the industry. The dark side is that many of the people who use design patterns fail to properly evaluate how applicable a particular design pattern or pattern language is to their specific set of design concerns. In addition, some developers, armed with their packaged knowledge, eagerly rush in to classify everything as a design pattern or solvable by a specific set of design patterns before attempting to perform and complete their domain analysis.

Along comes Michael Akroyd, who prepared a presentation for the 1996 Object World West conference entitled "AntiPatterns: Vaccinations against Object Misuse" [Akroyd 96]. His presentation was based upon a detailed analysis of the object-oriented literature in the industry and was an attempt to define a convergence of ideas about object orientation. The presentation focused on recognizing harmful software constructs, which were reoccurring across several software projects. This is the antithesis of the "Gang of Four (GoF)" patterns that emphasize the use of proven good designs, which can be applied in constructing new software.

Prior to Akroyd were others who mentioned the notion of AntiPatterns in hallways and around water coolers, but he was the first with a formal model. The discussion of the usefulness of AntiPatterns began almost in parallel with the introduction of patterns. Similar work on providing software guidance based on identifying dysfunctional behavior and refactoring a solution has been documented by Fred Brooks [Brooks 79], Bruce Webster [Webster 95], James Coplien [Coplien 95], and Andrew Koenig.

Because AntiPatterns have had so many contributors, it would be unfair to assign the original idea for AntiPatterns to a single source. Rather, AntiPatterns are a natural step in complementing the work of the design pattern movement, and extending the design pattern model. Our AntiPatterns attempt to bridge the gap between the academic formalisms of the GoF design patterns and the fledgling software developers who need more contextual information in order to evaluate and determine whether a particular technique is appropriate to their particular situation.

AntiPatterns Research

> "The study of AntiPatterns is an important research activity. The presence of 'good' patterns in a successful system is not enough; you also must show that those patterns are absent in unsuccessful systems. Likewise, it is useful to show the presence of certain patterns (AntiPatterns) in unsuccessful systems, and their absence in successful systems."
>
> —Jim Coplien

The concept of AntiPatterns is the first major software research initiative to focus on negative solutions. Given the frequency of software defects and project failures, negative solutions are probably a much richer field to study (a so-called target-rich environment). In AntiPatterns research, we are attempting to categorize, label, and describe recurring negative solutions. We do not stop there. With each AntiPattern, we attach one or more design patterns that provide constructive alternatives for resolving the root causes.

We present AntiPatterns from three perspectives: developer, architect, and manager:

- *Development AntiPatterns* comprise technical problems and solutions that are encountered by programmers.
- *Architectural AntiPatterns* identify and resolve common problems in how systems are structured.
- *Managerial AntiPatterns* address common problems in software processes and development organizations.

These three viewpoints are fundamental to software development, and many problems exist in each.

AntiPatterns: The Book

This chapter delineated the evolution of AntiPatterns and how they relate to improving the software industry. *AntiPatterns* provides an effective way to describe the problematic development and organizational issues found in software development, and details a course for resolution. To that end, the remaining chapters of the book are as follows:

- Chapter 2 introduces the AntiPatterns reference model. The reference model defines all of the common concepts used to define the AntiPatterns in the descriptions found in Part II.
- Chapter 3 presents AntiPatterns in two forms: the mini-AntiPattern template and the full AntiPattern template. Mini-AntiPatterns appear as shaded sidebars.
- Chapter 4 explains the implications of AntiPatterns in the software organization. This chapter provides essential guidance and etiquette for AntiPattern usage. We also describe the process for writing your own AntiPatterns.
- Part II presents the specifics of AntiPatterns and mini-AntiPatterns.
- Chapter 5 defines software development AntiPatterns.
- Chapter 6 defines software architecture AntiPatterns.
- Chapter 7 defines software project management AntiPatterns.
- Part III, comprising the Appendices, provides resources, including acronyms and a glossary, AntiPatterns summaries, and a bibliography.

C H A P T E R

AntiPatterns
Reference Model

This chapter overviews the reference model and template used for the AntiPatterns contained in Chapters 5 through 7, and presents the common definitions and concepts for the AntiPatterns in this book.

Patterns and AntiPatterns are related concepts, as shown in Figure 2.1. The essence of a design pattern is a problem and a solution. The problem is usually elaborated in terms of its context and applicable design forces. The role of the solution is to resolve the design forces in a way that generates some benefits, consequences, and follow-on problems. These new problems lead to the applicability of other patterns. Patterns are commonly occurring solutions that are frequently observed in practice. To be considered a pattern, the solution needs to be observed at least three times. Because no three occurrences can be identical, the design pattern is an abstraction of these experiences.

What distinguishes a design pattern from other forms of software knowledge is the use of a *template*, a consistent outline for the pattern documentation that ensures consistent and adequate coverage of the solution, design forces, and other consequences. The template contains useful,

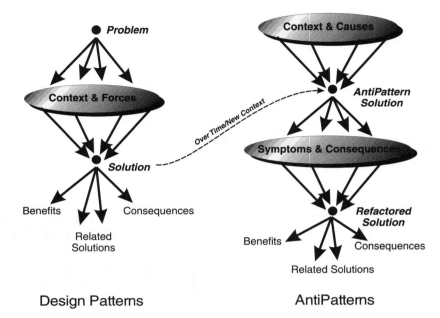

Design Patterns   AntiPatterns

FIGURE 2.1 Design pattern and AntiPattern concepts.

prewritten arguments that justify the application of the pattern and predict its consequences.

The essence of an AntiPattern is two solutions, instead of a problem and a solution for ordinary design patterns. The first solution is *problematic.* It is a commonly occurring solution that generates overwhelmingly negative consequences. The second solution is called the *refactored solution.* The refactored solution is a commonly occurring method in which the AntiPattern can be resolved and reengineered into a more beneficial form. Ralph Johnson, one of the primary proponents of patterns, has led much of the work in this area. For further information, try the URL, st-www.cs.uiuc.edu/users/droberts/tapos/TAPOS.html.

Patterns and AntiPatterns are related. Design patterns can often evolve into an AntiPattern. A popular pattern, such as procedural programming, can be the popular paradigm of one era, and fall out of favor in the next as its consequences are better understood. The difference between patterns solutions and AntiPatterns solutions is that of context: An AntiPattern is a pattern in an inappropriate context. When a pattern becomes an AntiPattern, it is useful to have an approach for evolving the solution into a better one. This process of change, migration, or evolution is called *refactoring.* In refactoring, we change one solution to another solution with an improved structure, a structure that provides increased benefits.

One of the key issues in patterns is readability. Pattern write-ups often begin with a tedious description of the context and design forces. The solution often seems rather obvious compared to the lengthy discussion of forces preceding its introduction. In our book, *CORBA Design Patterns,* we addressed this issue by organizing the pattern template for rapid understanding of the pattern purpose and solution concept. This was made possible through the use of a reference model, defining a conceptual framework and common concepts across all patterns in the language.

AntiPatterns take this concept several steps further. In an AntiPattern, the problem is depicted as a commonly occurring mistake. The mistaken solution maximizes the catastrophe that may underlie a fundamental problem. This maximization of the problem is an essential step in many fields of endeavor. For example, in software testing, the tester often maximizes a bug to the level of a system crash in order to gain the attention of developers [Beizer 97].

Since the first step toward recovery is admitting that you have a problem, the AntiPattern problem helps readers to clarify the problem in dramatic terms. They can then assess the applicability of the problem's symptoms and consequences to their own situation. Many people also find AntiPatterns entertaining. To err is human. We all laugh at our mistakes and the mistakes of others when no insult is intended.

Both design patterns and AntiPatterns are written by starting with the solution. The context, problem, and forces in a design pattern are written to lead uniquely to one solution. In order to ensure a unique mapping to one solution, design patterns often contain lengthy explanations of design forces. AntiPatterns are based on a different rhetorical structure. AntiPatterns begin with a compelling, problematic solution, then offer an alternative solution that refactors the problem. The refactored solution is not guaranteed to be unique; it is an effective way to resolve the forces that ensure more benefits. Any significant variations of the solution are included in a separate template section.

In practice, we have found AntiPatterns to be a much more powerful and effective form for describing recurring solutions than design patterns. We hope that you will too. An AntiPattern starts with an existing solution (or legacy approach), where most patterns assume a green-field problem (from-scratch programming). We find situations with legacy and existing problems to be more commonplace in practice. The AntiPattern amplifies the problem in a way that helps organizations to recognize the problematic structure, symptoms, and consequences. It then presents a common solution that refactors the system toward improved benefits and minimized consequences.

Viewpoints

This book presents AntiPatterns from three major viewpoints: the software developer, the software architect, and the software manager (Figure 2.2). *Development AntiPatterns* describe situations encountered by the programmer when solving programming problems (Chapter 5). *Architectural AntiPatterns* focus on common problems in system structure, their consequences, and solutions (Chapter 6). Many of the most serious unresolved problems in software systems occur from this perspective. *Management AntiPatterns* describe common problems and solutions due to the software organization (Chapter 7). Management AntiPatterns affect people in all software roles, and their solutions directly affect the technical success of the project.

We use a reference model for terminology common to all three viewpoints. The reference model is based upon three topics that introduce the key concepts of AntiPatterns:

FIGURE 2.2 Principal AntiPattern viewpoints.

- Root causes.
- Primal forces.
- Software design-level model (SDLM).

Root causes provide the fundamental context for AntiPatterns. *Primal forces* are the key motivators for decision making. The relative importance of these forces varies significantly with architectural scale. The architectural scales are defined by the *SDLM*. An understanding of the architectural levels defines the different scales for pattern applicability. Each pattern has a most-applicable scale, where it is presented in Chapters 5–7, but may also have applicability to other scales (also described in each pattern). The pattern template provides the outline for pattern definition.

Root Causes

Root causes are mistakes in software development that result in failed projects, cost overruns, schedule slips, and unfulfilled business needs [Mowbray 97]. The root causes identified here are pervasive: One-third out of all software projects are canceled; five out of six software projects are unsuccessful [Johnson 95]. Unfortunately, object-oriented technology has not changed this overall prognosis. In fact, each new technology wave (such as client/server) tends to increase software risk and the likelihood of falling prey to these root causes. The root causes are based upon the "seven deadly sins," a popular analogy that has been used successfully to identify ineffective practices [Bates 96].

Haste

Hasty decisions lead to compromises in software quality, as shown in Figure 2.3. Software projects are often subjected to severe schedule-related stress. At project inception, managers are pressured to trim budgets and schedules to make unrealistic targets. As successive project deadlines are missed, anything that appears to work is considered acceptable, regardless of quality. The usual victim of a slip in project delivery is testing.

- Unit test coverage for each component.
- Repeated testing of success paths and error states for integrated components.
- Regression testing.

FIGURE 2.3 Haste makes waste.

In this environment, long-term architectural benefits are sacrificed for expedience.

Quality, object-oriented architecture is the product of careful study, decision making, and experimentation. At a minimum, the object-oriented architecture process includes farming of requirements, architecture mining, and hands-on experience. Ideally, object-oriented architecture comprises a set of high-quality design decisions that provide benefits throughout the life cycle of the system.

Significant domain experience for the architect is essential as object-oriented architectures are competently defined and defended. With appropriate domain experience and design patterns, quality object-oriented architectures are defined rapidly. However, it's always a mistake to make object-oriented architectural decisions hastily.

Apathy

Apathy is not caring about solving known problems. That is not to say that all solutions are known or fully achievable, but apathy is a basic unwillingness to attempt a solution (Figure 2.4). Apathy about object-oriented architecture leads to a lack of partitioning. A key aspect of object-oriented architecture is proper partitioning. For example, object-oriented architecture partitions the system into class categories and defines their interfaces and connections.

FIGURE 2.4 Apathy is the worst form of flattery.

The critical partitioning decision in OO architecture is between stable reusable design and replaceable design. The stable design remains with the system throughout its life cycle, as individual software modules are modified, replaced, and added. Replaceable design details are best allocated to profiles, vertical specializations, and metadata.

Neglecting the critical partitioning means that the core of the architecture must change in response to subsystem level changes. This means that subsystem-level changes impact all of the modules in the entire system. Thus, the sin of apathy leads to poor support for change. In addition, poorly partitioned architectures make application interoperability and reuse difficult.

Narrow-Mindedness

Narrow-mindedness is the refusal to practice solutions that are otherwise widely known to be effective (Figure 2.5). An example of this is the use of metadata in software systems. *Metadata* is self-descriptive information in a software system that enables the system to change dynamically.

Many object-oriented systems are built with virtually no metadata. Without metadata, the application software contains hard-coded bindings, relationships, and assumptions about system configuration. For example, the number of servers or clients and their locations can be made transparently variable with straightforward use of metadata services. CORBA stan-

FIGURE 2.5 The Unteachables.

dards include various public metadata services, such as the Naming Service, the Trader Service, and the Interface Repository.

Sloth

Sloth is the "healthy sign" of a lazy developer or manager, who makes poor decisions based upon an "easy answer" (Figure 2.6). Distributed object technology enables application developers to define system-level interfaces quickly using the ISO Interface Definition Language (ISO IDL). Automatically generated interface stubs and skeletons make the task of constructing a distributed system relatively easy. The ease of creating and changing interfaces leads to the deadly sin of sloth—lack of configuration control.

Although sloth is more commonplace in small-scale, object-oriented projects, the habit of frequent interface change is difficult to overcome.

FIGURE 2.6 Sloth usually ends with sudden clarity.

The more interfaces change, the more the interface semantics become unclear to developers. Ultimately, developers and maintainers spend more than half of their time performing system discovery—trying to understand how the system works. The system loses any notion of architecture long before this point is reached.

Proper configuration control starts with the first phase of prototyping. Ideally, system-level interfaces are kept stable during active software development and modified only infrequently. Stable interfaces enable parallel development, effective documentation, and reduced software obsolescence.

Avarice

Greed can take many forms, but it leads to inappropriate software development decisions. Architectural avarice means the modeling of excessive details, which results in excessive complexity due to insufficient abstraction (Figure 2.7).

Excess complexity leads to many software problems and project challenges. Overly complex systems are expensive to develop, integrate, test, document, maintain, and extend. In some cases, development steps are skipped (such as testing) in order to make up for the lost time and money. This can lead very quickly to project failure.

FIGURE 2.7 Addicted to complexity.

Ignorance

Ignorance is intellectual sloth. It's the result of failing to seek understanding. It keeps people stupid (Figure 2.8), and eventually leads to long-term software problems. The sin of ignorance (implementation dependency) often occurs in the migration of applications to distributed architectures. In ignorance, one assumes that system-level interfaces are extracted from fine-grain definitions of existing application objects. For example, when an IDL interface is reverse-engineered from existing C++ header files, implementation-dependent interfaces are created and promulgated throughout a system and its subsystems.

If an object's interface is unique and there are no other implementations that support the same interface, then the interface is implementation-dependent. Every client or object that uses this interface is dependent upon unique implementation details. When this occurs repeatedly on a systemwide scale, a brittle system is created. This sin is also evident when vendor-proprietary interfaces are used without proper layering and wrapping for isolation.

Pride

The sin of pride is the not-invented-here syndrome (Figure 2.9). Object technology supports many reuse opportunities through the integration of commercial packages, freeware, and wrapped legacy applications.

FIGURE 2.8 Some people are too ignorant to change.

FIGURE 2.9 Pride goeth before the fall.

Often, developers unnecessarily invent new designs when knowledge from preexisting systems, products, and standards are readily applied through architecture mining. Reinvention involves many unnecessary risks and costs. New software must be designed, coded, debugged, tested, and documented. New architecture must be prototyped and evolved before it is proven to provide software benefits.

Primal Forces

Software design involves making choices. For example, some of the key choices that present themselves when designing software architecture include:

- Which details to expose and which details to abstract.
- Which features to include and which features to exclude.
- Which aspects to make flexible and extensible.
- Which aspects to constrain and guarantee.

Software design choices are often complex, with numerous issues (or forces) to consider, such as security, cost, adaptability, reliability, and so on. In order to make good choices, it's very important to clarify the context of the decision. Choices are clarified in several ways, such as:

- Separation of concerns.
- Establishing priorities.

To separate concerns, we need to limit the scope of each choice. Partitions in a software architecture are used to allocate and delineate the boundaries of concerns. Each partition is responsible for resolving a limited set of issues, which simplify decision making. The architecture represents the union of the partitions and provides coverage of all the relevant issues. This separation of concerns is a fundamental role of architecture.

Decisions are also clarified by an understanding of priorities. If we know what is important and what is not, it's much easier to choose what to include and what to exclude in a design. Decisions are difficult because they include some items and exclude many others, and we must be able to justify such choices. This is another fundamental role of architecture, to explain significant decisions and design choices.

Risk is a force that is always present in software decisions. Software projects are amazingly prone to failure. As noted, approximately one-third of all software projects are canceled, and approximately only one-sixth of software projects are considered successful. The remaining projects are typically over-budget and over-schedule by factors of two or more. The unsuccessful projects are also incapable of delivering the desired features. Once the systems are delivered, there is high risk involved in changing the system. Correction or extensions are likely to cause new software problems.

Considering these statistics, five out of six software projects are destined to fail. These figures are essentially unchanged by new technologies and approaches such as client/server and object orientation. As software professionals, the outlook is grim, unless something significant changes. We believe that significant changes are necessary in the way that software systems are architected and the way that risks are managed.

We see risk as a generalized force, which is an underlying factor in most other forces. To various degrees, management of risk is a universal force that motivates the patterns and solutions described here.

What Is a Primal Force?

Forces are concerns or issues that exist within a decision-making context. In a design solution, forces that are successfully addressed (or resolved) lead to benefits, and forces that are unresolved lead to consequences. For any given software problem, there are a number of forces that can influence a given solution. The application of a design pattern leads to a solution that resolves the forces in a particular way. In the solution, some forces are resolved more completely than others. The choice of a design solution establishes a priority on the forces, to the extent that the highest-priority forces are resolved the most completely.

Some forces are domain-specific. Domain-specific forces (called *vertical forces*) are unique to a particular situation due to the domain or problem addressed. Since vertical forces are unique (or local) to one software situation, resolution of vertical forces usually results in unique solutions for each software problem.

Another class of forces, *horizontal forces,* are applicable across multiple domains or problems. Horizontal forces are those that influence design choices across several software modules or components. With horizontal forces, design choices made elsewhere may have a direct or indirect impact on design choices made locally. For example, if the horizontal force is "design consistency," it is necessary to coordinate software designs across multiple software modules to ensure such consistency.

A certain class of horizontal forces are pervasive in software architecture and development. These are the *primal forces,* and are present in nearly all design situations, and should be considered part of the contextual forces driving most solutions. One role of the primal forces is to keep architecture and development on track. For example, a software decision that seems to be local can have a cumulative impact when there are other software groups making conflicting choices elsewhere in the same enterprise. The primal forces represent the pervasive forces, which arise from the interrelatedness of software decisions.

The primal forces are an important part of the guidelines presented in this pattern language. Each primal force is horizontally applicable across many domains of software architecture and development. The primal forces represent the common-sense basic considerations, which are necessary for successful software architecture and development. Primal forces comprise a fundamental *value system* for software architects and developers that are independent of particular situational forces.

The primal forces include:

- Management of functionality: meeting the requirements.
- Management of performance: meeting required speed of operation.
- Management of complexity: defining abstractions.
- Management of change: controlling evolution of software.
- Management of IT resources: controlling use and implementation of people and IT artifacts.
- Management of technology transfer: controlling technology change.

The primal forces have different relative importance at different scales. Functionality and performance are critical forces at application-level and finer grains, whereas management of IT resources and technology transfer are enterprise and global in scope. Before we can discuss these fully, we need to define the scales through the scalability model.

Table 2.1 identifies the degrees of impact of forces at the different levels of scale:

- *Critical.* The impact is fundamental, as it affects all of the software.
- *Important.* The impact must be seriously considered, as it affects a significant amount of the software.
- *Marginal.* The impact can often be ignored, as it affects a minimal portion of the software.
- *Unimportant.* The impact should not be considered.

TABLE 2.1 Degrees of Impact

	Global Industry	*Enterprise*	*System*	*Application*
Management of Functionality	unimportant	marginal	important	critical
Management of Performance	important	important	critical	critical
Management of Complexity	important	critical	important	marginal
Management of Change	unimportant	critical	critical	important
Management of IT Resources	unimportant	critical	important	marginal
Management of Technology Transfer	critical	important	important	marginal

- *Management of functionality* is a force best addressed at the application level. Developers are better able to effect functionality at its lowest level in response to (functional) requirements.
- *Management of performance* is best addressed at both the application and the system levels. Frequently, performance at the system level involves performing coarse-grained optimizations within a domain model. The domain model is used by application models, which contain localized, finer-grained optimizations.
- *Management of complexity* is important at all levels; however, complexity becomes exponentially worse at the higher scalability levels. In any case, it never becomes an unimportant consideration at any level.
- *Management of change* is critical at the enterprise and system levels, where the rate of change of individual products is moderate. Applications and external concerns change quite rapidly, generating new requirements and alterations in existing implementations. Therefore, it is important at the system and enterprise levels to plan an adaptable system capable of managing change. While, admittedly, change is even more rapid at the global level, it is less of a concern as there is little an organization can do about it.
- *Management of IT resources* is critical at the enterprise level because of the need for strategic planning. This includes people, time, hardware and software artifacts. It's also important at a system level to ensure that major software developments are successful.
- *Management of technology transfer* is important at the global industry level so as to stay abreast of technology advancements and be able to

reuse experience and knowledge across organizational boundaries. It is important at the enterprise level to make the most of the available resources within an organization and at a system level to gain tactical advantages of software advancements.

Table 2.2 identifies the roles in the software development and the level of their responsibility for each scale. Each role has a critical impact because that is the scale where they can be most effective, as Table 2.3 illustrates.

A developer is primarily concerned with optimizing functionality and performance. However, if a software project is going to be successful, the primal force of management of change must also be dealt with at this level. At the architect level, the same concerns are shared as the developer level, with the additional force of managing the complexity of the overall system. The architect must design the system such that the system interfaces are manageable, regardless of the complexity of its parts. A project

TABLE 2.2 Level of Responsibility

	Global Industry	*Enterprise*	*System*	*Application*
CIO	critical	critical	marginal	unimportant
Project Manager	unimportant	critical	important	marginal
Architect	marginal	important	critical	important
Developer	unimportant	marginal	important	critical

TABLE 2.3 Scale of Effectiveness

	Global Industry	*Enterprise*	*System*	*Application*
Management of Functionality			architect	developer
Management of Performance			architect	developer
Management of Complexity		project manager	architect	
Management of Change		project manager	architect	developer
Management of IT Resources	CIO	project manager		
Management of Technology Transfer	CIO			

manager has to aid the architect in the management of complexity and change and successfully deal with the management of IT resources, such as people, time, and budgets. Finally, at the CIO level, a plan must be in place for managing internal IT resources and for managing the technology transfer to and from other organizations in the industry.

MANAGEMENT OF FUNCTIONALITY

Managing functionality is making sure that software meets end-user requirements. Software provides a mapping from the world of end-user objects to the world of computer technology objects. The functionality of the software provides the mechanism for this mapping and for all of the operations performed on technology objects.

Interoperability is an important part of management of functionality, comprising the exchange of information and services between software modules. Interoperability enables multiple software modules to collaborate to provide functionality.

MANAGEMENT OF PERFORMANCE

The second primal force, and the one sometimes overlooked by software architects, is the management of performance. It is not sufficient for software to meet only its functionality requirements; the system must also meet performance needs. End users have changing perceptions throughout the lifetime of a system, which can impact these needs. A system is implicitly required to perform at least as fast as comparable systems developed using other technologies.

In the case of CORBA, the performance of an ORB product out of the box is only as good as the underlying technologies used to implement it. The ORB's built-in client-service decoupling enables the astute developer to perform many performance enhancements without changing application software. Because the performance enhancements are transparent to application software, they may be phased in over time, or added as needed as determined by the growth of the system. This results in a high degree of scalability in CORBA systems, which has been proven in the success of companies migrating from prototypes to enterprisewide operational implementations. The best-known performance enhancement supported by CORBA is load balancing. Since CORBA uses dynamic binding to connect clients with services, it is possible to insert algorithms in the binding process to ensure that the services are used optimally. Since many implementations can support an interface, services are often replicated to optimize load balancing.

Managing performance also involves application software optimizations. Application implementations control the details of processing, which is where the greatest amount of flexibility is available to tune the performance of the application. The majority of performance issues involve compute-bound application bottlenecks, not I/O-bound or network-bound performance. Specifically, an application developer controls the application's data structure selection, algorithms, and often, language implementation. Performance optimization is an expensive and time-consuming activity, and few projects are willing to incur the additional, often considerable, costs associated with application speed-up.

MANAGEMENT OF COMPLEXITY

In developing systems, it is important not to lose sight of the value of good software abstractions. Abstraction leads to simpler interfaces, uniform architectures, and improved object models. It is the lack of effective abstractions that results in excessive system complexity. Commonality between components is often not recognized and sufficiently exploited. Without proper design abstraction, needless component differences are created, resulting in redundant software and multiple points of maintenance for fundamentally similar code.

Managing complexity is a matter of analyzing a design and properly identifying the hot spots and problem areas that may be most affected by future changes; for example, the anticipation of changes that have the potential for a performance bottleneck in an implementation. Once hot spots have been correctly identified, a recursive process of redesign revision is appropriate, to provide simplicity and robustness. Developing abstractions that simplify individual interfaces provides cost savings across the overall system design. This can result in savings in the internal implementation of a software component, and in each of the clients that access the component services.

MANAGEMENT OF CHANGE

Adaptability is a highly desired but elusive software characteristic. Most organizations would prefer to have adaptable systems, but few realize the full implications of what it means to develop a flexible system. When developing a distributed system, it is not sufficient to simply include adaptability as a goal; rather, the system architect must consider the evolution of the system and decide how and where the system needs to be adaptable. When the system architect designs interface specifications, he or she is making decisions about where the areas of greatest adaptability exist and which are the areas of greatest stability. IDL can be used to define the software boundaries. If properly specified, it is the set of interfaces that provide decoupling between components in the system. A good set of IDL interfaces specifies the exposed functionality of a software component in order to make multiple implementations capable of satisfying the constraints of the interfaces. It is in the software interfaces where system stability and adaptability are realized. A system that can support component implementation changes and still maintain stability is much more adaptable than one whose interfaces must constantly be modified to support new component implementations. Minimizing the dependency of clients to particular component implementations is the role of the software architect. This is accomplished by abstracting the key functional elements of categories of components and defining them in an implementation-independent manner. IDL is an ideal notation because it is language-independent. With an ORB, the IDL interfaces can support location and platform independence as well.

Portability is an important aspect of management of change, for it is the ability to migrate application software from one product or platform to another. Many standards reduce risk by facilitating portability. Unfortunately, the portability provided by COTS products is imperfect, as vendors increase and decrease other COTS and platform support.

MANAGEMENT OF IT RESOURCES

Management of information technology (IT) resources concerns the ability to manage the assets of the enterprise on a large scale. A typical large-scale enterprise would have many different kinds of hardware (hardware heterogeneity), many different software products (software heterogeneity), and multiple releases of each technology. Managing the large volume of machines and software in a changing organization becomes a major issue in its own right. The management of IT resources involves many aspects, such as hardware/software acquisition, inventory, training, maintenance, upgrade, and support.

The majority of end users are incapable of providing their own technical support, so this support burden falls on the enterprise. If the support burden is unresolved, significant costs are associated with lost time and productivity, estimated by *Information Week* to be $40,000 per end-user PC per year (April 1996).

Security is an important aspect of management of IT resources. The secure control of information and services is becoming more important as systems become increasingly networked and interoperable.

MANAGEMENT OF TECHNOLOGY TRANSFER

Management of technology transfer comprises some of the key forces at the external boundary of the enterprise. It includes the formal and informal relationships established by the use and transfer of software and other technologies. Management of technology transfer is also an issue impacting many software developers because of the popularity and the availability of the Internet. It is relatively easy to disseminate technology information globally across enterprise boundaries through e-mail, the World Wide Web, and other services. These information exchanges impact the control of intellectual property and the changing dependencies of internal systems on external technologies.

Management of technology transfer also includes the possibility of creating and influencing standards. In essence, standards are technical agreements between enterprises; they represent the minimal technology transfer that occurs between organizations in order to establish commonality and cooperation. CORBA IDL makes the creation of interface specifications accessible to virtually all architects and developers. This same IDL is the accepted notation of the formal standards community and other consortia and alliances. It is now possible for most organizations to create technical agreements for software interfaces as a way to manage the technology transfer environment.

Software Design-Level Model

If an attempt is made to develop a system on a piecemeal basis without an overall architecture, the system will become increasingly unmanageable as the system evolves due to requirements changes and new technology adoptions. One of the key benefits of architecture is the separation of concerns, which means, rather than tackling all of the problems at once, partitioning the problem into solvable elements. In this pattern language, we present the scalability model that separates concerns based upon scale of software solutions. The model clarifies the key levels inherent in software systems and the problems and solutions available at each level.

In a typical small software system, there are two levels of scale (Figure 2.10). The first is the external model (or *application level*), which directly addresses the end-user requirements. This level includes the user interfaces and associated functionality. The applications are typically driven by interactive user control through graphical user interfaces (GUIs) or user commands. The applications implement the external model of the system that

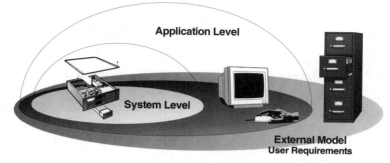

FIGURE 2.10 The existence of both external and internal models in software systems illustrates the need for multiple levels of software concerns.

interacts directly with the human organization. The applications contain the software needed to address the functional requirements of the organization.

The second level is the internal model (or *system level*). The system level comprises the connections between the applications; it does not directly interface with the end users, nor it is readily observable to end users. The system level provides an architecture for the software system. This level is charged with providing an infrastructure for the application level, and generates interoperability, communication, and coordination between applications. Access to data stores, auditing, and the management of interprocess resources also occur at the system level.

A similar partition exists at several other scales of software implementation; for example, when software solutions span multiple systems across organizations. There is another, related set of concerns at the enterprise level. The scalability model explains the differing priorities at each scale, and the pattern language includes a set of possible solutions. This resolves a key guidance challenge: ensuring that appropriate solutions are applied at their correct level so that the chances of developing an effective, maintainable system are maximized.

The pattern language is organized by architectural levels, which define a comprehensive framework in which to examine the patterns and principles of object-oriented architecture. Although we have identified seven architectural levels, our focus will be on the larger-scale levels of object-oriented architecture (Figure 2.11). The smaller-scale levels have been covered, to various extents, by other authors. Specifically, the object level is addressed by the current reusable component libraries and standards such as C++, Smalltalk, the CORBA object model, and CORBAservices. At the micro-architecture level, the Gamma Pattern Language (GPL) and additional design patterns research present the structures necessary to develop component micro-architectures [Gamma 95]. Significant work has also been done at the macro-component (frameworks) level. For example, Taligent Corporation was quite active in developing software and guidelines at the macro-component level in the development of its OO frameworks. Until now, the higher architectural levels have been mostly neglected, and as a result, general interoperability principles across applications, systems, and organizational enterprises have suffered from proprietary solutions and nonreusable, unscalable technological solutions. By defining the scalability model, the field of design patterns can be advanced to apply to larger-scale problems, which before now have absorbed significant resources and resulted in less reusable and extensible solutions.

Figure 2.11 shows the seven architectural levels: global, enterprise, system, application, macro-component, micro-component, and object. The

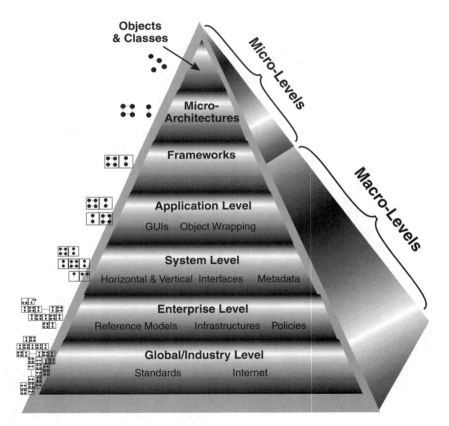

FIGURE 2.11 Software design-level model.

global level contains the design issues that are globally applicable across all systems. This level is concerned with coordination across all organizations, which participate in cross-organizational communications and information sharing. The *enterprise level* is focused upon coordination and communication across a single organization. The organization can be distributed across many locations and heterogeneous hardware and software systems. The *system level* deals with communications and coordination across applications and sets of applications. The *application level* is focused upon the organization of applications developed to meet a set of user requirements. The *macro-component levels* are focused on the organization and development of application frameworks. The *micro-component level* is centered on the development of software components that solve recurring software problems. Each solution is relatively self-contained and

---

Design Reuse versus Code Reuse

Design patterns are focused on providing reusable design guidance for developing large-scale systems. The reusability of design itself has a significant effect on the overall development cost of a system, far greater than the reuse of individual software components [Mowbray 95]. To illustrate this, Figure 2.12 shows a system on the left that is able to take advantage of several reusable components at the framework and microarchitectural levels. Note that the overall design of the system still has to occur and that the bulk of the overall tree is in the nodes in the nonleaf node parts of the design. Reducing components does effectively save time in that the prefabricated "leaf nodes" can be plugged into the design rather than custom constructed, but there is still a large outlay required to build the overall system. The right side of Figure 2.12 shows a system that is able to reuse much of the design of an existing system. Although the system is constrained to the domain of the previously built system, the level of reuse is far greater [Yourdon 93]. By reusing the design, any pieces that are identical to the previous system may be plugged in with minimal modifications. Still, there are many leaf nodes that must be customized to the new base of users to meet their specific requirements. Note that the cost of changing the leaf nodes is far less than the cost of changing the higher-level design. Therefore, optimizing the amount of design that is reused in a system provides a framework for minimizing the overall system costs far more than if the emphasis is on reusing individual components.

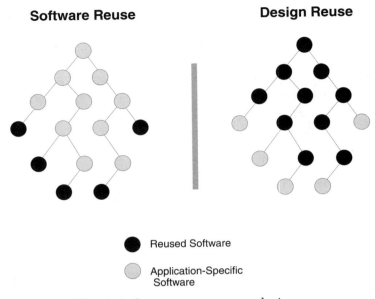

FIGURE 2.12 Software reuse versus design reuse.

often solves just part of an even larger problem. The *object level* is concerned with the development of reusable objects and classes. The object level is more concerned with code reuse than design reuse. Each of the levels is discussed in detail along with an overview of the patterns documented at each level.

Object Level

The finest-grain level is the object level. Here, a software developer is concerned with the definition and management of object classes and object instances. Decisions made at this level include selection of specific object attributes and proper signatures for each operation. At this level, the goal is to build primitive functionality to address application requirements. Secondary goals include reuse of existing software and documentation for the decisions used in making the decisions about what is included or excluded from the class description. Typically, discussions on the object level are so specific and detailed that they are used only to describe the specifics of a system's implementation.

At a business level, an object may represent the behavior and data of an account or customer. At an implementation level, an object may represent the methods and attributes of a Java GUI to edit, validate, and display account or customer data.

At the object level, in the case of class libraries and programming frameworks, objects and classes are language-dependent. Language independence is possible, for example, when they have their class definitions expressed in OMG IDL. A standard object model defined in CORBA defines the semantics of object interactions. Also, CORBAservices interfaces define basic object-level interfaces for the management and control of objects.

The CORBAservices are often used as building blocks for larger-scale software components, which may contain policy and rules as to how the services are used by a specific set of components. Language-dependent class definitions are written in a specific programming language, such as C, C++, Smalltalk, ADA, Java, and others, and are usually not sharable by other programming languages. Language-dependent classes may take advantage of shared run-time libraries so that they are capable of use by multiple applications.

Micro-Architecture Level

The micro-architecture level involves patterns that combine multiple objects or object classes. This might be a collection of cooperating business objects for the purpose of calculating air miles from a month of credit card transactions. At an implementation level, this might be the collection of cooperating objects that provide the GUI screens, business (processing rules), and persistence and query interfaces for a customer or an account object. This level is concerned with the development of small designs used to tackle a limited problem with a software application. The distinguishing characteristics of this level are a limited group of cooperating objects whose interrelationships with other objects are well-defined and understood by the implementers of the component. The goal of patterns at the micro-architectural level is to reuse the encapsulation of components so that they are isolated enough to handle future system changes. The Gamma Pattern Language was primarily concerned with the development of effective design patterns for applications at this level.

Framework Level

The framework level is concerned with the development of design patterns at the macro-component level, involving one or more micro-architectures. This could be a container-based framework used to store information on groups of customers and their accounts. Often, the solution presupposes several architectural issues such as the presence of object request broker

(ORB) architecture, or that certain capabilities are available within a system. At the framework level, the goal is to allow the reuse of both software code and the design used in writing the code. Patterns, which are unique to a specific framework model or macro-component architecture, would be included at this level. Effective patterns at this level can reduce the cost of building applications, which share the framework's domain, and their maintenance costs. Many of the patterns and much of the guidance from Taligent and Siemens are at this level [Buschmann 96]. Frameworks attempt to use large portions of design and software when applied to solve problems within a specialized domain.

Application Level

The application level is the next scale above frameworks. Applications typically involve numerous object classes, multiple micro-architectures, and one or more frameworks. The application level is concerned with the design patterns used in a single application program. Often, a single developer has control over how an application (at this level) is structured, controlled, and managed. At the application level, the primary goal is to implement a specific set of functionalities defined by the software requirements. Their functionality must be conformant with performance goals. This level contains diverse arrangements of structure and design techniques. Because the scope is limited to a single program, there is far less risk involved in experimentation at this level than at larger scales (which impact multiple applications, systems, or enterprises). If the higher scales are architected properly, the scope of impact of changes within an application is limited to a single-application program and the data on which it operates.

The application level contains programs that implement the external model of a software system; that is, an operational model of the real world. Specifically, the external requirements of the end user are satisfied at the application level; this includes issues relating to user interface and visible system functionality. Application-level software activities include object wrapping of legacy systems and new application development. Commercial off-the-shelf (COTS) applications reside in the model at this level, as well as groups of collaborating frameworks.

Since the finer-grain levels are covered adequately by other works, the pattern language is focused only upon the problem sets that occur at the application and larger scales. The work in design patterns at the application and higher levels has been minimal until now; however, it is precisely at these levels where object-oriented architecture is most important.

Application patterns cover a diverse set of solutions, and innovation at the application level in COTS software and development support environments is occurring rapidly. The chosen application patterns in the pattern language include libraries, frameworks, interpreters, event-driven, persistence, and others. This comprises a robust set of application patterns that explain the principles behind most application-level architectures.

System Level

A system comprises several integrated applications, which provide the functionality; the system level adds interoperation between the applications. The system is also responsible for managing life-cycle issues, such as system evolution. The system-level architecture is the enduring structure that survives the modification and replacement of component applications over the life cycle of the system. This could be an insurance system, for example, integrating marine, home, and automobile insurance applications, or a flight system for the centralized control of aircraft systems monitoring, Instrument Landing System (ILS), proximity warning, and autopilot.

The system level is interesting because the forces vary significantly compared to the application level. As we move to larger scales, the impact of change and complexity increase dramatically. Within one application there may be infrequent changes; at the system level, these application-level changes comprise cumulative changes with possible systemwide impacts. For example, if a dozen cooperating applications were upgraded once a year on a staggered schedule, the overall system would experience monthly upgrades, with an associated risk of the required changes to existing software affecting the rest of the applications.

Each application may be a complex program with hundreds of classes and thousands of methods. As we scale to the system level, the system complexity increases faster than that of the individual applications. From one perspective, the system resembles a large program that is the union of the individual applications. Since the applications must communicate, additional software implements application-to-application interconnections. If this complexity is not managed properly, the system with N applications resembles a much larger program with N complex modules and $N \times N$ interconnections (Figure 2.13). Complexity at the system level also includes communications mechanisms and distributed processing.

The apparent complexity also leads to a wide range of diversity in solutions. Many system-level solutions are ad hoc, or uniquely crafted for particular application implementations. Within an enterprise, there may

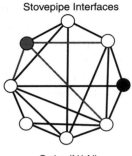

Stovepipe Interfaces

Order *(N*N)*

FIGURE 2.13 If every subsystem has a unique interface, then the system is overly complex.

be many software systems with varying software architectures. At the system level, the goal is to provide an infrastructure that applications may easily "plug in" in order to achieve some interoperability benefit. Here, the goal is to reuse architecture so that applications benefit from commonality between systems, which includes interoperability and software reuse.

At the system level, managing change and complexity are the two most important primal forces. Managing functionality and performance have more importance at the application level where they are directly controlled. Managing complexity is achieved through arriving at the right amount of abstraction for system architecture. Management of change is focused on the development of common interfaces. This defines how services are accessed. Common interfaces allow for component replacement of applications and systems. Good architecture is about matching the right amount of abstraction with the appropriate set of common interfaces.

The system level implements the system's internal model and provides the cohesiveness needed to allow applications to interoperate effectively with one another (refer back to Figure 2.10). Three key principles at this level include horizontal interfaces, vertical interfaces, and metadata. *Horizontal interfaces* are common interfaces designed for reuse across an organization; for example, horizontal interfaces may contain generic operations for data transfer and access. They can provide mechanisms for reuse, interoperability, and management of applications. *Vertical interfaces* are customized with respect to domain-specific requirements and vertical forces. Providing functionality to end users and optimizing performance are the key motivations behind vertical interfaces. *Metadata* is self-descriptive information, which defines services and data available within a system. Metadata enables system flexibility, with dynamic capabilities for managing change. Together, horizontal and vertical interfaces, along with metadata, comprise system-level software architecture.

Within the system level, patterns are categorized into either a structural or behavioral patterns. *Structural patterns* are those that possess a specific structure or set of related components. Structural design patterns at the system level include gateways, a repository, and component and domain object-oriented architecture. *Behavioral patterns* define how a system behaves under various conditions. The behavioral patterns are reuse categories, client/server, multitier, and automation.

Enterprise Level

The enterprise level is the largest architectural scale within an organization. Enterprise-level software comprises multiple systems, where each system comprises several applications (see Figure 2.14). This could be financial services for banking, mortgages, and insurance, or underground railway systems for ticketing, accounting, signaling, and track control. Unlike the global level, within the enterprise level, an organization has control of its resources and policies. The enterprise is responsible for

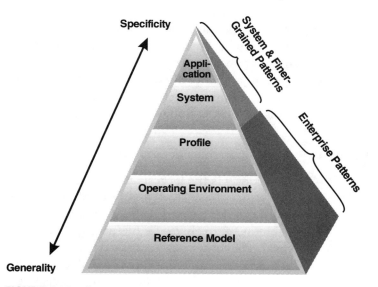

FIGURE 2.14 The enterprise architecture defines the technology utilization policies, including the standards reference model, the common operating environment, and the application profiles.

establishing policies and procedures that are in place throughout an organization. The enterprise-level patterns include guidance for making architectural design decisions that affect the structure, style, and future growth of enterprise software. The patterns help define the necessary policies that need to be in place at the enterprise level, balanced with autonomy at lower levels. The enterprise level is also differentiated from the global level by being limited to a definable scope of influence. The goal of the enterprise level is to provide software access and minimize costs through a consistent set of polices and services usable throughout the organization. By establishing organizational procedure in accordance with the design patterns, many typical enterprise problems in organizations can be minimized. For example, an organization that establishes a policy for particular file formats or network standards can avoid many related problems of procurement flexibility for state-of-the-art products and product incompatibilities without a means of data transfer between them.

At the enterprise level are four categories of software information management to consider: the organizational operating environment, distributed interprocess communications, resource management, and organizational profiles. In addition, certain decisions must be made at this level that are unique for a particular organization type. Some general characteristics of enterprise-level decisions will be presented as a guide toward identifying and applying some of these less common patterns.

Included at the enterprise level are the various organizational models, which direct an organization as to how to utilize various standards, for example, organizational policies, security and data access policies, and organizational infrastructures issues, such as the available communication protocols or the location of shared resources.

Global Level

The global level is the largest scale of the architectural levels, comprising multiple enterprises. The boundaries of global systems are difficult, if not impossible, to define, and include a mixture of de facto and formal standards that are actively in use by the multitude of organizations throughout the world. The key issues addressed involve the impact of software, which cross enterprise boundaries. The global level includes languages, standards, and policies that affect multiple enterprises. Global systems are those that bridge enterprises, and can be jointly controlled by multiple enterprises. The goals of the global level are the joint goals of multiple enterprises. For example, the global level may provide a set of leveragable standards and protocols that benefit organizations by allowing a general means of interoperability and communicating across different enterprises.

The best example of a global system is the Internet, which is defined through a collection of related standards and policies that exist throughout the world to enable the sharing of information. An important aspect of the Internet is the collection of standards that can be supported by anyone who wishes to share and access information in other organizations. The usage is beyond the control of any particular organization and is open to any person or group who wishes to participate.

Also included at the global level are the software standards. There are four major categories of standards in the computer industry: formal, de jure, de facto, and consortium standards.

1. *Formal standards* are those advocated by accredited formal standards bodies such as the International Standards Organization (ISO), ANSI, and IEEE.
2. *De jure standards* are mandated by law and endorsed by a government authority, including such standards as Ada95 and GOSIP.
3. *De facto standards* are those that enjoy the status through popular use. Currently, popular de facto standards include Microsoft Windows and Office, TCP/IP, and the various Internet protocols (IIOP).
4. *Consortium standards* are created by a wide variety of groups such as OMG and the Open Group. Typically, formal and de jure standards are specifications only, whereas de facto and consortium standards may also include an implementation.

Level Summary

A summary of the levels that are the focus of the pattern language is presented in Figure 2.15. The application level is where the functionality and performance that meet user requirements occurs. At the next larger scale, the system level defines the software interconnections between applications. The development of vertical interfaces and horizontal interfaces for interoperability between applications occurs at the system level. Along with the horizontal and vertical interfaces, metadata is defined for run-time flexibility to allow many types of system modifications without requiring changes to application software. The next larger scale is the enterprise level where organizational level policies, guidelines, and procedures are defined. At this level, the enterprise controls reference models

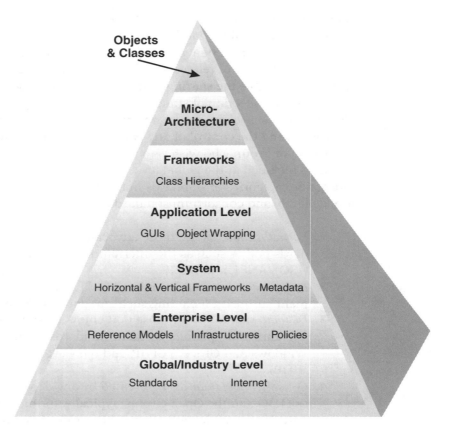

FIGURE 2.15 The software design-level model shows the levels addressed in the AntiPatterns found in Chapters 5–7.

and operating environments and makes choices to further the needs of the organization. At the global level, standards are generated as technology agreements are reached through consensus with other enterprises.

Architectural Scale and Primal Forces

The primal forces are persuasive concerns that influence most software choices. The trade-offs between these concerns will affect the overall quality of software architecture at all levels. In order to simplify decision making and clarify the separation of issues, we have estimated the relative importance of the primal forces at each architectural scale (Figure 2.16).

	Application "Programmer"	System "Architect"	Enterprise "CIO"	Global "CEO"
Management of Functionality	1			
Management of Performance	2			
Management of Complexity		2		
Management of Change		1	2	
Management of Resources			1	2
Management of Technology Transfer				1

FIGURE 2.16 The primal forces have varying relative priorities at each architectural scale.

On an application level, software developers are concerned primarily with managing functionality and performance when developing software to meet the functional needs of their user base. The system level is focused on developing an infrastructure that can effectively manage complexity and change in order to reduce the overall life-cycle costs of developing and maintaining an organization's software system. The system-level architect is responsible for providing adaptability and ensuring that the overall system design is sufficient to adapt to the evolving needs of an organization.

On the enterprise level, the emphasis is on managing resources, as large-scale systems often involve thousands of interacting components and services. Additionally, the management of change overshadows other primal forces that are addressed at lower levels. The management of resources becomes a major concern as the enterprise scale increases.

At a global level, the emphasis is on leveraging existing standards and effectively utilizing the existing knowledge base to enhance enterprise-level development. However, the enterprise's control over solutions is reduced as an organization has limited influence of external technologies. Keeping up to date on new technologies and use of IT resources are the primary concerns at the global level.

The pattern language will examine the recurring structures at each level and present detailed solutions for the major problems inherent at each architectural scale. Design patterns excel in establishing reusable architectural designs that balance the primal forces. A natural side effect of good object-oriented architecture, which effectively balances the forces, is that overall software development costs are reduced as maintenance costs are reduced, and services can be used during a major portion of the life cycle.

3

Templates for Patterns and AntiPatterns

The use of templates is what makes design patterns and AntiPatterns different from other forms of technical discussion. The template assures that important questions are answered about each pattern in a pattern language, pattern catalog, or pattern system. Without a template, a pattern is just somebody's unstructured prose, or someone saying, "It's a pattern because I'm an expert and I say so." We don't buy this argument and neither should you. Without structure, it's difficult to determine what is a pattern and what is not. This is because there is no recognizable form or distinction between ordinary technical discussion and patterns literature.

A pattern language (or catalog) is a collection of interrelated patterns. Each pattern has a consistent, *rhetorical structure*—a pattern template. By rhetorical structure, we mean that there is a well-conceived logic to the pattern descriptions. This consistent, logical structure is a direct result of the use of the template. Each section of the template has a rhetorical purpose. It's part of a technical line of reasoning, and each section answers some key questions about the pattern involved.

The intent and extent of the rhetorical structure varies between pattern catalogs. The structure of the template is chosen to match the audience's need and authors' resources. Some of the major template forms are described in the following sections.

Degenerate Form

Degenerate patterns are without discernible templates. Compared to *templated patterns*, a degenerate pattern contains only a single content section. Here is an example of a degenerate pattern form.

Degenerate Pattern Form

Technical Discussion: What does the author have to say about this set of concepts?

Is it a pattern? It's a subjective judgment. One can call it a pattern because the author has chosen to do so. We choose not to believe it's a pattern solely based upon the author's reputation or other subjective assessments.

Degenerate form provides no particular conventions or guidance upon which practitioners can rely. The readers have to analyze the author's prose to determine what is problem, intent, context, forces, solution, benefits, consequences, examples, and so forth. In practice, it is likely that one or more of these elements are missing.

Alexanderian Form

Christopher Alexander's traditional template comprises three sections: name, problem, and solution. The word THEREFORE partitions the discussion. THEREFORE appears between the discussion of issues and the discussion of a design approach. Here is an example of an Alexanderian pattern form.

Alexanderian Pattern Form

Name: What does the author call this concept?

Technical Discussion: What are some related issues?

THEREFORE

What is a common solution for resolving these issues?

The Alexanderian form contains an essential partitioning between motivations and actions. By convention, a diagram is included in the Alexanderian form. This is an important spatial abstraction of the ideas presented in prose. The Alexanderian form is the minimum one should expect for the description of any design pattern.

Minimal Template (Micro-Pattern)

The minimal, rhetorical structure of a software-engineering design pattern includes name, problem, and solution. The name defines unique terminology; the problem lists the context, forces, and/or applicability; and the solution is the pattern content (what to do about solving the problem). This structure is appropriate for low-overhead pattern documentation such as workshop-pattern development or on-site consulting, where expedience and content are key, and formality is not necessary. It's also concise, which is a requirement of some publication media. Here is the standard template for a micro-pattern.

Micro-Pattern Template

> **Name:** What shall this pattern be called by practitioners?
> **Problem:** What is motivating us to apply this pattern?
> **Solution:** How do we solve the problem?

Mini-Pattern Template

A mini-pattern decomposes the problem or solution to expose the teaching elements. The next most important rhetorical aspects of a pattern are the "teaching" elements. In particular, the context and forces and/or the benefits of consequences. Most important, these sections answer the why questions about the solution, as well as provide information about when to use the pattern. Here are two examples of mini-pattern templates.

Inductive Mini-Pattern

> **Name:** What shall this pattern be called by practitioners?
> **Context:** What are the assumed environment or a priori assumptions for applying this pattern?

Forces: What are the different design motivations that must be balanced?

Solution: How do we solve the problem?

Deductive Mini-Pattern

Name: What shall this pattern be called by practitioners?

Problem: What is motivating us to apply this pattern?

Solution: How do we solve the problem?

Benefits: What are the potential positive outcomes of applying this pattern?

Consequences: What are potential shortcomings and consequences of applying this pattern?

We describe two template forms for mini-patterns: inductive and deductive. The *inductive mini-pattern* focuses on the applicability of the pattern. The *deductive mini-pattern* focuses on the outcomes of the solution—benefits and consequences.

Formal Templates

There are many other potential sections added to a pattern and Anti-Pattern write-up. Citations that include reference to other related patterns and nonpattern technical concepts are also useful and necessary for a full formal treatment. Some of the formal templates used in publications are summarized here. Note that the following are paraphrased summaries of the authors' original template definitions. The Gang-of-Four (GoF) template is a formal template appropriate for micro-architecture-level patterns [Gamma 94].

Gang-of-Four Pattern

Pattern Name: What is the pattern called?

Pattern Classification: Is the pattern creational, structural, or behavioral?

Intent: What problem does this pattern solve?

Also Known As: What are other names for this pattern?

Motivation: What is an example scenario for applying this pattern?

Applicability: When does this pattern apply?

Structure: What are the class hierarchy diagrams for the objects in this pattern?

Participants: What are the objects that participate in this pattern?

Collaborations: How do these objects interoperate?

Consequences: What are the trade-offs of using this pattern?

Implementation: Which techniques or issues arise in applying this pattern?

Sample Code: What is an example of the pattern in source code?

Known Uses: What are some examples of real systems using this pattern?

Related Patterns: What other patterns from this pattern collection are related to this pattern?

System of Patterns Template

The system of patterns template is a formal template appropriate for multiple levels of patterns, such as idioms level, application level, and system level [Buschmann 96].

Name: What is this pattern called?

Also Known As: What are other names for this pattern?

Example: What is an example of the need for this pattern?

Context: When does this pattern apply?

Problem: What is the problem solved by this pattern?

Solution: What is the underlying principal underlying this pattern?

Structure: What objects are involved and related (structural diagram)?

Dynamics: How does this object collaborate (interaction diagram)?

Implementation: What are some guidelines for implementing this pattern?

Example Resolved: Show how the previous example is resolved using the pattern.

Variants: What are important variations of this pattern?

Known Uses: What are real-world systems using this pattern?

Consequences: What are the benefits and liabilities of using this pattern?

See Also: What are related patterns and how do they differ?

Rethinking the Design Pattern Template

Many practical experiences with formal templates were less than satisfactory for early pattern readers and practitioners. Patterns usually convey a fairly simple idea. However, many readers found the write-ups to be overly concerned with verbose details, issues, and preliminary discussion. This is an interesting reaction, given that pattern templates have come a long way from the enigmatic "degenerate templates."

What was needed was a way to convey the information quickly and conveniently. One key approach that we used was to leverage the templates upon a robust reference model. Instead of having each pattern be completely independent (in terms of context and forces), the *CORBA Design Patterns* reference model allowed us to define the horizontal (common) context and forces that occur at each scale of software design. By addressing this commonality in a separate reference-model chapter, we eliminated several pages of verbose preliminary discussion from virtually every pattern.

In addition, we wanted to structure the template for quick comprehension. Given that there are many patterns to learn and assimilate, and most practitioners are under extreme time pressures on the job, we organized the template sections to enable readers to learn a great deal about a pattern, before being subjected to a rambling, free-text discussion.

The CORBA Design Patterns template is organized so that the most concise information-packed sections are first and the free-form sections are last. The template begins with keywords defined in the reference model, followed by a summarized intent and a diagram abstraction of the solution. Applicability is a priority-ordered, bulleted list that quickly covers the most important motivations for using the pattern. The solution summary explains the patterns' technical approach crisply. Sections following the solution summary make this feasible.

In practice, we found that discussion of variations in the solution section really confuses some readers. A separate section is dedicated to the variations of the solution, so that the solution is explained without the confusing appearance of ambivalence or caveats. Another section that covers alternative software scale describes the patterns' differences when applied at another level of software design.

CORBA Design Pattern Template

Solution Name:

Solution Type: Is it a software pattern, technology pattern, process pattern, or role pattern (keyword only)?

Intent: What is this pattern all about, in 25 words or less?

Primal Forces: Which of the horizontal forces from the reference model are best resolved by this pattern?

Applicability at this Scale: When does this pattern apply; what are the significant motivations behind this pattern (ordered bullet list)?

Solution Summary: What is the pattern solution and approach (stated clearly, without verbose embellishment)?

Benefits: What are the primary positive results of applying this pattern (bulleted list)?

Other Consequences: What are the primary negative consequences of applying this pattern (bulleted list)?

Rescaling this Solution to Other Levels: How does this pattern differ if applied at other software scales?

Related Solutions: Cross-references and citations to other patterns (including other patterns from other pattern publications) and other technology examples, publication citations, and resources. Basically, point to anything outside this pattern write-up that may be of use to the reader.

Example: A practical example of this pattern in an application context, with source code listing if applicable.

Background: Any other relevant information?

AntiPattern Templates

AntiPatterns are a new form of patterns. A fundamental difference between a pattern and an AntiPattern is that with an AntiPattern a solution has negative consequences. Some consequences may be apparent now (the symptoms) and some may be anticipated (the consequences). There are basic forms of AntiPatterns.

To be useful, AntiPatterns also include a solution. So another way to differentiate between a pattern and an AntiPattern is that there are two solutions (instead of a problem and a solution). The first solution generates negative consequences (forces that must be resolved). The second solution is a migration (or refactoring) from the first solution that provides dramatically improved benefits and much-reduced consequences.

In an ordinary design pattern, the convention is that at least three known uses of the solution must exist. Because there are two solutions, the "rule of three" for AntiPatterns is different from patterns. Since no three solutions are identical, the pattern solution is a best-practices abstraction of the known uses.

AntiPatterns are different because they have two solutions. The first solution, "the AntiPattern," must conform to the rule-of-three occurrences just as with ordinary patterns. Unfortunately, it's very unlikely that each of these known occurrences of the AntiPattern were resolved in exactly the same way. The second solution is a best-practices solution, based upon the known solutions to the AntiPattern, if multiple solutions are known to exist. They can be identified in the template as well.

Pseudo-AntiPattern Template

This is a form of degenerate template in which the author describes a bad solution in disparaging terms. Some of the earliest AntiPatterns posted on the Internet had this form. This is not a particularly useful form, because it's subjective and quite one-sided in its pejorative tone.

> **Name:** What is the AntiPattern called?
>
> **Problem:** What are its derogatory characteristics?

Mini-AntiPattern

As we discussed, an AntiPattern template differs from a pattern in that it presents two solutions. The first solution is called the *AntiPattern problem;* the second solution is called the *refactored solution.* This minimal form can be extended with other template sections as appropriate.

> **Name:** What shall this AntiPattern be called by practitioners (pejorative)?
>
> **AntiPattern Problem:** What is the recurrent solution that causes negative consequences?
>
> **Refactored Solution:** How do we avoid, minimize, or refactor the AntiPattern problem?

A mini-AntiPattern can include a cartoon or an anecdote in a sidebar format, along with a discussion of how the AntiPattern is resolved. It's similar in purpose to micro-patterns and mini-patterns that provide a concise pattern description with a little less formality.

Full AntiPattern Template

The following AntiPattern template is used throughout the remainder of this book to fully document AntiPatterns. A number of simpler AntiPatterns are contained in sidebars in a minimal format called a mini-AntiPattern (previous template). The full AntiPattern template comprises a number of required and optional sections. The core sections are the *general form* of the AntiPattern and the *refactored solution*. They provide the solution/solution pair that comprises an AntiPattern.

- *AntiPattern Name.* The AntiPattern name is a unique noun phrase. It's intended to be pejorative. The solution name of the pattern introduces new terminology. The name is used for future reference to the principles contained in the AntiPattern. It's important that every AntiPattern have a name, in order to uniquely identify it. Names are critical as they form the basis for an organization's terminology when members discuss and document software and architectures.
- *Also Known As.* This identifies additional popular or descriptive names and phrases for this AntiPattern.
- *Most Frequent Scale.* Scale is indicated via a keyword from the reference model. This section identifies where this AntiPattern fits into the software design-level model (refer back to Figure 2.7). Each pattern is logically placed where the AntiPattern is most applicable. A secondary consideration for placement concerns the scale of the resulting solution. You can choose from idiom, micro-architecture, framework, application, system, enterprise, or global/industry. Scale also scopes the dimensions of the solution. Some patterns define useful solutions at several scales. The form of the rescaled solutions is also described in the AntiPattern template.
- *Refactored Solution Name.* This identifies the refactored solution pattern.
- *Refactored Solution Type.* This section contains keywords from the reference. From SDLM, it identifies the type of action that results from the AntiPattern solution. You can choose from software, technology, process, or role. *Software* indicates that new software is created by the solution. *Technology* indicates that the solution entails acquisition of a technology or product. *Process* indicates that the solution entails pursuing a process. *Role* indicates that the solution entails assigning responsibility to an individual or group. These four different kinds of solution types are detailed as follows:

1. *Software* patterns comprise the overwhelming majority of the patterns included in the AntiPatterns catalog. Software patterns involve the creation of new software. The vast majority of the design patterns currently available in the industry are software patterns.

2. *Technology* patterns solve software problems through adoption of a technology such as Java, as opposed to programming the capability from scratch. Technology patterns are also design patterns in that they result in software design and implementation, although the method of acquisition is different. Technology patterns may involve some programming, for example, creating an object wrapper for a commercial software module.

3. *Process* patterns provide the definition of activities that are consistently repeatable for a given solution.

4. *Role* patterns solve software problems by allocating clear responsibilities to organizational stakeholders. Process and role patterns are included because of the significant effect that communication and the human organization have upon software problem solving. Occasionally, we have found that a simple process or clarification of responsibilities provides the most effective *action lever* for solving a technical problem.

- *Root Causes.* This section contains keywords from the reference model. These are the general causes for this AntiPattern. Derived from the section on root causes in Chapter 2, choose from: haste, apathy, narrow-mindedness, sloth, avarice, ignorance, pride, or responsibility (the universal cause).

- *Unbalanced Forces.* This section contains keywords from the reference model, and identifies the primal forces that are ignored, misused, or overused in this AntiPattern. The choices include management of functionality, management of performance, management of complexity, management of change, management of IT resources, and management of technology transfer. Risk is an underlying force for all of these options. Note that management of IT resources pertains to general resource tracking and allocation issues, including finances.

- *Anecdotal Evidence.* This is an optional section. Often-heard phrases and comedic material associated with this AntiPattern appear in this section.

- *Background.* This is an optional section. The background can contain further examples of where problems occur or general background information that is useful or interesting.

- *General Form of this AntiPattern.* This section often includes a diagram, which identifies the general characteristics of this AntiPattern. This is not an example, but a generic version. A prose description explains the diagram (if any) and gives the general description of this AntiPattern. The refactored solution resolves the general AntiPattern posed by this section.

- *Symptoms and Consequences.* This is a bulleted list of symptoms and consequences that result from this AntiPattern.

- *Typical Causes.* This is a bulleted section in which the unique causes of this AntiPattern are identified (in addition to the root cases identified previously).

- *Known Exceptions.* AntiPattern behaviors and processes are not always wrong, and often there are specific occasions when this is the case. This section briefly identifies the primary exceptions to each full AntiPattern.

- *Refactored Solutions.* This section explains a refactored solution that resolves the forces in the AntiPattern identified in the general form section. This solution is described without variations; those are addressed in the variations section. The solution is structured in terms of solution steps.

- *Variations.* This is an optional section that lists any known major variations of this AntiPattern. In addition, if there are alternative solutions, they are described here as well. The variations section exists partly in order to enhance clarity in the general form and refactored solution sections. The solutions are explained clearly, without caveats about major options and alternative design points. The variations section includes these extensions, which expand upon the capabilities of the solution.

- *Example.* The example demonstrates how the solution is applied to the problem by paralleling the details of the solution. This section typically includes the following elements: problem diagram, problem description, solution diagram, and solution description. This section includes one or more examples of the AntiPattern abstracted from experience.

- *Related Solutions.* This section identifies any citations or cross-references that are appropriate. Any AntiPatterns that are closely related to this one are listed and the differences are explained. Relationships with design patterns from other pattern languages are identified and explained. Detailed citations are contained in the bibliography in the back of the book. The references to related patterns are an important aspect of the AntiPatterns. Each AntiPattern resolves some forces and creates new ones. The new forces can be resolved by related patterns, either at the same or another level. This section also highlights differences between similar patterns.

This section also includes related terminology, references, and resources. Related terminology is explained for two reasons: to distinguish our definitions from other terms using similar names, and to connect related concepts referred to by different names. These two ambiguities are the source of much confusion in software engineering circles. References include well-known terminology, example technologies, and relevant research. The references are particularly useful to experts who can use this information to rapidly relate this pattern to other known work. If an expert reviewer fully understands one or more of the references, then the core ideas of the pattern are already known by a different terminology. (We have encountered this effect in the use of other pattern languages. It sometimes takes significant time to resolve these terminology differences without this useful section.) This section serves as both a reference list and as an "also-known-as" list of synonyms with respect to other work. Resources include pointers to other kinds of information and organizations that address the problem.

- *Applicability to Other Viewpoints and Scales.* This section defines how the AntiPattern impacts the remaining viewpoints: managerial, architectural, or developer. It also describes the relevancy of the pattern to other levels. If a pattern assumes a different "name" at different levels, then it should be mentioned here. Some key questions addressed in this section include: What happens when the AntiPattern is applied at different levels? How effectively does it resolve the forces at the other scales? What new forces are introduced, and are they resolved as well? How do the key forces influencing the design patterns change with scale? How do the roles of the key design elements change with scale?

The AntiPatterns in Chapters 5–7 utilize this template to document the common dysfunctional practices in the software industry and suggests practical solutions that have been proven effective on at least three known occasions. These chapters discuss software development AntiPatterns, architectural AntiPatterns and managerial AntiPatterns. These levels were chosen to provide a comprehensive coverage of the critical issues involved in software projects.

Advice for Using AntiPatterns

There is a danger in using AntiPatterns to change existing organizational practices. Some early adopters used AntiPatterns in a destructive manner. Although they identified similarities with several of the AntiPatterns discussed in this work, rather than serving as a catalyst for change, these anti-social practices resulted in early retirement or reassignment to distant corporate offices. While assigning blame and pointing fingers may provide a temporary rush of satisfaction, this is not the intended use of software AntiPatterns.

It's important to remember that every company may be suffering from several AntiPatterns at any given moment. However, the absence of AntiPatterns does not guarantee that an organization will be successful. In fact, many organizations are successful despite repeated violations of common sense—that is, AntiPatterns. Certainly, resolving an AntiPattern can result in software improvement, but you don't have to address every AntiPattern to be successful. AntiPatterns are most appropriate for resolving chronic problems, especially when they must be proactively addressed in order to meet the organizational goals. Heed the advice: "If it's not broken, don't fix it; leave well enough alone."

The purpose of AntiPatterns is not to focus on dysfunctional software practices. Rather, the purpose is the development and implementation of strategies to fix the problems that arise. Improvements to software projects are best done incrementally. A plan that involves the simultaneous correction of several AntiPatterns is risky and ill-advised. By focusing on improving processes on a case-by-case basis, according to a well-conceived plan, the chances of successfully implementing a viable solution are markedly increased. Furthermore, implementing a solution is feasible only when the technical staff has the necessary skills to address the problem. When the technical knowledge is not sufficient to fully implement an AntiPattern solution, the cure can cause problems that are as bad or worse than the original malady.

Dysfunctional Environments

A dysfunctional work environment in the software industry is one in which discussions of organizational politics, controversy, and negativity dominate technical discourse. We have worked in and survived this type of environment in several software development organizations. We hate working in dysfunctional environments, and you should, too.

AntiPatterns are not intended to exacerbate dysfunctional work environments. Quite the contrary, the more dysfunctional an environment becomes, the less sophisticated, less enjoyable, and less productive the technical discourse is. More sophisticated technical discourse is necessary for software engineering to evolve. AntiPatterns are intended to create awareness. Using AntiPatterns, you can clearly see when dysfunctional practices lead to negative consequences. AntiPatterns give bad practices clear-cut names and characteristics. They enable you to quickly detect their presence, avoid or resolve them, and move on to more interesting and productive issues.

AntiPatterns cannot completely change the way you work. You are probably already successful in your software engineering career. AntiPatterns are meant to generate new awareness. They are intellectual tools to help you work through difficult situations and the inherent contradictions of the software business.

AntiPatterns and Change

Obviously, change is necessary in software development. When five out of six corporate software projects are unsuccessful, something is seriously wrong [Johnson 95]. And when something is wrong in an organization, the reason is almost always the same: People are not taking responsibility [Block 81]. Therefore, the most important change is to motivate people to take responsibility for problems. To help people to recognize their responsibilities, a form of intervention is required.

A classic intervention pattern is called Peeling the Onion. It's an interview technique that involves three questions (in this sequence):

1. What is the problem?
2. What are other people doing to contribute to this problem?
3. What are you doing to contribute to this problem?

This technique is used to gather information in an organization. Answering these questions builds awareness of individual responsibilities.

The first step in intervention is for the participants to admit that there is a problem. This is called consciousness raising. Software Anti-Patterns clearly define the most common problems, and the descriptions of their symptoms and consequences provide the means to detect problems and foresee their outcomes.

A key aspect of problem resolution is awareness of alternatives. Optimists will tell you there are always alternatives, and never, never, never be negative. Understanding that there are many alternatives to problematic practices is an important enabler in the implementation of change. In other words, the suggested AntiPattern solutions are only some of the many possible alternatives. Certain of the AntiPattern solutions may even be applicable to other AntiPatterns. Therefore, it's helpful to read all of the solutions, even if the AntiPattern's general form may not seem immediately applicable at first glance.

Fixed and Improvisational Responses

Patterns and AntiPatterns document some of the known alternative solutions. In response to stimuli, there are really only two kinds of responses: improvisational and fixed. An *improvisational response* involves making something up on the spur of the moment. It's *not* a pattern. A *fixed response* is something learned or practiced. It *is* a pattern or AntiPattern. Whether the response leads to positive or negative consequences depends upon the context and the execution of the pattern. If the context implies negative consequences, it's an AntiPattern. If the context implies positive outcomes, it's a pattern.

A pattern can become an AntiPattern if applied in the wrong context. This happens all the time in technology through built-in obsolescence terms such as "structured programming" and "Altair 8080." As a technology paradigm (pattern) ages, its shortcomings become well known. Eventually, the technology paradigm is perceived by most practitioners as an AntiPattern. This designation provides an important rationale for its replacement by new technology.

Writing New AntiPatterns

This book establishes the field of AntiPatterns research, but it does not define all possible software AntiPatterns. The analysis in Chapters 5–7, while reasonably comprehensive, barely scratches the surface of the number of AntiPatterns in the software development culture. Amazingly, some experienced people have not heard of the most basic AntiPatterns (Spaghetti Code and Stovepipe System). This book addresses that deficiency.

Software culture is full of isolated processes, and there is a great deal to learn from. AntiPatterns are an effective way to capture knowledge, transfer ideas, and foster communications. It's important that AntiPattern identification and documentation, along with a prescribed solution, be performed by software practitioners throughout the industry. The documentation of AntiPatterns is critical in disseminating information to others and arriving at industry consensus regarding what constitutes a dysfunctional practice and how to effectively engineer a solution. There are several key observations that will aid in your future work on patterns and AntiPatterns:

1. *Design patterns start with a recurring solution.* Design patterns are usually written from the bottom up; in other words, design patterns start with a recurring solution. The pattern author later adds context and forces. These context and forces are carefully crafted to lead you to a unique solution; the solution they started with. This explains why many design patterns are hard to read. As a design pattern reader, your first task is to decipher the logic behind the context and forces. Often, this logic leads you to one predetermined conclusion, rather than a real understanding of the forces, symptoms, and consequences of the real situation. The solution often seems obvious and simple, especially after the detailed, in-depth examination. AntiPatterns are an attempt to discuss the material appropriate for design patterns in a form much more palatable to the reader.

2. *AntiPatterns start with a recurring problem.* AntiPatterns are written from the top down. The AntiPattern starts with a commonly recurring design or practice. In typical, current context, the design or practice has obvious negative consequences. Select one or more pejorative names to identify the AntiPattern; the best names are those in popular use. The AntiPattern description includes learning elements such as symptoms, consequences, and causes. We choose to list symptoms and consequences together. Symptoms are in the past and present; consequences are in the future. Separating symptoms and consequences would establish a time frame for the state of the AntiPattern.

3. *Use study groups.* It is useful to discuss a written description of the AntiPattern and its refactored solution in a group environment; writer's workshops are one form. We have also found that less formal discussion groups made up of software peers, like book study clubs, are effective forums. The group can tell you whether the write-up is really an AntiPattern by recalling instances of the AntiPattern's occurrence.

   From our experience reviewing many design patterns and AntiPatterns in group situations, we find AntiPatterns much more fun! (than ordinary patterns) A good AntiPattern gets people involved in the discussion. Good AntiPatterns tend to inspire people to contribute their experiences and ideas.

4. *Become an AntiPattern author.* New AntiPattern authors can focus on recurring problems that are observed in several distinct contexts (at least three, similar to the rationale for describing software design patterns). To fully describe an AntiPattern, it's important to supplement the AntiPattern problem description and solution with a discussion of causes, symptoms, and one or more concrete examples to provide a clear context. In the solution, one of the examples should discuss the successful refactoring of a situation that uses the guidance given in the solution. This does not necessarily have to be from a current project, but it can relate to experience on other projects and in other companies, even when there was no direct involvement. The refactored solution does not have to be a unique solution, but it should be highly relevant.

Descriptions of related AntiPatterns and alternative solutions are included in the Variations section of each AntiPattern. In *CORBA Design Patterns* [Mowbray 97c], we found it useful to separate the variations in order to clarify the solution; in this way, the refactored solution is presented without caveats that can cause confusion.

Summary

Software AntiPatterns comprise a new research area, which is a derivative of design patterns. When this research began, it was assumed that it would be difficult to identify software AntiPatterns. But AntiPatterns were already commonplace in the software industry; in fact, the industry had created and employed AntiPatterns since the invention of programmable computers.

We believe AntiPatterns are a more effective way to communicate software knowledge than ordinary design patterns because:

- AntiPatterns clarify problems for software developers, architects, and managers by identifying the symptoms and consequences that lead to the dysfunctional software development processes.
- AntiPatterns convey the motivation for change and the need for refactoring poor processes.
- AntiPatterns are necessary to gain an understanding of common problems faced by most software developers. Learning from other developers' successes and failures is valuable and necessary. Without this wisdom, AntiPatterns will continue to persist.

5

Software Development
AntiPatterns

Our first exposure to software development AntiPatterns was through the presentations of Mike Akroyd, a hands-on software consultant to Motorola and other major firms [Akroyd 96]. The Akroyd AntiPatterns define classic problems in object-oriented software design. Some of the development AntiPatterns in this chapter are extensions of his concepts (see references). One attractive feature of all Akroyd AntiPatterns is the inclusion of a *refactored solution*, the incorporation of which gives AntiPatterns a valuable purpose: Not only do they point out trouble, but they also tell you how to get out of it.

Proper AntiPatterns define a migration (or refactoring) from negative solutions to positive solutions. AntiPatterns that describe only the negative solution are called *pseudo-AntiPatterns*. Think of pseudo-AntiPatterns as flaming e-mail diatribes. After working with the Akroyd AntiPatterns, we discovered examples of AntiPatterns and pseudo-AntiPatterns on the Internet. The Pattern Languages of Program Design (PLoP) conference also discussed some AntiPattern-related papers, such as the "Big Ball of Mud" [Foote 97].

Software Refactoring

A key goal of development AntiPatterns is to describe useful forms of software refactoring. *Software refactoring* is a form of code modification, used to improve the software structure in support of subsequent extension and long-term maintenance. In most cases, the goal is to transform code without impacting correctness.

Good software structure is essential for system extension and maintenance. Software development is a chaotic activity, therefore the implemented structure of systems tends to stray from the planned structure as determined by architecture, analysis, and design. Software refactoring is an effective approach for improving software structure. The resulting structure does not have to resemble the original planned structure. The structure changes because programmers learn constraints and approaches that alter the context of the coded solutions. When used properly, refactoring is a natural activity in the programming process. For example, the solution for the Spaghetti Code AntiPattern discussed later in this chapter defines a software development process that incorporates refactoring.

Refactoring is strongly recommended prior to performance optimization. Optimizations often involve compromises to program structure. Ideally, optimizations affect only small portions of a program. Prior refactoring helps partition optimized code from the majority of the software.

Formal Refactoring Transformations

Formal refactoring transformations include superclass abstraction, conditional elimination, and aggregate abstraction. These formal refactorings originated in Opdyke's PhD thesis [Opdyke 92]. They are called formal refactorings because implementations can be proven not to affect program correctness. It's also possible to automate these transformations. The following refactorings involve changes to object classes, implementations, and relationships.

- *Superclass abstraction.* This refactoring applies to two or more similar classes. A superclass abstraction creates an abstract class that merges the common implementations of several concrete classes. To perform a superclass abstraction, the program transformation involves: (a) transformation of similar method signatures to common method signatures, (b) creation of an abstract superclass, (c) code modification to merge selected implementations, and (d) migration of common methods to the abstract superclass.

- *Conditional elimination.* This refactoring applies when the structure and behavior of a class is heavily dependent upon a conditional statement. The steps are: (a) create new subclasses corresponding to each condition, (b) migrate the action code from the conditional to the new subclasses, and (c) redirect class references to refer to the subclass types as appropriate. This last change can affect constructors, type declarations, and invocations of overloaded methods. The modified references should maintain the original logical states from the conditional, as invariant assertions on the new classes.
- *Aggregate abstraction.* An aggregate abstraction reorganizes class relationships to improve their structure and extensibility. This transformation can take several forms: (a) conversion of inheritance relationships to aggregate relationships, (b) migration of aggregated classes to component relationships, or (c) migration of component relationships to aggregate relationships.

These three, large-grain refactorings are dependent upon dozens of small-grain program transformations [Opdyke 92], which are familiar to virtually all programmers. Examples of small-grain transformations include: (a) renaming classes, methods, and attributes; (b) creating new classes; (c) migrating functionality between classes; (d) converting direct references to indirect pointers, and so forth. For a complete list, consult Opdyke (1992).

Development AntiPattern Summaries

Development AntiPatterns utilize various formal and informal refactoring approaches. The following summaries provide an overview of the Development AntiPatterns found in this chapter and focus on the development AntiPattern problem. Included are descriptions of both development and mini-AntiPatterns. The refactored solutions appear in the appropriate AntiPattern templates that follow the summaries.

The Blob: Procedural-style design leads to one object with a lion's share of the responsibilities, while most other objects only hold data or execute simple processes. The solution includes refactoring the design to distribute responsibilities more uniformly and isolating the effect of changes.

Continuous Obsolescence: Technology is changing so rapidly that developers often have trouble keeping up with current versions of software and finding combinations of product releases that work together. Given that every commercial product line evolves through new releases, the situation is becoming more difficult for developers to cope with. Finding compatible releases of products that successfully interoperate is even harder.

Lava Flow: Dead code and forgotten design information is frozen in an ever-changing design. This is analogous to a Lava Flow with hardening globules of rocky material. The refactored solution includes a configuration management process that eliminates dead code and evolves or refactors design toward increasing quality.

Ambiguous Viewpoint: Object-oriented analysis and design (OOA&D) models are often presented without clarifying the viewpoint represented by the model. By default, OOA&D models denote an implementation viewpoint that is potentially the least useful. Mixed viewpoints don't allow the fundamental separation of interfaces from implementation details, which is one of the primary benefits of the object-oriented paradigm.

Functional Decomposition: This AntiPattern is the output of experienced, nonobject-oriented developers who design and implement an application in an object-oriented language. The resulting code resembles a structural language (Pascal, FORTRAN) in class structure. It can be incredibly complex as smart procedural developers devise very "clever" ways to replicate their time-tested methods in an object-oriented architecture.

Poltergeists: Poltergeists are classes with very limited roles and effective life cycles. They often start processes for other objects. The refactored solution includes a reallocation of responsibilities to longer-lived objects that eliminate the Poltergeists.

Boat Anchor: A Boat Anchor is a piece of software or hardware that serves no useful purpose on the current project. Often, the Boat Anchor is a costly acquisition, which makes the purchase even more ironic.

Golden Hammer: A Golden Hammer is a familiar technology or concept applied obsessively to many software problems. The solution involves expanding the knowledge of developers through education, training, and book study groups to expose developers to alternative technologies and approaches.

Dead End: A Dead End is reached by modifying a reusable component if the modified component is no longer maintained and supported by the supplier. When these modifications are made, the support burden transfers to the application system developers and maintainers. Improvements in the reusable component are not easily integrated, and support problems can be blamed upon the modification.

Spaghetti Code: Ad hoc software structure makes it difficult to extend and optimize code. Frequent code refactoring can improve software structure, support software maintenance, and enable iterative development.

Input Kludge: Software that fails straightforward behavioral tests may be an example of an input kludge, which occurs when ad hoc algorithms are employed for handling program input.

Walking through a Minefield: Using today's software technology is analogous to walking through a high-tech mine field [Beizer 97a]. Numerous bugs are found in released software products; in fact, experts estimate that original source code contains two to five bugs per line of code.

Cut-and-Paste Programming: Code reused by copying source statements leads to significant maintenance problems. Alternative forms of reuse, including black-box reuse, reduce maintenance issues by having common source code, testing, and documentation.

Mushroom Management: In some architecture and management circles, there is an explicit policy to keep system developers isolated from the system's end users. Requirements are passed second-hand through intermediaries, including architects, managers, or requirements analysts.

In addition to the preceding AntiPatterns, this chapter includes a number of mini-AntiPatterns that represent other common problems and solutions.

THE BLOB

AntiPattern Name: The Blob
Also Known As: Winnebago [Akroyd 96] and The God Class [Riel 96]
Most Frequent Scale: Application
Refactored Solution Name: Refactoring of Responsibilities
Refactored Solution Type: Software
Root Causes: Sloth, Haste
Unbalanced Forces: Management of Functionality, Performance, Complexity
Anecdotal Evidence: "This is the class that is really the *heart* of our architecture."

BACKGROUND

Do you remember the original black-and-white movie The Blob? Perhaps you saw only the recent remake. In either case, the story line was almost the same: A drip-sized, jellylike alien life form from outer space somehow makes it to Earth. Whenever the jelly thing eats (usually unsuspecting earthlings), it grows. Meanwhile, incredulous earthlings panic and ignore the one crazy scientist who knows what's happening. Many more people are eaten before they come to their senses. Eventually, the Blob grows so large that it threatens to wipe out the entire planet. The movie is a good analogy for the Blob AntiPattern, which has been known to consume entire object-oriented architectures (see Figure 5.1).

GENERAL FORM

The Blob is found in designs where one class monopolizes the processing, and other classes primarily encapsulate data. This AntiPattern is character-

FIGURE 5.1 The Blob.

ized by a class diagram composed of a single complex controller class surrounded by simple data classes, as shown in Figure 5.2. The key problem here is that the majority of the responsibilities are allocated to a single class.

In general, the Blob is a procedural design even though it may be represented using object notations and implemented in object-oriented languages. A procedural design separates process from data, whereas an object-oriented design merges process and data models, along with partitions. The Blob contains the majority of the process, and the other objects contain the data. Architectures with the Blob have separated process from data; in other words, they are procedural-style rather than object-oriented architectures.

The Blob can be the result of inappropriate requirements allocation. For example, the Blob may be a software module that is given responsibilities that overlap most other parts of the system for system control or system management. The Blob is also frequently a result of iterative development where proof-of-concept code evolves over time into a prototype, and eventually, a production system. This is often exacerbated by the use of primarily GUI-centric programming languages, such as Visual Basic, that allow a simple form to evolve its functionality, and therefore purpose, dur-

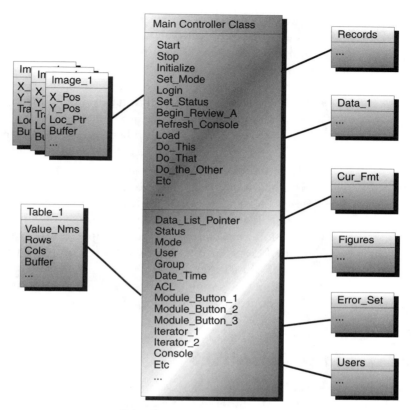

FIGURE 5.2 Controller Class.

ing incremental development or prototyping. The allocation of responsibilities is not repartitioned during system evolution, so that one module becomes predominant. The Blob is often accompanied by unnecessary code, making it hard to differentiate between the useful functionality of the Blob Class and no-longer-used code (see the Lava Flow AntiPattern).

SYMPTOMS AND CONSEQUENCES

- Single class with a large number of attributes, operations, or both. A class with 60 or more attributes and operations usually indicates the presence of the Blob [Akroyd 96].
- A disparate collection of unrelated attributes and operations encapsulated in a single class. An overall lack of cohesiveness of the attributes and operations is typical of the Blob.

- A single controller class with associated simple, data-object classes.
- An absence of object-oriented design. A program main loop inside the Blob class associated with relatively passive data objects. The single controller class often nearly encapsulates the applications entire functionality, much like a procedural main program.
- A migrated legacy design that has not been properly refactored into an object-oriented architecture.
- The Blob compromises the inherent advantages of an object-oriented design. For example, The Blob limits the ability to modify the system without affecting the functionality of other encapsulated objects. Modifications to the Blob affect the extensive software within the Blob's encapsulation. Modifications to other objects in the system are also likely to have impact on the Blob's software.
- The Blob Class is typically too complex for reuse and testing. It may be inefficient, or introduce excessive complexity to reuse the Blob for subsets of its functionality.
- The Blob Class may be expensive to load into memory, using excessive resources, even for simple operations.

TYPICAL CAUSES

- *Lack of an object-oriented architecture.* The designers may not have an adequate understanding of object-oriented principles. Alternatively, the team may lack appropriate abstraction skills.
- *Lack of (any) architecture.* The absence of definition of the system components, their interactions, and the specific use of the selected programming languages. This allows programs to evolve in an ad hoc fashion because the programming languages are used for other than their intended purposes.
- *Lack of architecture enforcement.* Sometimes this AntiPattern grows accidentally, even after a reasonable architecture was planned. This may be the result of inadequate architectural review as development takes place. This is especially prevalent with development teams new to object orientation.
- *Too limited intervention.* In iterative projects, developers tend to add little pieces of functionality to existing working classes, rather than add new classes, or revise the class hierarchy for more effective allocation of responsibilities.
- *Specified disaster.* Sometimes the Blob results from the way requirements are specified. If the requirements dictate a procedural solution,

then architectural commitments may be made during requirements analysis that are difficult to change. Defining system architecture as part of requirements analysis is usually inappropriate, and often leads to the Blob AntiPattern, or worse.

KNOWN EXCEPTIONS

The Blob AntiPattern is acceptable when wrapping legacy systems. There is no software partitioning required, just a final layer of code to make the legacy system more accessible.

REFACTORED SOLUTION

As with most of the AntiPatterns in this section, the solution involves a form of refactoring. The key is to move behavior away from the Blob. It may be appropriate to reallocate behavior to some of the encapsulated data objects in a way that makes these objects more capable and the Blob less complex. The method for refactoring responsibilities is described as follows:

1. Identify or categorize related attributes and operations according to contracts. These contracts should be cohesive in that they all directly relate to a common focus, behavior, or function within the overall system. For example, a library system architecture diagram is represented with a potential Blob class called LIBRARY. In the example shown in Figure 5.3, the LIBRARY class encapsulates the sum total of all the system's functionality. Therefore, the first step is to identify cohesive sets of operations and attributes that represent contracts. In this case, we could gather operations related to catalog management, like Sort_Catalog and Search_Catalog, as shown in Figure 5.4. We could also identify all operations and attributes related to individual items, such as Print_Item, Delete_Item, and so on.

2. The second step is to look for "natural homes" for these contract-based collections of functionality and then migrate them there. In this example, we gather operations related to catalogs and migrate them from the LIBRARY class and move them to the CATALOG class, as shown in Figure 5.5. We do the same with operations and attributes related to items, moving them to the ITEM class. This both simplifies the LIBRARY class and makes the ITEM and CATALOG classes more than simple encapsulated data tables. The result is a better object-oriented design.

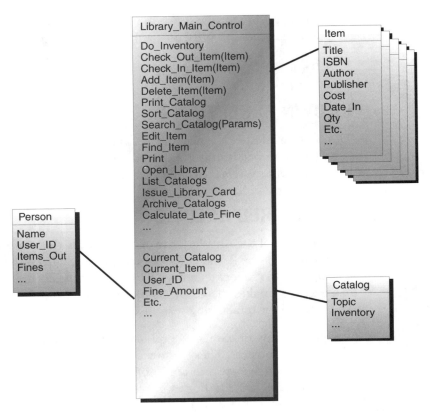

FIGURE 5.3 The Library Blob.

3. The third step is to remove all "far-coupled," or redundant, indirect associations. In the example, the ITEM class is initially far-coupled to the LIBRARY class in that each item really belongs to a CATALOG, which in turn belongs to a LIBRARY.

4. Next, where appropriate, we migrate associates to derived classes to a common base class. In the example, once the far-coupling has been removed between the LIBRARY and ITEM classes, we need to migrate ITEMs to CATALOGs, as shown in Figure 5.6.

5. Finally, we remove all transient associations, replacing them as appropriate with type specifiers to attributes and operations arguments. In our example, a Check_Out_Item or a Search_For_Item would be a transient process, and could be moved into a separate transient class with local attributes that establish the specific location or search criteria for a specific instance of a check-out or search. This process is shown in Figure 5.7.

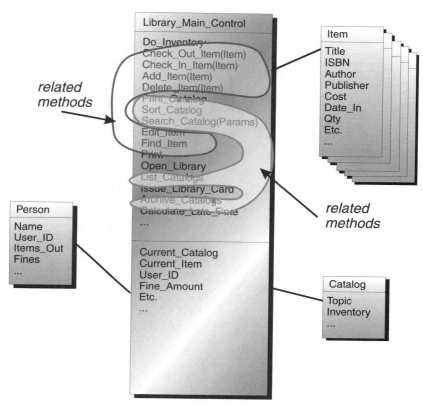

FIGURE 5.4 Regrouping the Blob by contracts.

VARIATIONS

Sometimes, with a system composed of the Blob class and its supporting data objects, too much work has been invested to enable a refactoring of the class architecture. An alternative approach may be available that provides an "80%" solution. Instead of a bottom-up refactoring of the entire class hierarchy, it may be possible to reduce the Blob class from a controller to a coordinator class. The original Blob class manages the system's functionality; the data classes are extended with some of their own processing. The data classes operate at the direction of the modified coordinator class. This process may allow the retention of the original class hierarchy, except for the migrations of processing functionality from the Blob class to some of the encapsulated data classes.

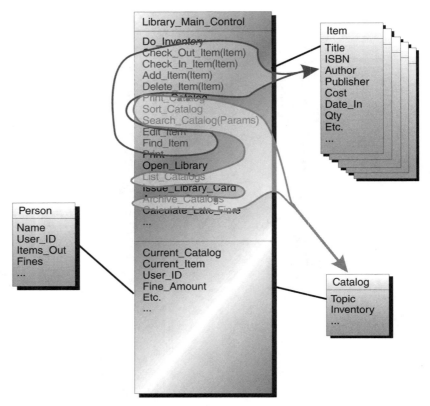

FIGURE 5.5 Migrating the contracted collections.

Riel identifies two major forms of the Blob AntiPattern. He calls these two forms God Classes: *Behavioral Form* and *Data Form* [Riel 96]. The Behavioral Form is an object that contains a centralized process that interacts with most other parts of the system. The Data Form is an object that contains shared data used by most other objects in the system. Riel introduces a number of object-oriented heuristics for detecting and refactoring God Class designs.

APPLICABILITY TO OTHER VIEWPOINTS AND SCALES

Both architectural and managerial viewpoints play key roles in the initial prevention of the Blob AntiPattern. Avoidance of the Blob may require

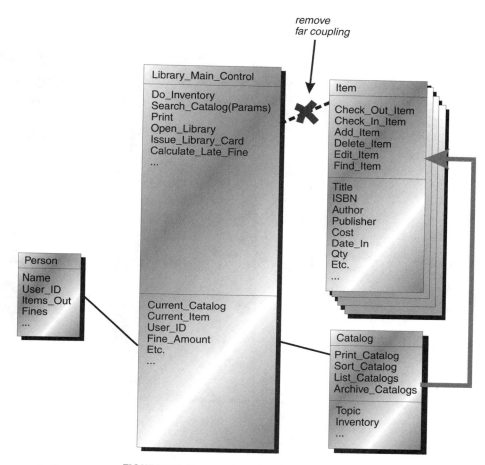

FIGURE 5.6 Removing the far couplings.

ongoing policing of the architecture to assure adequate distribution of responsibilities. It is through an architectural viewpoint that an emerging Blob is recognized. With a mature object-oriented analysis and design process, and an alert manager who understands the design, developers can prevent the cultivation of a Blob.

The most important factor is that, in most cases, it's much less expensive to create appropriate design than to rework design after implementation. Up-front investment in good architecture and team education can ensure a project against the Blob and most other AntiPatterns. Ask any insurance salesperson, and he or she may tell you that most insurance is purchased *after* it was needed by people who are poorer but wiser.

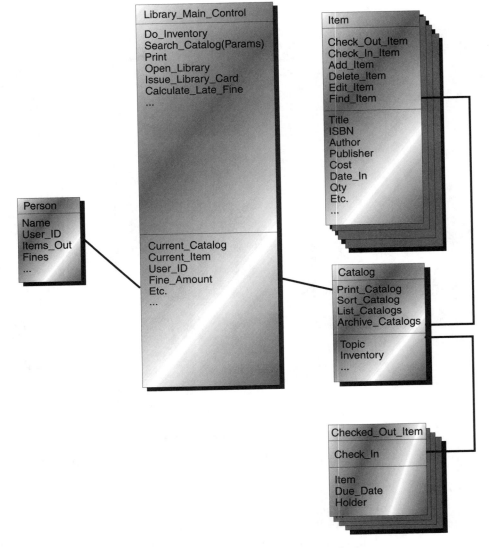

FIGURE 5.7 Removing transient associations.

EXAMPLE

A GUI module that is intended to interface to a processing module gradually takes on the processing functionality of background-processing modules. An example of this is a PowerBuilder screen for customer data entry/retrieval. The screen can:

1. Display data.
2. Edit data.
3. Perform simple type validation. The developer then adds functionality to what was intended to be the decision engine:

   - Complex validation.
   - Algorithms that use the validated data to assess next actions.

4. The developer then gets new requirements to:

   - Extend the GUI to three forms.
   - Make it script-driven (including the development of a script engine).
   - Add new algorithms to the decision engine.

The developer extends the current module to incorporate all of this functionality. So instead of developing several modules, a single module is developed, as shown in Figure 5.8. If the intended application is architected and designed, it is easier to maintain and extend. This would look like Figure 5.9.

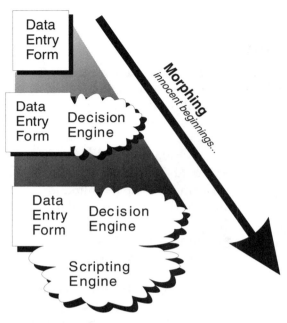

FIGURE 5.8 Life of a protoype GUI.

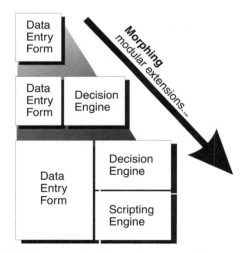
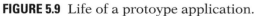

FIGURE 5.9 Life of a protoype application.

Mini-AntiPattern: Continuous Obsolescence

AntiPattern Problem

Technology is changing so rapidly that developers have trouble keeping up with the current versions of software and finding combinations of product releases that work together. Given that every commercial product line evolves through new product releases, the situation has become increasingly difficult for developers to cope with. Finding compatible releases of products that successfully interoperate is even harder.

Java is a well-known example of this phenomenom, with new versions coming out every few months. For example, by the time a book on Java 1.X goes to press, a new Java Development Kit obsoletes the information. Java is not alone; many other technologies also participate in Continuous Obsolescence. The most flagrant examples are products that embed the year in their brand names, such as Product98. In this way, these products flaunt the progression of their obsolescence. Another example is the progression of Microsoft dynamic technologies:

DDE

OLE 1.0

OLE 2.0

COM

ActiveX

DCOM

COM+

From the technology marketers' perspective, there are two key factors: *mindshare* and *marketshare*. Rapid innovation requires the dedicated attention of consumers to stay current with the latest product features, announcements, and terminology. For those following the technology, rapid innovation contributes to mindshare; in other words, there is always new news about technology X. Once a dominant marketshare is obtained, the suppliers' primary income is through obsolescence and replacement of earlier product releases. The more quickly technologies obsolesce (or are perceived as obsolete), the higher the income.

Refactored Solution

An important stabilizing factor in the technology market is *open systems standards*. A consortium standard is the product of an industry concensus that requires time and investment. Joint marketing initiatives build user awareness and acceptance as the technologies move into the mainstream. There is an inherent inertia in this process that benefits consumers, for once a vendor product is conformant to a standard, the manufacturer is unlikely to change the conformant features of the product.

The advantages of a rapidly obsolescing technology are transitive. Architects and developers should depend upon interfaces that are stable or that they control. Open systems standards give a measure of stability to an otherwise chaotic technology market.

Variations

The Wolf Ticket Mini-AntiPattern (Chapter 6) describes various approaches that consumers can use to influence product direction toward improved product quality.

LAVA FLOW

AntiPattern Name: Lava Flow
Also Known As: Dead Code
Most Frequent Scale: Application
Refactored Solution Name: Architectural Configuration Management
Refactored Solution Type: Process
Root Causes: Avarice, Greed, Sloth
Unbalanced Forces: Management of Functionality, Performance, Complexity
Anecdotal Evidence: "Oh *that!* Well Ray and Emil (they're no longer with the company) wrote that routine back when Jim (who left last month) was trying a workaround for Irene's input processing code (she's in another department now, too). I don't think it's used anywhere now, but I'm not really sure. Irene didn't really document it very clearly, so we figured we would just leave well enough alone for now. After all, the bloomin' thing works doesn't it?!"

BACKGROUND

In a data-mining expedition, we began looking for insight into developing a standard interface for a particular kind of system. The system we were mining was very similar to those we hoped would eventually support the standard we were working on. It was also a research-originated system and highly complex. As we delved into it, we interviewed many of the developers concerning certain components of the massive number of pages of code printed out for us. Over and over, we got the same answer: "I don't know what that class is for; it was written before I got here." We gradually realized that between 30 and 50 percent of the actual code that comprised this complex system was not understood or documented by any one currently working on it. Furthermore, as we analyzed it, we learned that the questionable code really served no purpose in the current system; rather, it was there from previous attempts or approaches by long-gone developers. The current staff, while very bright, was loath to modify or delete code that they didn't write or didn't know the purpose of, for fear of breaking something and not knowing why or how to fix it.

At this point, we began calling these blobs of code "lava," referring to the fluid nature in which they originated as compared to the basaltlike hardness and difficulty in removing it once it had solidified. Suddenly, it dawned on us that we had identified a potential AntiPattern.

Nearly a year later, and after several more data-mining expeditions and interface design efforts, we had encountered the same pattern so frequently that we were routinely referring to Lava Flow throughout the department (see Figure 5.10).

GENERAL FORM

The Lava Flow AntiPattern is commonly found in systems that originated as research but ended up in production. It is characterized by the lavalike "flows" of previous developmental versions strewn about the code landscape, which have now hardened into a basaltlike, immovable, generally useless mass of code that no one can remember much, if anything, about (see Figure 5.11). This is the result of earlier (perhaps Jurassic) developmental times when, while in a research mode, developers tried out several ways of accomplishing things, typically in a rush to deliver some kind of demonstration, thereby casting sound design practices to the winds and sacrificing documentation.

The result is several fragments of code, wayward variable classes, and procedures that are not clearly related to the overall system. In fact, these flows are often so complicated in appearance and spaghettilike that they seem important, but no one can really explain what they do or why they exist. Sometimes, an old, gray-haired hermit developer can remember certain details, but typically, everyone has decided to "leave well enough alone" since the code in question "doesn't really cause any harm, and might actually be critical, and we just don't have time to mess with it."

"Architecture is the art of how to waste space."

—Phillip Johnson

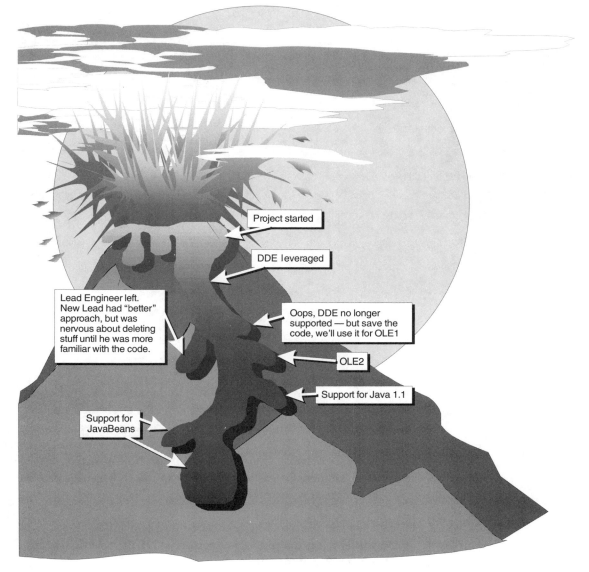

FIGURE 5.10 The Lava Flow of obsolete technologies and forgotten extensions leaves hardened globules of dead code in its wake.

```
...
// This class was written by someone earlier (Alex?) to manage the indexing
// or something (maybe). It's probably important. Don't delete. I don't
// think it's used anywhere - at least not in the new MacroINdexer module which
// may actually replace whatever this was used for...
class IndexFrame extends Frame
{
    // IndexFrame constructor
    //------------------------------------------------------------------------------
    public IndexFrame(String index_parameter_1)
    {
    // Note: need to add additional stuff here...
    super (str);
    }
    //------------------------------------------------------------------------------
...
```

FIGURE 5.11 Lava Flow source code listing.

Though it can be fun to dissect these flows and study their anthropology, there is usually not enough time in the schedule for such meanderings. Instead, developers usually take the expedient route and neatly work around them.

This AntiPattern is, however, incredibly common in innovative design shops where proof-of-concept or prototype code rapidly moves into production. It is poor design, for several key reasons:

- Lava Flows are expensive to analyze, verify, and test. All such effort is expended entirely in vain and is an absolute waste. In practice, verification and test are rarely possible.
- Lava Flow code can be expensive to load into memory, wasting important resources and impacting performance.
- As with many AntiPatterns, you lose many of the inherent advantages of an object-oriented design. In this case, you lose the ability to leverage modularization and reuse without further proliferating the Lava Flow globules.

SYMPTOMS AND CONSEQUENCES

- Frequent unjustifiable variables and code fragments in the system.
- Undocumented complex, important-looking functions, classes, or segments that don't clearly relate to the system architecture.
- Very loose, "evolving" system architecture.
- Whole blocks of commented-out code with no explanation or documentation.
- Lots of "in flux" or "to be replaced" code areas.
- Unused (dead) code, just left in.
- Unused, inexplicable, or obsolete interfaces located in header files.
- If existing Lava Flow code is not removed, it can continue to proliferate as code is reused in other areas.
- If the process that leads to Lava Flow is not checked, there can be exponential growth as succeeding developers, too rushed or intimidated to analyze the original flows, continue to produce new, secondary flows as they try to work around the original ones, this compounds the problem.
- As the flows compound and harden, it rapidly becomes impossible to document the code or understand its architecture enough to make improvements.

TYPICAL CAUSES

- R&D code placed into production without thought toward configuration management.
- Uncontrolled distribution of unfinished code. Implementation of several trial approaches toward implementing some functionality.
- Single-developer (lone wolf) written code.
- Lack of configuration management or compliance with process management policies.
- Lack of architecture, or non-architecture-driven development. This is especially prevalent with highly transient development teams.
- Repetitive development process. Often, the goals of the software project are unclear or change repeatedly. To cope with the changes, the project must rework, backtrack, and develop prototypes. In response to demonstration deadlines, there is a tendency to make hasty

changes to code on the fly to deal with immediate problems. The code is never cleaned up, leaving architectural consideration and documentation postponed indefinitely.

■ Architectural scars. Sometimes, architectural commitments that are made during requirements analysis are found not to work after some amount of development. The system architecture may be reconfigured, but these inline mistakes are seldom removed. It may not even be feasible to comment-out unnecessary code, especially in modern development environments where hundreds of individual files comprise the code of a system. "Who's going to look in all those files? Just link em in!"

KNOWN EXCEPTIONS

Small-scale, throwaway prototypes in an R&D environment are ideally suited for implementing the Lava Flow AntiPattern. It is essential to deliver rapidly, and the result is not required to be sustainable.

REFACTORED SOLUTION

There is only one sure-fire way to prevent the Lava Flow AntiPattern: Ensure that sound architecture precedes production code development. This architecture must be backed up by a configuration management process that ensures architectural compliance and accommodates "mission creep" (changing requirements). If architectural consideration is short-changed up front, ultimately, code is developed that is not a part of the target architecture, and is therefore redundant or dead. Over time, dead code becomes problematic for analysis, testing, and revision.

In cases where Lava Flow already exists, the cure can be painful. An important principle is to avoid architecture changes during active development. In particular, this applies to computational architecture, the software interfaces defining the systems integration solution. Management must postpone development until a clear architecture has been defined and disseminated to developers. Defining the architecture may require one or more system discovery activities. System discovery is required to locate the components that are really used and necessary to the system. System discovery also identifies those lines of code that can be safely deleted. This activity is tedious; it can require the investigative skills of an experienced software detective.

As suspected dead code is eliminated, bugs are introduced. When this happens, resist the urge to immediately fix the symptoms without fully understanding the cause of the error. Study the dependencies. This will help you to better define the target architecture.

To avoid Lava Flow, it is important to establish system-level software interfaces that are stable, well-defined, and clearly documented. Investment up front in quality software interfaces can produce big dividends in the long run compared to the cost of jackhammering away hardened globules of Lava Flow code.

Tools such as the Source-Code Control System (SCCS) assist in configuration management. SCCS is bundled with most Unix environments and provides a basic capability to record histories of updates to configuration-controlled files.

EXAMPLE

We recently participated in a data-mining expedition site where we attempted to identify evolutionary interfaces that resulted from preliminary interface architectures that we originated and were in the process of updating. The system we mined was targeted because the developers had utilized our initial architecture in a unique way that fascinated us: Essentially, they constructed a quasi-event service out of our generic inter-application framework.

As we studied their system, we encountered large segments of code that baffled us. These segments didn't seem to contribute to the overall architecture that we had expected to find. They were somewhat incohesive and only very sparsely documented, if at all. When we asked the current developers about some of these segments, the reply was, "Oh that? Well we're not using that approach anymore. Reggie was trying something, but we came up with a better way. I guess some of Reggie's other code may depend on that stuff though, so we didn't delete anything." As we looked deeper into the matter, we learned that Reggie was no longer even at the site, and hadn't been there for some time, so the segments of code were several months old.

After two days of code examination, we realized that the majority of the code that comprised the system was most likely similar to that code that we already examined: completely Lava Flow in nature. We gleaned very little that helped us articulate how their architecture actually was constructed; therefore, it was nearly impossible to mine. At this point, we essentially gave up trying to mine the code and instead focused on the current developer's explanations of what was "really" going on, hoping to somehow codify their work into interface extensions that we could incorporate into our upcoming revisions to our generic interapplication framework.

One solution was to isolate the single, key person who best understood the system they had developed, and then to jointly write IDL with that person. On the surface, the purpose of the IDL we were jointly writing was to support a crisis demonstration that was weeks away. By utilizing the Fire Drill Mini-AntiPattern, we were able to get the systems developers to validate our IDL by using it to rapidly build a CORBA wrapper for their product for the demonstration. Many people lost a lot of sleep, but the demonstration went well. There was, of course, one side effect to this solution: We ended up with the interface, in IDL, which we had set out to discover in the first place.

RELATED SOLUTIONS

In today's competitive world, it is often desirable to minimize the time delay between R&D and production. In many industries, this is critical to a company's survival. Where this is the case, inoculation against Lava Flow can sometimes be found in a customized configuration-management (CM) process that puts certain limiting controls in place at the prototyping stage, similar to "hooks" into a real, production-class development without the full restraining impact on the experimental nature of R&D. Where possible, automation can play a big role here, but the key lies in the customization of a quasi-CM process that can be readily scaled into a full-blown CM control system once the product moves into a production environment. The issue is one of balance between the costs of CM in hampering the creative process and the cost of rapidly gaining CM control of the development once that creative process has birthed something useful and marketable.

This approach can be facilitated by periodic mapping of a prototyping system into an updated system architecture, including limited, but standardized inline documentation of the code.

 ## APPLICABILITY TO OTHER VIEWPOINTS AND SCALES

The architectural viewpoint plays a key role in preventing Lava Flows initially. Managers can also play a role in early identification of Lava Flows or the circumstances that can lead to Lava Flows. These managers must also have the authority to put the brakes on when Lava Flow is first identified, postponing further development until a clear architecture can be defined and disseminated.

As with most AntiPatterns, prevention is always cheaper than correction, so up-front investment in good architecture and team education can typically ensure a project against this and most other AntiPatterns. While this initial cost does not show immediate returns, it is certainly a good investment.

Mini-AntiPattern: Ambiguous Viewpoint

AntiPattern Problem

Object-oriented analysis and design (OOA&D) models are often presented without clarifying the viewpoint represented by the model. By default, OOA&D models denote an implementation viewpoint that is potentially the least useful. Mixed viewpoints don't allow the fundamental separation of interfaces from implementation details, which are one of the primary benefits of the object-oriented paradigm.

Refactored Solution

There are three fundamental viewpoints for OOA&D models: the business viewpoint, the specification viewpoint, and the implementation viewpoint. The business viewpoint defines the user's model of the information and processes. This is a model that domain experts can defend and explain (commonly called an analysis model). Analysis models are some of the most stable models of the information system and are worthwhile to maintain.

Models can be less useful if they don't focus on the required perspective(s). A perspective applies filters to the information. For example, defining a class model for a telephone exchange system will vary significantly depending upon the focus provided by the following perspectives:

- Telephone user, who cares about the ease of making calls and receiving itemized bills.
- Telephone operator, who cares about connecting users to required numbers.
- Telephone accounting department, which cares about the formulae for billing and records of all calls made by users.

Some of the same classes will be identified, but not many; where there are, the methods will not be the same.

The specification viewpoint focuses on software interfaces. Because objects (as abstract data types) are intended to hide implementation details behind interfaces, the specification viewpoint defines the exposed abstractions and behaviors in the object system. The specification viewpoint defines the software boundaries between objects in the system.

The implementation viewpoint defines the internal details of the objects. Implementation models are often called design models in practice. To be an accurate model of the software, design models must be maintained continuously as the software is developed and modified. Since an out-of-date model is useless, only selected design models are pertinent to maintain; in particular, those design models that depict complex aspects of the system.

FUNCTIONAL DECOMPOSITION

AntiPattern Name: Functional Decomposition
Also Known As: No Object-Oriented AntiPattern "No OO" [Akroyd 96]
Most Frequent Scale: Application
Refactored Solution Name: Object-Oriented Reengineering
Refactored Solution Type: Process
Root Causes: Avarice, Greed, Sloth
Unbalanced Forces: Management of Complexity, Change
Anecdotal Evidence: "This is our 'main' routine, here in the class called LISTENER."

BACKGROUND

Functional Decomposition is good in a procedural programming environment. It's even useful for understanding the modular nature of a larger-scale application. Unfortunately, it doesn't translate directly into a class hierarchy, and this is where the problem begins. In defining this Anti-Pattern, the authors started with Michael Akroyd's original thoughts on this topic. We have reformatted it to fit in with our template, and extended it somewhat with explanations and diagrams.

GENERAL FORM

This AntiPattern is the result of experienced, nonobject-oriented developers who design and implement an application in an object-oriented language. When developers are comfortable with a "main" routine that calls numerous subroutines, they may tend to make every subroutine a class, ignoring class hierarchy altogether (and pretty much ignoring object orientation entirely). The resulting code resembles a structural language such as Pascal or FORTRAN in class structure. It can be incredibly complex, as smart procedural developers devise very clever ways to replicate their time-tested methods in an object-oriented architecture.

You will most likely encounter this AntiPattern in a C shop that has recently gone to C++, or has tried to incorporate CORBA interfaces, or has just implemented some kind of object tool that is supposed to help them. It's usually cheaper in the long run to spend the money on object-oriented training or just hire new programmers who think in objects.

SYMPTOMS AND CONSEQUENCES

- Classes with "function" names such as Calculate_Interest or Display_Table may indicate the existence of this AntiPattern.
- All class attributes are private and used only inside the class.
- Classes with a single action such as a function.
- An incredibly degenerate architecture that completely misses the point of object-oriented architecture.
- Absolutely no leveraging of object-oriented principles such as inheritance and polymorphism. This can be extremely expensive to maintain (if it ever worked in the first place; but never underestimate the ingenuity of an old programmer who's slowly losing the race to technology).
- No way to clearly document (or even explain) how the system works. Class models make absolutely no sense.
- No hope of ever obtaining software reuse.
- Frustration and hopelessness on the part of testers.

TYPICAL CAUSES

- *Lack of object-oriented understanding.* The implementers didn't "get it." This is fairly common when developers switch from programming in a nonobject-oriented programming language to an object-oriented programming language. Because there are architecture, design, and implementation paradigm changes, object-orientation can take up to three years for a company to fully achieve.
- *Lack of architecture enforcement.* When the implementers are clueless about object orientation, it doesn't matter how well the architecture has been designed; they simply won't understand what they're doing.

And without the right supervision, they will usually find a way to fudge something using the techniques they do know.

- *Specified disaster.* Sometimes, those who generate specifications and requirements don't necessarily have real experience with object-oriented systems. If the system they specify makes architectural commitments prior to requirements analysis, it can and often does lead to AntiPatterns such as Functional Decomposition.

KNOWN EXCEPTIONS

The Functional Decomposition AntiPattern is fine when an object-oriented solution is not required. This exception can be extended to deal with solutions that are purely functional in nature but wrapped to provide an object-oriented interface to the implementation code.

REFACTORED SOLUTION

If it is still possible to ascertain what the basic requirements are for the software, define an analysis model for the software, to explain the critical features of the software from the user's point of view. This is essential for discovering the underlying motivation for many of the software constructs in a particular code base, which have been lost over time. For all of the steps in the Functional Decomposition AntiPattern solution, provide detailed documentation of the processes used as the basis for future maintenance efforts.

Next, formulate a design model that incorporates the essential pieces of the existing system. Do not focus on improving the model but on establishing a basis for explaining as much of the system as possible. Ideally, the design model will justify, or at least rationalize, most of the software modules. Developing a design model for an existing code base is enlightening; it provides insight as to how the overall system fits together. It is reasonable to expect that several parts of the system exist for reasons no longer known and for which no reasonable speculation can be attempted.

For classes that fall outside of the design model, use the following guidelines:

1. If the class has a single method, try to better model it as part of an existing class. Frequently, classes designed as helper classes to

another class are better off being combined into the base class they assist.

2. Attempt to combine several classes into a new class that satisfies a design objective. The goal is to consolidate the functionality of several types into a single class that captures a broader domain concept than the previous finer-grained classes. For example, rather than have classes to manage device access, to filter information to and from the devices, and to control the device, combine them into a single device controller object with methods that perform the activities previously spread out among several classes.

3. If the class does not contain state information of any kind, consider rewriting it as a function. Potentially, some parts of the system may be best modeled as functions that can be accessed throughout various parts of the system without restriction.

Examine the design and find similar subsystems. These are reuse candidates. As part of program maintenance, engage in refactoring of the code base to reuse code between similar subsystems (see the Spaghetti Code solution for a detailed description of software refactoring).

EXAMPLE

Functional Decomposition is based upon discrete functions for the purpose of data manipulation, for example, the use of Jackson Structured Programming. Functions are often methods within an object-oriented environment. The partitioning of functions is based upon a different paradigm, which leads to a different grouping of functions and associated data.

The simple example in Figure 5.12 shows a functional version of a customer loan scenario:

1. Adding a new customer.
2. Updating a customer address.
3. Calculating a loan to a customer.
4. Calculating the interest on a loan.
5. Calculating a payment schedule for a customer loan.
6. Altering a payment schedule.

Figure 5.13 then shows the object-oriented view of a customer loan application. The previous functions map to object methods.

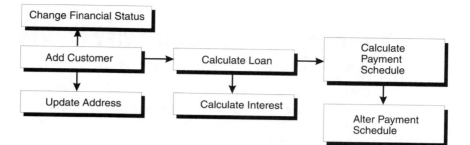

FIGURE 5.12 Functional decomposition of a customer loan system.

RELATED SOLUTIONS

If too much work has already been invested in a system plagued by Functional Decomposition, you may be able to salvage things by taking an approach similar to the alternative approach addressed in the Blob AntiPattern.

Instead of a bottom-up refactoring of the whole class hierarchy, you may be able to extend the "main routine" class to a "coordinator" class that manages all or most of the system's functionality. Function classes can then be "massaged" into quasi-object-oriented classes by combining them and beefing them up to carry out some of their own processing at the direction of the modified "coordinator" class. This process may result in a class hierarchy that is more workable [Fowler 97].

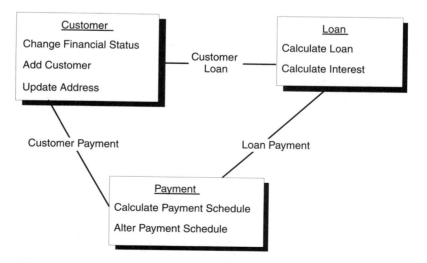

FIGURE 5.13 Object-oriented model of a customer loan system.

APPLICABILITY TO OTHER VIEWPOINTS AND SCALES

Both architectural and managerial viewpoints play key roles in either initial prevention or ongoing policing against the Functional Decomposition AntiPattern. If a correct object-oriented architecture was initially planned and the problem occurred in the development stages, then it is a management challenge to enforce the initial architecture. Likewise, if the cause was a general lack of incorrect architecture initially, then it is still a management challenge to recognize this, put the brakes on, and get architectural help—the sooner the cheaper.

POLTERGEISTS

AntiPattern Name: Poltergeists

Also Known As: Gypsy [Akroyd 96], Proliferation of Classes [Riel 96], and Big DoIt Controller Class [Fowler 97]

Most Frequent Scale: Application

Refactored Solution Name: Ghostbusting

Refactored Solution Type: Process

Root Causes: Sloth, Ignorance

Unbalanced Force: Management of Functionality, Complexity

Anecdotal Evidence: "I'm not exactly sure what this class does, but it sure is important!"

 ## BACKGROUND

When Michael Akroyd presented the Gypsy AntiPattern at Object World West in 1996, he likened the transient appearance and then discrete vanishing of the gypsy class to a "Gypsy Wagon" that is there one day and gone the next. As we studied Akroyd's model, we wanted to convey more of the Gypsy's invoking function in the overall AntiPattern name. Thus, we felt that since poltergeists represent "restless ghosts" that cause "bump-in-the-night types of phenomena," that term better represented the "pop in to make something happen" concept of this AntiPattern while retaining the "here now then suddenly vanished" flavor of the initial Gypsy name (see Figure 5.14).

In the LISP language, as in many others, certain pure-evil programmers exist who take great glee in leveraging the "side effects" of certain language functions to mysteriously perform key functionality in their systems. Analysis and understanding of such systems is virtually impossible, and any attempt at reuse is considered insane.

FIGURE 5.14 Poltergeists: ghostly classes.

Like the Poltergeist "controller" class, the use of "side effects" to accomplish any principle task in an implementation is an incorrect utilization of the language or architecture tool, and should be avoided.

 GENERAL FORM

Poltergeists are classes with limited responsibilities and roles to play in the system; therefore, their effective life cycle is quite brief. Poltergeists clutter software designs, creating unnecessary abstractions; they are excessively complex, hard to understand, and hard to maintain.

This AntiPattern is typical in cases where designers familiar with process modeling but new to object-oriented design define architectures. In this AntiPattern, it is possible to identify one or more ghostlike apparition classes that appear only briefly to initiate some action in another more permanent class. Akroyd calls these classes "Gypsy Wagons" [Akroyd 96]. Typically, Gypsy Wagons are invented as controller classes that exist only to invoke methods of other classes, usually in a predetermined sequence. They are usually obvious because their names are often suffixed by _manager or _controller.

The Poltergeist AntiPattern is usually intentional on the part of some greenhorn architect who doesn't really understand the object-oriented concept. Poltergeist classes constitute bad design artifacts for three key reasons:

1. They are unnecessary, so they waste resources every time they "appear."
2. They are inefficient because they utilize several redundant navigation paths.
3. They get in the way of proper object-oriented design by needlessly cluttering the object model.

SYMPTOMS AND CONSEQUENCES

- Redundant navigation paths.
- Transient associations.
- Stateless classes.
- Temporary, short-duration objects and classes.
- Single-operation classes that exist only to "seed" or "invoke" other classes through temporary associations.
- Classes with "control-like" operation names such as start_process_alpha.

TYPICAL CAUSES

- *Lack of object-oriented architecture.* "The designers don't know object orientation."
- *Incorrect tool for the job.* Contrary to popular opinion, the object-oriented approach isn't necessarily the right solution for every job. As a poster once read, "There is no right way to do the wrong thing." That is to say, if object orientation isn't the right tool, there's no right way to implement it.

■ *Specified disaster.* As in the Blob, management sometimes makes architectural committments during requirements analysis. This is inappropriate, and often leads to problems like this AntiPattern.

KNOWN EXCEPTIONS

There are no exceptions to the Poltergeists AntiPattern.

REFACTORED SOLUTION

Ghostbusters solve Poltergeists by removing them from the class hierarchy altogether. After their removal, however, the functionality that was "provided" by the poltergeist must be replaced. This is easy with a simple adjustment to correct the architecture.

The key is to move the controlling actions initially encapsulated in the Poltergeist into the related classes that they invoked. This is explained in detail in the next section.

EXAMPLE

In order to more clearly explain the Poltergeist, consider the peach-canning example in Figure 5.15. We see that the class PEACH_CANNER _CONTROLLER is a Poltergeist because:

■ It has redundant navigation paths to all other classes in the system.
■ All of its associations are transient.
■ It has no state.
■ It is a temporary, short-duration class that pops into existence only to invoke other classes through temporary associations.

In this example, if we remove the Poltergeist class, the remaining classes lose the ability to interact. There is no longer any ordering of processes. Thus, we need to place such interaction capability into the remaining hierarchy, as shown in Figure 5.16. Notice that certain operations are added to each process such that the individual classes interact and process results.

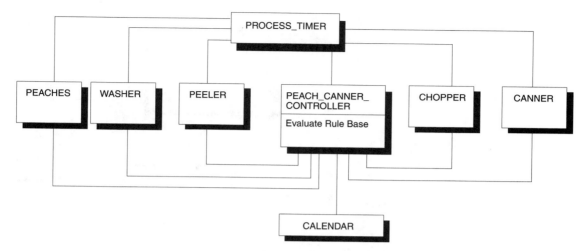

FIGURE 5.15 Controller class.

RELATED SOLUTIONS

The "80% solution" discussed in the Blob AntiPattern results in something that looks very similar to a Poltergeist. The "coordinator" class presented still manages all or most of the system's functionality and typically exhibits many of the features of a Poltergeist.

APPLICABILITY TO OTHER VIEWPOINTS AND SCALES

We elected to place this AntiPattern in the development chapter, rather than with the architectural AntiPatterns, because it usually occurs when developers are designing a system as they implement it (typically by the seat of their pants!) although certainly it may come as a result of failure to properly architect a system. Whether this presents evidence that Poltergeists are really a case of failed management is left to the reader.

As with most development AntiPatterns, both architectural and managerial viewpoints play key roles in initial prevention and ongoing policing against them. It's through an architectural viewpoint that an emerging AntiPattern is often recognized, and through effective management that it is properly addressed when not prevented outright.

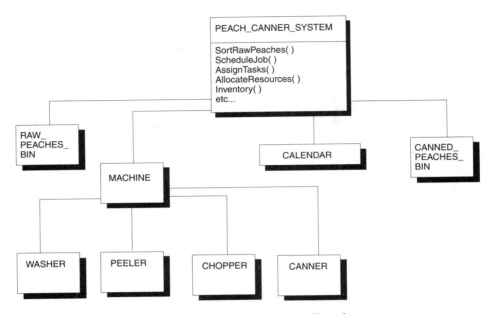

FIGURE 5.16 Refactored controller class.

Managers should take great care to ensure that object-oriented architectures are evaluated by qualified object-oriented architects as early as possible and then on an ongoing basis to prevent novice-induced errors such as this AntiPattern. Pay the price for good architecture up front!

Mini-AntiPattern: Boat Anchor

AntiPattern Problem

A Boat Anchor is a piece of software or hardware that serves no useful purpose on the current project. Often, the Boat Anchor is a costly acquisition, which makes the purchase even more ironic.

The reasons for acquiring a Boat Anchor are usually compelling at the time. For example, a policy or programmatic relationship may require the purchase and usage of a particular piece of hardware or software. This is a starting assumption (or constraint) of the software project. Another compelling reason is when a key manager is convinced of the utility of the acquisition. A sales practice called "very important person (VIP) marketing" targets the sales pitch at senior decision makers who have buying authority. VIP marketing often focuses on chief executive officers of small- to medium-size corporations. A commitment to the product is made without proper technical evaluation.

The consequences for managers and software developers are that significant effort may have to be devoted to making the product work. After a significant investment of time and resources, the technical staff realizes that the product is useless in the current context, and abandons it for another technical approach. Eventually, the Boat Anchor is set aside and gathers dust in some corner (if it's hardware).

Refactored Solution

Good engineering practice includes the provision for technical backup, an alternative approach that can be instituted with minimal software rework. The selection of technical backup is an important risk-mitigation strategy. Technical backups should be identified for most infrastructure technologies (upon which most software depends), and for other technologies in high-risk areas. Technical backups should be evaluated along with critical-path technologies in the selection process. Prototyping with evaluation licenses (available from most vendors) is recommended for both critical-path and back-up technologies.

Related AntiPatterns

Rational decision making is explained in the solution to the Irrational Management AntiPattern. Rational decision making can be used as an objective technology selection process to identify Boat Anchors prior to acquisition. The solution to the Smoke and Mirrors AntiPattern describes the practices for prepurchase technology evaluation, including review of product documentation and train-before-you-buy.

GOLDEN HAMMER

AntiPattern Name: Golden Hammer
Also Known As: Old Yeller, Head-in-the sand
Most Applicable Scale: Application
Refactored Solution Name: Expand your horizons
Refactored Solution Type: Process
Root Causes: Ignorance, Pride, Narrow-Mindedness
Unbalanced Forces: Management of Technology Transfer
Anecdotal Evidence: "I have a hammer and everything else is a nail (Figure 5.17)." "Our database is our architecture." "Maybe we shouldn't have used Excel macros for this job after all."

BACKGROUND

This is one of the most common AntiPatterns in the industry. Frequently, a vendor, specifically a database vendor, will advocate using its growing product suite as a solution to most of the needs of an organization. Given the initial expense of adopting a specific database solution, such a vendor often provides extensions to the technology that are proven to work well with its deployed products at greatly reduced prices.

GENERAL FORM

A software development team has gained a high level of competence in a particular solution or vendor product, referred to here as the Golden Hammer. As a result, every new product or development effort is viewed as something that is best solved with it. In many cases, the Golden Hammer is a mismatch for the problem, but minimal effort is devoted to exploring alternative solutions.

FIGURE 5.17 When your only tool is a hammer, everything else is a nail.

This AntiPattern results in the misapplication of a favored tool or concept. Developers and managers are comfortable with an existing approach and unwilling to learn and apply one that is better suited. This is typified by the common "our database is our architecture" mind-set, particularly common in the world's banking community.

Frequently, an advocate will propose the Golden Hammer and its associated product suite as a solution to most of the needs of an organization. Given the initial expense of adopting a specific solution, Golden Hammer advocates will argue that future extensions to the technology, which are designed to work with their existing products, will minimize risk and cost.

SYMPTOMS AND CONSEQUENCES

- Identical tools and products are used for wide array of conceptually diverse products.
- Solutions have inferior performance, scalability, and so on when compared to other solutions in the industry.
- System architecture is best described by a particular product, application suite, or vendor tool set.
- Developers debate system requirements with system analysts and end users, frequently advocating requirements that are easily accommo-

dated by a particular tool and steering them away from areas where the adopted tool is insufficient.

- Developers become isolated from the industry. They demonstrate a lack of knowledge and experience with alternative approaches.
- Requirements are not fully met, in an attempt to leverage existing investment.
- Existing products dictate design and system architecture.
- New development relies heavily on a specific vendor product or technology.

TYPICAL CAUSES

- Several successes have used a particular approach.
- Large investment has been made in training and/or gaining experience in a product or technology.
- Group is isolated from industry, other companies.
- Reliance on proprietary product features that aren't readily available in other industry products.
- "Corncob" proposing the solution (see Corncob AntiPattern in Chapter 7).

KNOWN EXCEPTIONS

The Golden Hammer AntiPattern sometimes works:

1. If the product that defines the architectural constraints is the intended strategic solution for the long term; for example, using an Oracle database for persistent storage and wrapped stored procedures for secure access to data.
2. If the product is part of a vendor suite that provides for most of the software needs.

REFACTORED SOLUTION

This solution involves a philosophical aspect as well as a change in the development process. Philosophically, an organization needs to develop a commitment to an exploration of new technologies. Without such a commitment, the lurking danger of overreliance on a specific technology or vendor tool set exists. This solution requires a two-pronged approach: A greater commitment by management in the professional development of their developers, along with a development strategy that requires explicit software boundaries to enable technology migration.

Software systems need to be designed and developed with well-defined boundaries that facilitate the replaceability of individual software components. A component should insulate the system from proprietary features in its implementation. If the system is developed using explicit software boundaries, the interfaces that make up the boundaries become points at which the software used in the implementation may be replaced with a new implementation, without affecting the other components in the system. An industry standard, such as the OMG IDL specification, is an invaluable tool for incorporating rigid software boundaries between components.

In addition, software developers need to be up to date on technology trends, both within the organization's domain and in the software industry at large. This can be accomplished through several activities that encourage the interchange of technical ideas. For example, developers can establish groups to discuss technical developments (design patterns, emerging standards, new products) that may impact the organization in the future. They can also form book study clubs to track and discuss new publications that describe innovative approaches to software development. In practice, we have found the book study club paradigm to be a very effective way to exchange ideas and new approaches. Even without full management buyin, developers can establish informal networks of technology-minded people to investigate and track new technologies and solutions. Industry conferences are also a great way to contact people and vendors and stay informed as to where the industries are headed and what new solutions are available to developers.

On the management side, another useful step is to adopt a commitment to open systems and architectures. Without it, developers often acquire the attitude that achieving short-term results by any means necessary is acceptable. Though this may be desirable in the short term, future results become problematic because rather than building upon a solid foundation of past successes, effort is expended reworking past software to conform to new challenges. Flexible, reusable code requires an investment in its initial development, otherwise long-term benefits will not be achieved [Jacobson 97]. Also, the danger of overreliance on a specific technology or vendor tool set is a potential risk in the product or project development. In-house research programs that develop proof-of-concept prototypes are effective for testing the feasibility of incorporating less risky open technologies into a development effort.

Another management-level way of eliminating or avoiding the Golden Hammer AntiPattern is to encourage the hiring of people from different areas and from different backgrounds. Teams benefit from having a broader experience base to draw upon in developing solutions. Hiring a database team whose members all have experience in using the same database product greatly limits the likely solution space, in comparison to a similar team whose experience encompasses a wide range of database technology solutions.

Finally, management must actively invest in the professional development of software developers, as well as reward developers who take initiative in improving their own work.

VARIATIONS

A common variation of Golden Hammer occurs when a developer uses a favorite software concept obsessively. For example, some developers learn one or two of the GoF patterns [Gamma 94] and apply them to all phases of software analysis, design, and implementation. Discussions about intent or purpose are insufficient to sway them from recognizing the applicability of the design pattern's structure and force-fitting its use throughout the entire development process. Education and mentoring is required to help people become aware of other available approaches to software system construction.

EXAMPLE

A common example of the Golden Hammer AntiPattern is a database-centric environment with no additional architecture except that which is provided by the database vendor. In such an environment, the use of a particular database is assumed even before object-oriented analysis has begun. As such, the software life cycle frequently begins with the creation of an entity-relationship (E-R) diagram that is produced as a requirements document with the customer. This is frequently destructive, because the E-R diagram ultimately is used to specify the database requirements; and detailing the structure of a subsystem before understanding and modeling the system presumes that the impact of the actual customer requirements on the system design is minimal. Requirements gathering should enable system developers to understand the user needs to the extent that the external behavior of the solution system is understood by the user as a black box [Davis 93]. Conceivably, many systems are built to satisfy user requirements without utilizing a database at all. However, with the Golden

Hammer AntiPattern in force, such possibilities are discounted up front, leading to every problem incorporating a database element.

Over time, the organization may develop several database-centric products that could have been implemented as independent systems. The database evolves into the basis for interconnectivity between applications, and it manages distribution and shared access to data. In addition, many implementation problems are addressed through using database proprietary features that commit future migrations to parallel the development of a technology of the implementation database. At some point, it may be necessary to interoperate with systems that either do not share the same database-centric architecture or are implemented using a different database that may not permit unrestricted access to their information. Suddenly, development becomes extremely expensive as unique, special-purpose connections are built to "bridge" between unique systems. If, however, some thought is given to the problem before the situation gets too far out of hand, a common framework can be developed, where products chosen for particular areas are selected based on standard interface specifications, such as CORBA, DCOM, or TCP/IP.

Another example is an insurance company with several stovepipe legacy systems that decided in its move to client/server that Microsoft Access should be the key part of the solution for persistence. The entire front end of the call-center system was architected around an early version of this product. Thereafter, the system's future was fully constrained by the development path of the database product because of a bad architecture decision. Needless to say, the system lasted less than six months.

RELATED SOLUTIONS

- *Lava Flow*. This AntiPattern results when the Golden Hammer Anti-Pattern is applied over the course of several years and many projects. Typically, older sections based on earlier versions of the Golden Hammer are delegated to remote, seldom-used parts of the overall application. Developers become reluctant to modify these sections, which build up over time and add to the overall size of the application while implementing functions that are seldom, if ever, used by the customer.
- *Vendor Lock-In*. Vendor lock-in is when developers actively receive vendor support and encouragement in applying the Golden Hammer AntiPattern. A software project is actively committed to relying upon

a single vendor's approach in designing and implementing an object-oriented system.

Mini-AntiPattern: Dead End

Also Known As

Kevorkian Component

AntiPattern Problem

A Dead End is reached by modifying a reusable component, if the modified component is no longer maintained and supported by the supplier. When these modifications are made, the support burden transfers to the application system developers and maintainers. Improvements in the reusable component cannot be easily integrated, and support problems may be blamed on the modification.

The supplier may be a commercial vendor, in which case this AntiPattern is also known as COTS Customization. When subsequent releases of the product become available, the special modifications will have to be made again, if possible. If fact, it may not be possible to upgrade the customized component, for various reasons such as cost and staff turnover.

The decision to modify a reusable component by a system's integrator is often seen as a workaround for the vendor's product inadequacies. As a short-term measure, this helps a product development progress, rather than slow it down. The longer-term support burden becomes untenable when trying to deal with the future application versions and the "reusable component" vendor's releases. The only time we saw this work was when the system's integrator arranged with the reusable component vendor that the SI modifications would be included in the next release of the vendor product. It was pure luck that their objectives were the same.

Refactored Solution

Avoid COTS Customization and modifications to reusable software. Minimize the risk of a Dead End by using mainstream platforms and

COTS infrastructure, and upgrading according to the supplier's release schedule. When customization is unavoidable, use an isolation layer (see Vendor Lock-In AntiPattern). Use isolation layers and other techniques to separate dependencies from the majority of the application software from customizations and proprietary interfaces.

A Dead End may be an acceptable solution in testbeds that support basic research such as throwaway code, and significant benefits are realized through the customization.

SPAGHETTI CODE

AntiPattern Name: Spaghetti Code
Most Applicable Scale: Application
Refactored Solution Name: Software Refactoring, Code Cleanup
Refactored Solution Type: Software
Root Causes: Ignorance, Sloth
Unbalanced Forces: Management of Complexity, Change
Anecdotal Evidence: "Ugh! What a mess!" "You *do* realize that the language supports more than one function, right?" "It's easier to rewrite this code than to attempt to modify it." "Software engineers don't write spaghetti code." "The quality of your software structure is an investment for future modification and extension."

BACKGROUND

The Spaghetti Code AntiPattern is the classic and most famous AntiPattern; it has existed in one form or another since the invention of programming languages. Nonobject-oriented languages appear to be more susceptible to this AntiPattern, but it is fairly common among developers who have yet to fully master the advanced concepts underlying object orientation.

GENERAL FORM

Spaghetti Code appears as a program or system that contains very little software structure. Coding and progressive extensions compromise the software structure to such an extent that the structure lacks clarity, even to the original developer, if he or she is away from the software for any length of time. If developed using an object-oriented language, the software may include a small number of objects that contain methods with very large implementations that invoke a single, multistage process flow. Furthermore, the object methods are invoked in a very predictable manner, and there is a negligible degree of dynamic interaction between the objects in the system. The system is very difficult to maintain and extend, and there is no opportunity to reuse the objects and modules in other similar systems.

SYMPTOMS AND CONSEQUENCES

- After code mining, only parts of object and methods seem suitable for reuse. Mining Spaghetti Code can often be a poor return on investment; this should be taken into account before a decision to mine is made.
- Methods are very process-oriented; frequently, in fact, objects are named as processes.
- The flow of execution is dictated by object implementation, not by the clients of the objects.
- Minimal relationships exist between objects.
- Many object methods have no parameters, and utilize class or global variables for processing.
- The pattern of use of objects is very predictable.
- Code is difficult to reuse, and when it is, it is often through cloning. In many cases, however, code is never considered for reuse.
- Object-oriented talent from industry is difficult to retain.
- Benefits of object orientation are lost; inheritance is not used to extend the system; polymorphism is not used.
- Follow-on maintenance efforts contribute to the problem.
- Software quickly reaches a point of diminishing returns; the effort involved in maintaining an existing code base is greater than the cost of developing a new solution from the ground up.

"First things first, second things never."

—Shirley Conran

TYPICAL CAUSES

- Inexperience with object-oriented design technologies.
- No mentoring in place; ineffective code reviews.
- No design prior to implementation.
- Frequently the result of developers working in isolation.

KNOWN EXCEPTIONS

The Spaghetti Code AntiPattern is reasonably acceptable when the interfaces are coherent and only the implementation is spaghetti. This is somewhat like wrapping a nonobject-oriented piece of code. If the lifetime of the component is short and cleanly isolated from the rest of the system, then some amount of poor code may be tolerable.

The reality of the software industry is that software concerns usually are subservient to business concerns, and, on occasion, business success is contingent on delivering a software product as rapidly as possible. If the domain is not familiar to the software architects and developers, it may be better to develop products to gain an understanding of the domain with the intention of designing products with an improved architecture at some later date [Foote 97].

REFACTORED SOLUTION

Software refactoring (or code cleanup) is an essential part of software development [Opdyke 92]. Seventy percent or more of software cost is due to extensions, so it is critical to maintain a coherent software structure that supports extension. When the structure becomes compromised through supporting unanticipated requirements, the ability of the code to support extensions becomes limited, and eventually, nonexistent. Unfortunately, the term "code cleanup" does not appeal to pointy-haired managers, so it may be best to discuss this issue using an alternative term such as "software investment." After all, in a very real sense, code cleanup is the maintenance of software investment. Well-structured code will have a longer life cycle and be better able to support changes in the business and underlying technology.

Ideally, code cleanup should be a natural part of the development process. As each feature (or group of features) is added to the code, code cleanup should follow what restores or improves the code structure. This can occur on an hourly or daily basis, depending on the frequency of the addition of new features.

Code cleanup also supports performance enhancement. Typically, performance optimization follows the 90/10 rule, where only 10 percent of the code needs modification in order to achieve 90 percent of the optimal performance. For single-subsystem or application programming, performance optimization often involves compromises to code structure. The first goal is to achieve a satisfactory structure; the second is to determine by measurement where the performance-critical code exists; the third is to carefully introduce necessary structure compromises to enhance performance. It is sometimes necessary to reverse the performance enhancement changes in software to provide for essential system extensions. Such areas merit additional documentation, in order to preserve the software structure in future releases.

The best way to resolve the Spaghetti Code AntiPattern is through prevention; that is, to think, then develop a plan of action before writing. If, however, the code base has already degenerated to the point that it is unmaintainable, and if reengineering the software is not an option, there are still steps that can be taken to avoid compounding the problem. First, in the maintenance process, whenever new features are added to the Spaghetti Code code base, do not modify the Spaghetti Code simply by adding code in a similar style to minimally meet the new requirement. Instead, always spend time refactoring the existing software into a more maintainable form. Refactoring the software includes performing the following operations on the existing code:

1. Gain abstract access to member variables of a class using accessor functions. Write new and refactored code to use the accessor functions.

2. Convert a code segment into a function that can be reused in future maintenance and refactoring efforts. It is vital to resist implementing the Cut-and-Paste AntiPattern (discussed next). Instead, use the Cut-and-Paste *refactored* solution to repair prior implementations of the Cut-and-Paste AntiPattern.

3. Reorder function arguments to achieve greater consistency throughout the code base. Even consistently bad Spaghetti Code is easier to maintain than inconsistent Spaghetti Code.

4. Remove portions of the code that may become, or are already, inaccessible. Repeated failure to identify and remove obsolete portions of code is one of the major contributors to the Lava Flow AntiPattern.

5. Rename classes, functions, or data types to conform to an enterprise or industry standard and/or maintainable entity. Most software tools provide support for global renaming.

In short, commit to actively refactoring and improving Spaghetti Code to as great an extent as resources allow whenever the code base needs to be modified. It's extremely useful to apply unit and system testing tools and applications to ascertain that refactoring does not immediately introduce any new defects into the code base. Empirical evidence suggests that the benefits of refactoring the software greatly outweigh the risk that the extra modifications may generate new defects.

If prevention of Spaghetti Code is an option, or if you have the luxury of fully engineering a Spaghetti Code application, the following preventative measures may be taken:

1. Insist on a proper object-oriented analysis process to create the domain model, regardless of how well the domain is understood. It is crucial that any moderate- or large-size project develop a domain model as the basis of design and development. If the domain is fully understood to the point that a domain model is not needed, counter with "If that's true, then the time to develop one would be negligible." If it actually is, then politely admit you were mistaken. Otherwise, the time that it takes justifies how badly it was needed.

2. After developing a domain model that explains the system requirements and the range of variability that must be addressed, develop a separate design model. Though it is valid to use the domain model as a starting point for design, the domain model must be maintained as such in order to retain useful information that would otherwise be lost if permitted to evolve directly into a design model. The purpose of the design model is to extract the commonality between domain objects and abstract in order to clarify the necessary objects and relationships in the system. Properly performed, it establishes the bounds for software implementation. Implementation should be performed only in order to satisfy system requirements, either explicitly indicated by the domain model or anticipated by the system architect or senior developers.

3. In the development of the design model, it is important to ensure that objects are decomposed to a level where they are fully understood by developers. It is the developers, not the designers, who must believe the software modules are easy to implement.

4. Once a first pass has been made at both the domain and design model, begin implementation based upon the plan established by the design. The design does not have to be complete; the goal is that the implementation of software components should always be according to some predefined plan. Once development begins,

proceed to incrementally examine other parts of the domain model and design other parts of the system. Over time, the domain model and the design model will be refined to accommodate discoveries in the requirements gathering, design decisions, and to cope with implementation issues. Again, Spaghetti Code is far less likely to occur if there is an overall software process in which the requirements and design are specified in advance of the implementation, instead of occurring concurrently.

EXAMPLE

This is a frequent problem demonstrated by people new to object-oriented development, who map system requirements directly to functions, using objects as a place to group related functions. Each function contains an entire process flow that completely implements a particular task. For example, the code segment that follows contains functions such as initMenus(), getConnection(), and executeQuery(), which completely execute the specified operation. Each object method contains a single process flow that performs all of the steps in sequence needed to perform the task. The object retains little or no state information between successive invocations; rather, the class variables are temporary storage locations to handle intermediate results of a single process flow.

• LINES 1–16

```
public class Showcase extends Applet
implements EventOutObserver {
//Globals
String
homeUrl="http://www.webserver.com
/images/"
;

int caseState;
String url="jdbc:odbc:WebApp";
Driver theDriver;
Connection con=null;
ResultSet rs,counter;
int theLevel;
int count=0;
String tino;
```

• LINES 17–32

```
int [] clickx;
int [] clicky;
String [] actions;
String [] images;
String [] spectra;
String showcaseQuery=null;
TextArea output=null;
Browser browser=null;
Node material=null;
EventInSFColor diffuseColor=null;
EventOutSFColor outputColor=null;
EventOutSFTime touchTime=null;
boolean error=false;
EventInMFNode addChildren;
Node mainGroup=null;
EventOutSFVec2f coord=null;
```

- LINES 33–80

```
EventInSFVec3f translation=null;
EventOutSFTime theClick=null;
Image test;
int rx,ry;
float arx,ary;
int b=0;
Graphics gg=null;

//Initialize applet
public void init() {
  super.init(); setLayout(null);
  initMenus();
  output=new TextArea(5, 40);
  add(output);
  browser=(Browser)
Browser.getBrowser((Applet)this);
  addNotify(); resize(920,800);
initUndoStack();
  caseState=0; theLevel=0;
  setClock(0);
 try { theDriver=new postgresql
 .Driver(); }
 catch(Exception e) {};
try { con=DriverManager
.getConnection(

"jdbc:postgresql://www.webserver
.com/WebApps",
    "postgres","");
    Statement stmt=con
    .createStatement();
    showcaseQuery="SELECT sid,
    case,
button,text , name, actions FROM
WebApp
WHERE case="+caseState+" and
level="+theLevel+";";
    rs=stmt.executeQuery
    (showcaseQuery);
    count=0; while (rs.next())
    count++;
    System.out.println("Count=
    "+count+"\n");
    rs=stmt.executeQuery
    (showcaseQuery);
  }
  catch(Exception e) {System.out
  .println(
```

- LINES 81–128

```
    "Error connecting and running:
    "+e);};
  nextButton=new
symantec.itools.awt.ImageButton();
  lastButton=new
symantec.itools.awt.ImageButton();
  try {
    nextButton.setImageURL(new
java.net.URL(

"http://www.webserver.com:8080/
images/next.jpg"));
    if (count<7) nextButton
    .setVisible(false);
    else nextButton.setVisible
    (true);
    lastButton.setImageURL(new
java.net.URL(

"http://www.webserver.com:8080/
images/last.jpg"));
  }
  catch(Exception e) {};
imageButtons=new
symantec.itools.awt.ImageButton[6];
l1=new
symantec.itools.awt.shape.Horizontal
Line();
l2=new
symantec.itools.awt.shape.Horizontal
Line();
v1=new
symantec.itools.awt.shape.Vertical
Line();
v2=new
symantec.itools.awt.shape.Vertical
Line();
bigspectralabel=new
java.awt.Label("Spectra");
gtruthlabel=new
java.awt.Label("GroundTruth");
clickx=new int[6];
clicky=new int[6];
actions=new String[6];
images=new String[6];
spectra=new String[6];
imageLabels =new java.awt.Label[6];
for (int I=0; i<6 ; i++) {
```

```
  imageButtons[i]=new
symantec.itools.awt.ImageButton();
  imageLabels[i]=new java.awt
  .Label();
  actions[i]=new String();
  images[i]=new String();
  spectra[i]=new String();

};
for (int i=0; i<6 ; i++) {
 try{
   rs.next();
   tino=rs.getString(4);
System.out.println(tino+"\n");
   actions[i]=rs.getString(6);}
  catch(Exception e) {System.out
  .println("SQL
Error :"+e);}
   try{
      System.out.print(tino+ln"\n");
      int len=tino.length();
      if (tino.startsWith
      ("INVISIBLE")) {
         imageButtons[i]
         .setVisible(false);
         imageLabels[i]
         .setVisible(false);}
      else {
      imageButtons[i].setImageURL(
         new java.net.URL
         (homeUrl+tino));
      imageButtons[i].setVisible
      (true);
      imageLabels[i].setText
      (rs.getString(5));
      imageLabels[i].setVisible
      (true);
   }
 } catch (Exception e) { System.out
 .println(
      "Died in accessor statement:
      "+e);
      }
}
11.reshape(0,6,775,1);add(11);
12.reshape(0,120,775,1);add(12);
v1.reshape(0,6,1,114);add(v1);
v2.reshape(775,6,1,114);add(v2);
```

```
bigspectralabel.reshape
(460,122,200,16);
bigspectralabel.setVisible(false);
gtruthlabel.reshape(124,122,200,16);
gtruthlabel.setVisible(false);
add(bigspectralabel);add
(gtruthlabel);
nextButton.reshape(2,12,84,40);
add(nextButton);
lastButton.reshape(2,56,84,40);
add(lastButton);
imageLabels[0].reshape
(124,12,84,16);
add(imageLabels[0]);
imageButtons[0].reshape(124,
30 ,84,84;)
add(imageButtons[0]);
imageLabels[1].reshape
(236,12,84,16);
add(imageLabels[1]);
imageButtons[1].reshape
(236,30,84,84);
add(imageButtons[1]);
imageLabels[2].reshape
(348,12,84,16);
add(imageLabels[2]);
imageButtons[2].reshape
(348,30 ,84,84);
add(imageButtons[2]);
imageLabels[3].reshape
(460,12,84,16);
add(imageLabels[3]);
imageButtons[3].reshape
(460,30 ,84,84);
add(imageButtons[3]);
imageLabels[4].reshape
(572,12,84,16);
add(imageLabels[4]);
imageButtons[4].reshape
(572,30 ,84,84);
add(imageButtons[4]);
imageLabels[5].reshape
(684,12,84,16);
add(imageLabels[5]);
imageButtons[5].reshape
(684,30 ,84,84);
add(imageButtons[5]);
 // Take out this line if you don't
```

• LINES 225-228 • LINES 229-232

```
use                                  getDocumentBase());
// symantec.itools.net.RelativeURL   //{{INIT_CONTROLS
symantec.itools.lang.Context         //}}
.setDocumentBase(                    }
```

RELATED SOLUTIONS

- *Analysis Paralysis.* This AntiPattern is the result of taking the solution to its logical extreme. Rather than developing code ad hoc without a design to guide the overall structure of the code, Analysis Paralysis produces a detailed design without ever reaching a point at which implementation can commence.
- *Lava Flow.* This AntiPattern frequently contains several examples of Spaghetti Code that discourage the refactoring of the existing code base. With Lava Flow, the code base had a logical purpose at some point in its life cycle, but portions became obsolescent, yet remained as part of the code base.

Mini-AntiPattern: Input Kludge

AntiPattern Problem

Software that fails straightforward behavioral tests may be an example of an Input Kludge, which occurs when ad hoc algorithms are employed for handling program input. For example, if the program accepts free text input from the user, an ad hoc algorithm will mishandle many combinations of legal and illegal input strings. The anecdotal evidence for an Input Kludge goes like this: "End users can break new programs within moments of touching the keyboard."

Refactored Solution

For nondemonstration software, use production-quality input algorithms. For example, lexical analysis and parsing software is readily available as freeware. Programs such as *lex* and *yacc* enable robust handling of text comprised of regular expressions and context-free language grammars. Employing these technologies for production-quality software is recommended to ensure proper handling of unexpected inputs.

Variation

Many software defects arise due to unexpected combinations of user-accesible features. Employing a *feature matrix* is recommended for sophisticated applications with graphical user interfaces. A feature matrix is state information in the program used to enable and disable features prior to user actions. When the user invokes a feature, the feature matrix indicates which other features must be disabled in order to avoid conflicts. For example, a feature matrix is often used to highlight and unhighlight menu commands prior to displaying the menu.

Background

Programmers are trained to avoid input combinations that cause program and system crashes. In a hands-on training course on OpenDoc, we used a preliminary alpha release of the technology that was not yet sufficiently robust for production-quality development. In other words, it was easy to crash the entire operating system with seemingly correct sequences of input commands and mouse operations. The students spent the first day experiencing numerous system crashes and waiting for system reboot. After attending the "crashing labs," we wondered whether the release was robust enough to enable any kind of sophisticated software development. By the end of the week, we had learned to work around the limitations and perform programming tasks and input operations that went well beyond our expectations formed the first day. We had internalized the input sequences that avoided system crashes.

FIGURE 5.18 The best way through a mine field is to follow some-body.

Mini-AntiPattern: Walking through a Mine Field

AntiPattern Problem

Using today's software technology is analogous to walking through a high-technology mine field [Beizer 97b]. (See Figure 5.18.) This mini-AntiPattern is also known as Nothing Works or Do You Believe in Magic? Numerous bugs occur in released software products; in fact, experts esti-mate that original source code contains two to five bugs per line of code. This means that the code will require two or more changes per line to remove all defects. Without question, many products are released well before they are ready to support operational systems. A knowledgeable software engineer states that, "There are no real systems, not even ours."

The location and consequences of software defects are unrelated to their apparent causes, and even a minor bug can be catastrophic. For example, operating systems (UNIX, Windows, etc.) contain many known and unknown security defects that make them vulnerable to attack; furthermore, the Internet has dramatically increased the likelihood of system attack.

End users encounter software bugs frequently. For example, approximately one in seven correctly dialed telephone numbers is not completed by the telephone system (a software-intensive application). And note, the rate of complaint is low compared to the frequency of software failures.

The purpose of commercial software testing is to limit risk, in particular, support costs [Beizer 97a]. For shrink-wrapped software products, each time an end user contacts a vendor for technical support, most or all of the profit margin is spent answering the call.

With simpler systems of the past, we were lucky. When a software bug occurred, the likely outcome was that nothing happened. With today's systems, including computer-controlled passenger trains and spacecraft control systems, the outcome of a bug can be catastrophic. Already, there have been half a dozen major software failures where financial losses exceeded $100 million.

Refactored Solution

Proper investment in software testing is required to make systems relatively bug-free. In some progressive companies, the size of testing staff exceeds programming staff [Cusumano 95]. The most important change to make to testing procedures is configuration control of test cases [Beizer 97a]. A typical system can require five times as much test-case software as production software. Test software is often more complex than production software because it involves the explicit management of execution timing to detect many bugs. When test software detects a bug, it is more likely to be the result of a bug in the test than in the code being tested. Configuration control enables the management of test software assets; for example, to support regression testing.

Other effective approaches for testing include automation of test execution and test design. Manual test execution is labor-intensive, and there is no proven basis for the effectiveness of manual testing. In contrast, automatic test execution enables running tests in concert with the build cycle. Regression tests can be executed without manual intervention, ensuring that software modifications do not cause defects in previously tested behaviors. Test design automation supports the generation of rigorous test suites, and dozens of good tools are available to support test design automation.

Variations

Formal verification is used in a number of applications to ensure an error-free design [Bowen 97]. Formal verification involves proving (in a mathematical sense) the satisfaction of requirements. Unfortunately, computer scientists trained to perform this form of analysis are relatively rare. In addition, the results of formal analysis are expensive to generate and may be subjective. Consequently, in general, we do not recommend this approach as feasible for most organizations.

Software inspection is an alternative approach that has been shown to be effective in a wide range of organizations [Gilb 95]. Software inspection is a formal process for review of code and documentation products. It involves careful review of software documentation in search of defects; for example, it is recommended that each inspector search for approximately 45 minutes per page of documentation. The defects discovered by multiple inspectors are then listed during an inspection logging meeting. The document editor can remove defects for subsequent review by the inspection team. Quality criteria are established for initial acceptance of the document by the inspection team and completion of the inspection process. Software inspection is a particularly useful process because it can be applied at any phase of development, from the writing of initial requirements documents through coding.

Background

"Do you believe in magic?" is a question sometimes posed by savvy computer professionals. If you believe that today's software systems are robust, you certainly do believe in magic.

The reality of today's software technology is analogous to an intriguing short story in Stephen Gaskin's *Mind at Play* [Gaskin 79]. In the story, people are driving shiny new cars and living comfortable lives. However, there is one man who wants to see the world as it really exists. He approaches an authority figure who can remove all illusions from his perception. Then, when he looks at the world, he sees people walking in the streets pretending to be driving fancy cars. In other words, the luxurious lifestyles were phony. In the end, the man recants, and asks to be returned to his prior state of disillusionment.

In one view, today's technology is very much like the Gaskin story. It is easy to believe that we are using mature software technologies on powerful, robust platforms. In fact, this is an illusion; software bugs are pervasive, and there are no robust platforms underneath.

CUT-AND-PASTE PROGRAMMING

AntiPattern Name: Cut-and-Paste Programming
Also Known As: Clipboard Coding, Software Cloning, Software Propagation
Most Applicable Scale: Application
Refactored Solution Name: Black Box Reuse
Refactored Solution Type: Software
Root Causes: Sloth
Unbalanced Forces: Management of Resources, Technology Transfer
Anecdotal Evidence: "Hey, I thought you fixed that bug already, so why is it doing this again?" "Man, you guys work fast. Over 400,000 lines of code in three weeks is outstanding progress!"

> "Never mind the quality, feel the width."
>
> —Vince Powell and Harry Driver

BACKGROUND

Cut-and-Paste Programming is a very common, but degenerate form of software reuse which creates maintenance nightmares. It comes from the notion that it's easier to modify existing software than program from scratch. This is usually true and represents good software instincts. However, the technique can be easily over used.

GENERAL FORM

This AntiPattern is identified by the presence of several similar segments of code interspersed throughout the software project. Usually, the project contains many programmers who are learning how to develop software by following the examples of more experienced developers. However, they are learning by modifying code that has been proven to work in similar situations, and potentially customizing it to support new data types or slightly customized behavior. This creates code duplication, which may have positive short-term consequences such as boosting line count metrics, which may be used in performance evaluations. Furthermore, it's easy to extend the code as the developer has full control over the code used in his or her application and can quickly meet short-term modifications to satisfy new requirements.

SYMPTOMS AND CONSEQUENCES

- The same software bug reoccurs throughout software despite many local fixes.
- Lines of code increase without adding to overall productivity.
- Code reviews and inspections are needlessly extended.
- It becomes difficult to locate and fix all instances of a particular mistake.
- Code is considered self-documenting.
- Code can be reused with a minimum of effort.
- This AntiPattern leads to excessive software maintenance costs.
- Software defects are replicated through the system.
- Reusable assets are not converted into an easily reusable and documented form.
- Developers create multiple unique fixes for bugs with no method of resolving the variations into a standard fix.
- Cut-and-Paste Programming form of reuse deceptively inflates the number of lines of code developed without the expected reduction in maintenance costs associated with other forms of reuse.

TYPICAL CAUSES

- It takes a great deal of effort to create reusable code, and organization emphasizes short-term payoff more than long-term investment.
- The context or intent behind a software module is not preserved along with the code.
- The organization does not advocate or reward reusable components, and development speed overshadows all other evaluation factors.
- There is a lack of abstraction among developers, often accompanied by a poor understanding of inheritance, composition, and other development strategies.

- The organization insists that code must be a perfect match to the new task to allow it to be reused. Code is duplicated to address perceived inadequacies in meeting what is thought to be a unique problem set.
- Reusable components, once created, are not sufficiently documented or made readily available to developers.
- A "not-invented-here" syndrome is in operation in the development environment.
- There is a lack of forethought or forward thinking among the development teams.
- Cut-and-Paste AntiPattern is likely to occur when people are unfamiliar with new technology or tools; as a result, they take a working example and modify it, adapting it to their specific needs.

KNOWN EXCEPTIONS

The Cut-and-Paste Programming AntiPattern is acceptable when the sole aim is to get the code out of the door as quickly as possible. However, the price paid is one of increased maintenance.

REFACTORED SOLUTION

Cloning frequently occurs in environments where white-box reuse is the predominant form of system extension. In white-box reuse, developers extend systems primarily though inheritance. Certainly, inheritance is an essential part of object-oriented development, but it has several drawbacks in large systems. First, subclassing and extending an object requires some knowledge of how the object is implemented, such as the intended constraints and patterns of use indicated by the inherited base classes. Most object-oriented languages impose very few restrictions, types of extensions can be implemented in a derived class and lead to nonoptimal use of subclassing. In addition, typically, white-box reuse is possible only at application compile time (for compiled languages), as all subclasses must be fully defined before an application is generated.

On the other hand, black-box reuse has a different set of advantages and limitations and is frequently a better option for object extension in moderate and large systems. With black-box reuse, an object is used as-is, through its specified interface. The client is not allowed to alter how the object interface is implemented. The key benefit of black-box reuse is that, with the support of tools, such as interface definition languages, the implementation of an object can be made independent of the object's interface. This enables a developer to take advantage of late binding by mapping an interface to a specific implementation at run time. Clients can be written to a static object interface yet benefit over time by more advanced services that support the identical object interface. Of course, the drawback is that the supported services are limited to those supported by the same interface. Changes to the interface typically must be made at compile time, similar to interface or implementation changes in white-box reuse.

The distinction between white-box and black-box reuse mirrors the difference between object-oriented programming (OOP) and component-oriented programming (COP), where the white-box subclassing is the traditional signature of OOP and the dynamic late binding of interface to implementation is a staple in COP.

Restructuring software to reduce or eliminate cloning requires modifying code to emphasize black-box reuse of duplicated software segments. In the case where Cut-and-Paste Programming has been used extensively throughout the lifetime of a software project, the most effective method of recovering your investment is to refactor the code base into reusable libraries or components that focus on black-box reuse of functionality. If performed as a single project, this refactoring process is typically difficult, long, and costly, and requires a strong system architect to oversee and execute the process and to mediate discussions on the merits and limitations of the various extended versions of software modules.

Effective refactoring to eliminate multiple versions involves three stages: code mining, refactoring, and configuration management. Code mining is the systematic identification of multiple versions of the same software segment. The refactoring process involves developing a standard version of the code segment and reinserting it into the code base. Configuration management is a set of policies drawn up to aid in the prevention of future occurrences of Cut-and-Paste Programming. For the most part, this requires monitoring and detection policies (code inspections, reviews, validation), in addition to educational efforts. Management buy-in is essential to ensure funding and support throughout all three stages.

EXAMPLE

There is one piece of code that we suspect has been cloned repeatedly throughout several organizations and probably is still cloned today. This piece of code has been observed several hundred times across dozens of organizations. It is a code file that implements a linked-list class without the use of templates or macros. Instead, the data structure stored by the linked list is defined in a header file, so each linked list is customized to operate only on the specified data structure. Unfortunately, the original author of the code (rumor has it he was originally a LISP programmer) introduced a flaw in the linked-list code: It failed to free the memory of an item when it was deleted; instead, it just rearranged the pointers. On occasion, this code has been modified to fix this defect; however, more often than not, it still exists. It's clearly the same code set; the variable names, the instructions, and even the formatting is exactly the same in each and every case. Even the file is typically named <prefix>link.c, where the prefix is one or two letters that cryptically refer to the data structure managed by the list.

RELATED SOLUTIONS

Spaghetti Code often contains several instances of the Cut-and-Paste Programming AntiPattern. Because Spaghetti Code is not structured for easy component reuse, in many cases, Cut-and-Paste Programming is the only means available for reusing existing segments of code. Of course, this leads to unnecessary code bloat and a maintenance nightmare, but empirical evidence suggests that Spaghetti Code without Cut-and-Paste Programming is typically an even worse mess than instances that make use of Cut-and-Paste Programming.

Cloning can be minimized in new development through the implementation of a software reuse process or organization [Jacobson 97]. Some degree of cloning is inevitable in large software development; however, when it occurs, there must be a formalized process for merging clones into a common baseline [Kane 97].

Mini-AntiPattern: Mushroom Management

Also known as Pseudo-Analysis and Blind Development, Mushroom Management is often described by this phrase: "Keep your developers in the dark and feed them fertilizer." An experienced system architect recently stated, "Never let software developers talk to end users." Furthermore, without end-user participation, "The risk is that you end up building the wrong system."

AntiPattern Problem

In some architecture and management circles, there is an explicit policy to isolate system developers from the system's end users. Requirements are passed second-hand through intermediaries, including architects, managers, or requirements analysts. Mushroom Management assumes that requirements are well understood by both end users and the software project at project inception. It is assumed that requirements are stable.

There are several mistaken assumptions in Mushroom Management:

- In reality, requirements change frequently and drive about 30 percent of development cost. In a Mushroom Management project, these changes are not discovered until system delivery. User acceptance is always a significant risk, which becomes critical in Mushroom Management.
- The implications of requirements documents are rarely understood by end users, who can more easily visualize the meaning of requirements when they experience a prototype user interface. The prototype enables end users to articulate their real needs in contrast to the prototype's characteristics.
- When developers don't understand the overall requirements of a product, they rarely understand the required component interaction and necessary interfaces. Because of this, poor design decisions are made and often result in stovepipe components with weak interfaces that do not fulfill the functional requirements.

Mushroom Management affects developers by creating an environment of uncertainty. Often, the documented requirements are not sufficiently detailed, and there is no effective way to obtain clarification. In order to do their job, developers must make assumptions, which may lead to pseudo-analysis, that is, object-oriented analysis that takes place without end-user participation. Some Mushroom Management projects eliminate analysis altogether and proceed directly from high-level requirements to design and coding.

Refactored Solution

Risk-driven development is a spiral development process based upon prototyping and user feedback. Risk-driven development is a specialization of iterative-incremental development process (see the Analysis Paralysis AntiPattern in Chapter 7). In this case, every increment is an external iteration. In other words, every project increment includes extensions to user-interface functionality. The increment includes a user-interface experiment, including hands-on experience. The experiment assesses the acceptability and usability of each extension, and the results of the experiment influence the direction of the project through the selection of the next iteration. Because the project frequently assesses user acceptance, and uses this input to influence the software, the risk of user rejection is minimized.

Risk-driven development is most applicable to applications, which are user-interface-intensive and require relatively simple infrastructure support. Personal computer applications that depend upon local files for storage infrastructure are strong candidates for risk-driven development.

Variations

Including a domain expert on the development team is a very effective way to have domain input on project decisions. Whenever there is a domain-specific question, team members have expertise on-hand. An important risk in this approach, however, is that the domain expert represents only one opinion from the domain community.

C H A P T E R

6

Software Architecture
AntiPatterns

Architecture AntiPatterns focus on the system-level and enterprise-level structure of applications and components. Although the engineering discipline of software architecture is relatively immature [Shaw 96], what has been determined repeatedly by software research and experience is the overarching importance of architecture in software development:

- Good architecture is a critical factor in the success of the system development [Booch 96, Shaw 96, Mowbray 95].
- Architecture-driven software development is the most effective approach to building systems [Booch 96, Horowitz 93]. Architecture-driven approaches are superior to requirements-driven, document-driven, and methodology-driven approaches. Projects often succeed in spite of methodology, not because of it [Mowbray 95].

Software architecture is a subset of the overall system architecture, which includes all design and implementation aspects, including hardware and technology selection. Important principles of architecture include the following:

- Architecture provides a view of the whole system [Hilliard 96]. This distinguishes architecture from other analysis and design models that focus on parts of a system.
- An effective way to model whole systems is through multiple viewpoints [ISO 96]. The viewpoints correlate to various stakeholders and technical experts in the system-development process [Hilliard 96].

Software architecture is distinguished from programming in several ways. First, the difference between an architect and a programmer is that the architect takes into account the cost of their decisions. Complexity is viewed by many in the architecture, management, and metrics fields as the key architecture design force [Shaw 96], and software complexity is related to software cost [Horowitz 93]. At a minimum, the architect is responsible for managing complexity.

Software architecture focuses on three aspects of software design [Shaw 96]:

1. *Partitioning.* The functional partitioning of software modules.
2. *Interfaces.* The software interfaces between modules.
3. *Connections.* The selection and characteristics of the technology used to implement the interface connections between software modules.

These architecture decisions are usually implemented by a much larger group of developers and maintainers. In order to manage these elements effectively, there are significant challenges for architects in managing the people and relationships. Some examples include: communicating the design to developers, achieving buy in from managers and developers, and managing the implementation and extension of the design.

Architecture AntiPatterns Summaries

The following AntiPatterns focus on some common problems and mistakes in the creation, implementation, and management of architecture. They are summarized here and explained in detail in the balance of the chapter.

Lack of commonality between systems in terms of design and technology is the cause of much frustration and the inability to provide interoperability and reuse between related systems. Improved enterprise architecture planning is used to align system developments.

Autogenerated Stovepipe: This AntiPattern occurs when migrating an existing software system to a distributed infrastructure. An Autogenerated Stovepipe arises when converting the existing software interfaces to distributed interfaces. If the same design is used for distributed computing, a number of problems emerge.

Stovepipe Enterprise: A Stovepipe System is characterized by a software structure that inhibits change. The refactored solution describes how to abstract subsystem and components to achieve an improved system structure. The Stovepipe Enterprise AntiPattern is characterized by a lack of coordination and planning across a set of systems.

Jumble: When horizontal and vertical design elements are intermixed, an unstable architecture results. The intermingling of horizontal and vertical design elements limits the reusability and robustness of the architecture and the system software components.

Stovepipe System: Subsystems are integrated in an ad hoc manner using multiple integration strategies and mechanisms, and all are integrated point to point. The integration approach for each pair of subsystems is not easily leveraged toward that of other subsystems. The Stovepipe System AntiPattern is the single-system analogy of Stovepipe Enterprise, and is concerned with how the subsystems are coordinated within a single system.

Cover Your Assets: Document-driven software processes often produce less-than-useful requirements and specifications because the authors evade making important decisions. In order to avoid making a mistake, the authors take a safer course and elaborate upon alternatives.

Vendor Lock-In: Vendor Lock-In occurs in systems that are highly dependent upon proprietary architectures. The use of architectural isolation layers can provide independence from vendor-specific solutions.

Wolf Ticket: A Wolf Ticket is a product that claims openness and conformance to standards that have no enforceable meaning. The products are delivered with proprietary interfaces that may vary significantly from the published standard.

Architecture by Implication: Management of risk in follow-on system development is often overlooked due to overconfidence and recent system successes. A general architecture approach that is tailored to each application system can help identify unique requirements and risk areas.

Warm Bodies: Software projects are often staffed with programmers with widely varying skills and productivity levels. Many of these people may be assigned to meet staff size objectives (so-called "warm bodies"). Skilled programmers are essential to the success of a software project. So-called heroic programmers are exceptionally productive, but as few as 1 in 20 have this talent. They produce an order of magnitude more working software than an average programmer.

Design by Committee: The classic AntiPattern from standards bodies, Design by Committee creates overly complex architectures that lack coherence. Clarification of architectural roles and improved process facilitation can refactor bad meeting processes into highly productive events.

Swiss Army Knife: A Swiss Army Knife is an excessively complex class interface. The designer attempts to provide for all possible uses of the class. In the attempt, he or she adds a large number of interface signatures in a futile attempt to meet all possible needs.

Reinvent the Wheel: The pervasive lack of technology transfer between software projects leads to substantial reinvention. Design knowledge buried in legacy assets can be leveraged to reduce time-to-market, cost, and risk.

The Grand Old Duke of York: Egalitarian software processes often ignore people's talents to the detriment of the project. Programming skill does not equate to skill in defining abstractions. There appear to be two distinct groups involved in software development: *abstractionists* and their counterparts the *implementationists*.

Mini-AntiPattern: Autogenerated Stovepipe

AntiPattern Problem

This AntiPattern occurs when migrating an existing software system to a distributed infrastructure. An Autogenerated Stovepipe arises when converting the existing software interfaces to distributed interfaces. If the same design is used for distributed computing, a number of problems emerge. For example, the existing interfaces may be using fine-grain operations to transfer information that may be inefficient in a distributed environment. Preexisting interfaces are usually implementation-specific, and will cause subsystem interdependencies when used in a larger-scale distributed system. Local operations often make various assumptions about location, including address space and access to the local file system. Excess complexity can arise when multiple existing interfaces are exposed across a larger-scale distributed system.

Refactored Solution

When designing distributed interfaces for existing software, the interfaces should be reengineered. A separate, larger-grained object model should be considered for the distributed interfaces. The interoperability functionality used by multiple subsystems should be the design center of the new interfaces. Design that is independent of particular subsystems can be achieved through architecture mining. The stability of the new interfaces is very important, given that separately compiled software will be dependent upon these new designs.

STOVEPIPE ENTERPRISE

AntiPattern Name: Stovepipe Enterprise

Also Known As: Islands of Automation

Most Frequent Scale: Enterprise

Refactored Solution Name: Enterprise Architecture Planning

Refactored Solution Type: Process

Root Causes: Haste, Apathy, Narrow-Mindedness

Unbalanced Forces: Management of Change, Resources, Technology Transfer

Anecdotal Evidence: "Can I have my own island (of automation)?" (See Figure 6.1.) "We're unique!"

BACKGROUND

Stovepipe is a popular term used to describe software systems with ad hoc architectures. It is a metaphor to the exhaust pipes of wood-burning stoves, so-called pot-bellied stoves. Since wood burning produces corrosive

FIGURE 6.1 Island of automation.

substances that erode metal, a stovepipe must be constantly maintained and repaired in order to avoid leakage. Often, the pipes are repaired with any materials at hand, thus wood-burning stovepipes quickly become a hodgepodge of ad hoc repairs—hence, the reference is used to describe the ad hoc structure of many software systems.

GENERAL FORM

Multiple systems within an enterprise are designed independently at every level. Lack of commonality inhibits interoperability between systems, prevents reuse, and drives up cost; in addition, reinvented system architecture and services lack quality structure supporting adaptability.

    At the lowest level are the standards and guidelines. These work like architectural building codes and zoning laws across enterprise systems. The next level up in the hierarchy is the operating environment [Mowbray 97c], which comprises infrastructure and object services. The top two layers include the value-added functional services and the mission-specific services. By selecting and defining all of these technologies independently, Stovepipe Enterprises "create islands of automation," isolated from the rest of the enterprise, as shown in Figure 6.2.

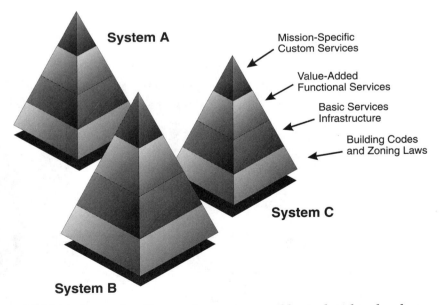

FIGURE 6.2 Stovepipe Enterprises are caused by isolated technology decisions at every level of coordination.

SYMPTOMS AND CONSEQUENCES

- Incompatible terminology, approaches, and technology between enterprise systems.
- Brittle, monolithic system architectures and undocumented architectures.
- Inability to extend systems to support business needs.
- Incorrect use of a technology standard.
- Lack of software reuse between enterprise systems.
- Lack of interoperability between enterprise systems.
- Inability of systems to interoperate even when using the same standards.
- Excessive maintenance costs due to changing business requirements; the need to extend the system to incorporate new products and technologies.
- Employee turnover, which causes project discontinuity and maintenance problems.

TYPICAL CAUSES

- Lack of an enterprise technology strategy, specifically:

    Lack of a standard reference model [Mowbray 97a].
    Lack of system profiles [Mowbray 97a].

- Lack of incentive for cooperation across system developments:

    Competing business areas and executives.

- Lack of communication between system development projects.
- Lack of knowledge of the technology standard being used.
- Absence of horizontal interfaces in system integration solutions.

KNOWN EXCEPTIONS

The Stovepipe Enterprise AntiPattern is unacceptable for new systems at an enterprise level in this day and age, particularly when most companies are facing the need to extend their business systems. However, when companies grow by takeover or merger, the Stovepipe AntiPattern is likely to occur; in which case, wrapping some systems can be an intermediate solution.

Another exception is when a common service layer is implemented across the enterprise systems. This is usually a manifestation of the Vendor Lock-In AntiPattern (discussed later in this chapter). These systems have a common horizontal component; for example, in banking, this is often true of databases such as DB2 and Oracle.

REFACTORED SOLUTION

Coordination of technologies at several levels is essential to avoid a Stovepipe Enterprise, as shown in Figure 6.3. Initially, the selection of standards can be coordinated through the definition of a standards reference model [Mowbray 97a]. The standards reference model defines the common standards and a migration direction for enterprise systems. The establishment of a common operating environment coordinates the selection of products and controls the configuration of product versions. Defining system profiles that coordinate the utilization of products and standards is essential to assure standards benefits, reuse, and interoperability. At least one system profile should define usage conventions across systems.

Through much experience, large enterprises have worked out some useful conventions for the definition of object-oriented architectures that can apply to many organizations. A key challenge of large-scale architecture is to define detailed interoperability conventions across systems while

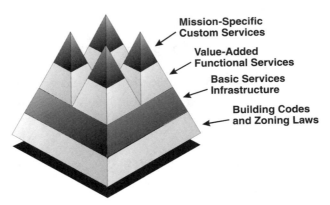

Mission-Specific
Custom Services

Value-Added
Functional Services

Basic Services
Infrastructure

Building Codes
and Zoning Laws

FIGURE 6.3 Coordinated technologies enable the establishment of common infrastructure and standards.

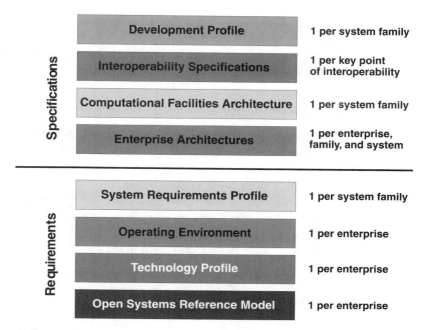

FIGURE 6.4 Multiple levels of coordination: Technology policies, requirements, and specifications may be necessary in large enterprises.

addressing technology strategy and requirements. For very large enterprises, experience has shown that four requirements models and four specification models are necessary to properly scope and resolve interoperability challenges, as shown in Figure 6.4.

The requirements models include:

1. Open Systems Reference Model.
2. Technology Profile.
3. Operating Environment.
4. System Requirements Profile.

The specification models include:

1. Enterprise Architectures.
2. Computational Facilities Architecture.
3. Interoperability Specifications.
4. Development Profile.

The following sections describe these models, each of which is part of an overall enterprise-architecture plan. The plan provides effective coordination between projects and reduces the need for point-to-point interoperability solutions.

OPEN SYSTEMS REFERENCE MODEL

An *open systems reference model* contains a high-level architecture diagram and a list of target standards for system development projects. The purpose of this model is to identify all of the candidate standards for projects, to coordinate open-systems strategies.

An off-the-shelf reference model of this type is the IEEE POSIX 1003.0 standard. This section of POSIX lists a wide range of open systems standards with respect to applicability, maturity, commercial support, and other factors. This POSIX standard is the starting point for many enterprise-specific reference models.

TECHNOLOGY PROFILE

When open-systems reference models were invented less than 10 years ago, they were thought to be the complete answer to systems interoperability. Unfortunately, developers were uncertain how these models affected their projects. A key problem is that reference models define future architecture goals with an unspecified time frame for implementation. Also, approximately a third of the items change status every year, due to the activities of standards bodies.

Technology profiles were invented to define the short-term standards plan for systems developers. A technology profile is a concise list of standards drawn from a reference model, which is considered a set of flexible guidelines; but technology profiles often mandate standards for current and new systems development projects. The technology profile clarifies what the developer has to do about the reference model standards; for example, the US-DOD Joint Technical Architecture is a technical profile that identifies standards for current implementation.

OPERATING ENVIRONMENT

Most large enterprises have heterogeneous hardware and software architectures, but even with a consistent infrastructure, varying installation practices can cause serious problems for enterprise interoperability, software reuse, security, and systems management.

An *operating environment* defines product releases and installation conventions that are supported by the enterprise, and establishes guidelines that must be flexible locally, to support R&D and unique systems requirements. The enterprise can encourage compliance with these conventions through technical support services and purchasing procedures; in other words, the enterprise can influence the adoption of the recommended environments by making them the easiest system configurations to obtain and support. Variations from the operating environment must be supported locally at extra cost.

SYSTEM REQUIREMENTS PROFILE

Enterprise architecture planning often produces broad, high-level requirements documents. For any particular family of systems, the requirements may be unclear to developers because of the sheer volume of information. A *system requirements profile* is a summary of key requirements for a family of related systems. The time frame is short term. Ideally, this document is only a few dozen pages in length, written to clarify the intended implementation goals for component systems and application development projects.

The system requirements profile identifies necessary scoping of system capabilities, and thus is the stepping-off point for enterprise requirements planning. The balance of the enterprise planning models are architecture and design specifications (described in subsequent sections), which are expressed through object-oriented models and comprise a set of object-oriented software architectures.

ENTERPRISE ARCHITECTURE

An *enterprise architecture* is a set of diagrams and tables that define a system or family of systems from various stakeholder viewpoints; thus, the enterprise architecture comprises views of the entire system. Current and future time frames are depicted, and each view addresses the issues posed by principal stakeholders, such as end users, developers, systems operators, and technical specialists.

Consistency of the architecture views and notations across projects is important, for enterprise architectures enable technical communication across projects. Reuse and interoperability opportunities can be identified when projects share their architectures. Since individual projects have the most knowledge of the technical details, project-specific architectures can be compiled into accurate, enterprisewide architectures.

COMPUTATIONAL FACILITIES ARCHITECTURE

As just explained, enterprise architectures are important communication tools for end users and architects. Each of the remaining specifications detail the computational architecture that defines interfaces for interoperability and reuse.

A *computational facilities architecture (CFA)* identifies and defines key points of interoperability for a family of systems. Each facility identifies a set of application program interfaces (APIs) and common data objects that are defined in detail in the interoperability specifications. A CFA partitions the enterprise's interoperability needs into manageable specifications; it also defines a road map of priorities and schedules for the facilities. This is necessary to initiate and guide the formulation of interoperability specifications.

Achieving consensus on the facilities in a CFA is a key challenge for many enterprises. Misunderstandings abound regarding the role of the facilities in relation to external requirements, the need for system independence, the definition of common abstractions, and the necessity of limiting the scope of the facilities.

INTEROPERABILITY SPECIFICATION

An *interoperability specification* defines the technical details of a computational facility. Typical interoperability specifications include APIs defined in IDL and common data object definitions.

Interoperability specifications establish key points of interoperability in a manner that is independent of any particular system of subsystem implementation. Architecture mining is a particularly effective process for creating these specifications [Mowbray 97c]. During system maintenance, the key points of interoperability become value-added entry points for system extension.

DEVELOPMENT PROFILE

An interoperability specification alone is not enough to assure successful integration, because the semantics of APIs can be interpreted differently by different implementors. Robust API designs have built-in flexibility that enable extension and reuse, and details of their usage are often discovered in the development process. Some of these details may be unique to a particular set of systems.

A *development profile* records the implementation plans and developer agreements that are necessary to assure interoperability and successful integration. A development profile identifies the parts of API specifications that are used, local extensions to the specification, and conventions that coordinate integration.

While it is important to configuration-control all of these models, development profiles are working documents that evolve throughout development and maintenance life cycles. Multiple development profiles may exist for a single API specification, each of which addresses the integration needs of a particular domain or family of systems.

EXAMPLE

System 1 and System 2 in Figure 6.5 represent two Stovepipe Systems in the same enterprise. While similar in many ways, these systems lack commonality; they use different database products, different office automation tools, have different software interfaces, and use unique graphical user interfaces (GUIs). The potential commonalities between these systems was not recognized and therefore not utilized by the designers and developers.

To resolve the AntiPattern, the enterprise starts by defining a standards reference model. This model, shown in Figure 6.6, selects some baseline standards for interchange across all systems. The next step is to choose products for an operating environment. In this case, both database products are selected, but only one of the office automation tools. This is the supported direction for future migration of the enterprise. The enterprise can facilitate this operating environment through enterprise product

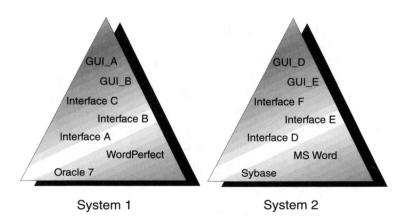

FIGURE 6.5 Stovepipe Enterprise with two systems.

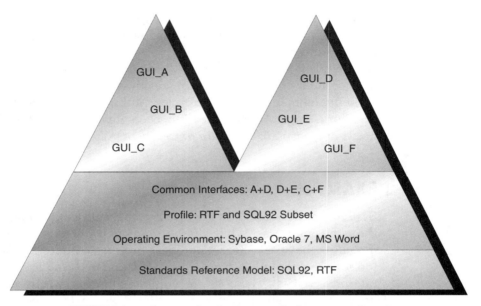

FIGURE 6.6 Refactored solution: techology coordination.

licensing, training, and technical support. This level also defines profiles for use of these technologies and common interfaces with reusable service implementations. The GUI applications comprise the remaining system-specific implementations.

RELATED SOLUTIONS

Reinvent the Wheel is an AntiPattern that comprises a subset of the overall problem of Stovepipe Systems. Reinvent the Wheel is focused upon the lack of maturity of designs and implementations caused by the lack of communication between development projects.

Standards reference model, operating environment, and profile are solutions from the book *CORBA Design Patterns* [Mowbray 97a]. They are all important components in the solution of Stovepipe Enterprises.

Examples of standards reference models include the IEEE POSIX.0, NIST Application Portability Profile (APP), and volume 7 of the U.S. Department of Defense's *Technical Architecture Framework for Information Management* (TAFIM). Examples of common interfaces and profiles can be found on www-ismc.itsi.disa.mil/ciiwg/ciiwg.html.

APPLICABILITY TO OTHER VIEWPOINTS AND SCALES

Stovepipe Enterprises are often the consequence of organizational boundaries imposed by management. Organizational structures that inhibit communication and the transfer of technology produce the kind of disconnects that result in the lack of coordination that characterizes Stovepipe Enterprises. The impact of the Stovepipe Enterprise AntiPattern on management is that every system development involves significant but unnecessary risk and cost. Since the systems do not interoperate and are difficult to integrate, the overall organizational effectiveness is impacted. The organization's ability to accommodate changing business requirements is greatly impeded by the Stovepipe Enterprise. An emerging requirement for enterprises is called *agile systems*, which are able to accommodate changes in business processes because they already support interoperability across most or all enterprise systems.

Developers, too, are affected by the Stovepipe Enterprise because they are often asked to create brittle solutions to bridge independently architected systems. These interfaces are difficult to maintain and reuse, and the absence of technology coordination makes the creation of these interfaces quite challenging. Often, combinations of middleware solutions and commercial products (database engines) must be bridged in order to achieve interoperability.

Mini-AntiPattern: Jumble

AntiPattern Problem

When horizontal and vertical design elements are intermixed, an unstable architecture results. Vertical design elements are dependent upon the individual application and specific software implementations. Horizontal design elements are those that are common across applications and specific implementations. By default, the two are mixed together by developers and architects. But doing this limits the reusability and robustness of the architecture and the system software components. Vertical elements cause software dependencies that limit extensibility and reuse. Intermingling makes all the software designs less stable and reusable.

Refactored Solution

The first step is to identify the horizontal design elements and delegate them to a separate architecture layer. Then use the horizontal elements to capture the common interoperability functionality in the architecture. For example, the horizontal elements are abstractions of the specific subsystem implementations:

1. Add vertical elements as extensions for specialized functionality and for performance.
2. Incorporate metadata into the architecture.
3. Trade off the static elements of the design (horizontal and vertical) with the dynamic elements (metadata).

Proper balance of horizontal, vertical, and metadata elements in an architecture leads to well-structured, extensible, reusable software.

Background

It takes some time to fully understand the meaning and implications of horizontal and vertical design elements. These topics are explored further in our companion book, *CORBA Design Patterns* [Mowbray 97c]. In particular, the Horizontal-Vertical-Metadata (HVM) pattern and related CORBA design patterns establish key principles for software architecture design. The Jumble AntiPattern describes the most common misuse of these principles.

STOVEPIPE SYSTEM

AntiPattern Name: Stovepipe System
Also Known As: Legacy System, Uncle Sam Special, Ad Hoc Integration
Most Frequent Scale: System
Refactored Solution Name: Architecture Framework
Refactored Solution Type: Software
Root Causes: Haste, Avarice, Ignorance, Sloth
Unbalanced Forces: Management of Complexity, Change
Anecdotal Evidence: "The software project is way over-budget; it has slipped its schedule repeatedly; my users still don't get the expected features; and I can't modify the system. Every component is a stovepipe."

BACKGROUND

Stovepipe System is a widely used derogatory name for legacy software with undesirable qualities. In this AntiPattern, we attribute the cause of these negative qualities to the internal structure of the system. An improved system structure enables the evolution of the legacy system to meet new business needs and incorporate new technologies seamlessly. By applying the recommended solution, the system can gain new capabilities for adaptability that are uncharacteristic of Stovepipe Systems.

GENERAL FORM

The Stovepipe System AntiPattern is the single-system analogy of Stovepipe Enterprise, which involves a lack of coordination and planning across a set of systems. The Stovepipe System AntiPattern addresses how the subsystems are coordinated within a single system. The key problem in this AntiPattern is the lack of common subsystem abstractions, whereas in a Stovepipe Enterprise, the key problem is the absence of common multi-system conventions.

Subsystems are integrated in an ad hoc manner using multiple integration strategies and mechanisms. All subsystems are integrated point to point, as shown in Figure 6.7, thus the integration approach for each pair of subsystems is not easily leveraged toward that of other subsystems. Furthermore, the system implementation is brittle because there are many implicit dependencies upon system configuration, installation details, and system state. The system is difficult to extend, and extensions add additional point-to-point integration links. As each new capability and alteration is integrated, system complexity increases, throughout the life cycle of the stovepipe system; subsequently, system extension and maintenance become increasingly intractable.

SYMPTOMS AND CONSEQUENCES

- Large semantic gap between architecture documentation and implemented software; documentation does not correspond to system implementation.
- Architects are unfamiliar with key aspects of integration solution.
- Project is over-budget and has slipped its schedule for no obvious reason.
- Requirements changes are costly to implement, and system maintenance generates surprising costs.
- System may comply with most paper requirements but does not meet user expectations.

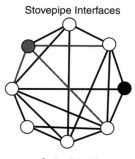

Stovepipe Interfaces

Order *(N∗N)*

FIGURE 6.7 Stovepipe interfaces require point-to-point integration, which leads to order $(N \times N)$ system cost and complexity.

- Users must invent workarounds to cope with limitations of the system.
- Complex system and client installation procedures are followed that defy attempts to automate.
- Interoperability with other systems is not possible, and there is an inability to support integrated system management and intersystem security capabilities.
- Changes to the systems become increasingly difficult.
- System modifications become increasingly likely to introduce new serious bugs.

TYPICAL CAUSES

- Multiple infrastructure mechanisms used to integrate subsystems; absence of a common mechanism makes the architecture difficult to describe and modify.
- Lack of abstraction; all interfaces are unique to each subsystem.
- Insufficient use of metadata; metadata is not available to support system extensions and reconfigurations without software changes.
- Tight coupling between implemented classes requires excessive client code that is service-specific.
- Lack of architectural vision.

KNOWN EXCEPTIONS

Research and development software production often institute the Stovepipe System AntiPattern to achieve a rapid solution. This is perfectly acceptable for prototypes and mockups; and sometimes, insufficient knowledge about a domain may require a Stovepipe System to be initially developed to gain domain information either for building a more robust system or for evolving the initial system into an improved version [Foote 97]. Or, the choice to use a vendor's product and not reinvent the wheel can lead to both the Stovepipe System AntiPattern and the Vendor Lock-In AntiPattern.

REFACTORED SOLUTION

The refactored solution to the Stovepipe System AntiPattern is a component architecture that provides for flexible substitution of software modules. Subsystems are modeled abstractly so that there are many fewer exposed interfaces than there are subsystem implementations. The substitution can be both static (compile-time component replacement) and dynamic (run-time dynamic binding). The key to defining the component interfaces is to discover the appropriate abstractions. The subsystem abstractions model the interoperability needs of the system without exposing unnecessary differences between subsystems and implementation-specific details, as shown in Figure 6.8.

In order to define a component architecture, you should choose a base level of functionality that the majority of applications will support. In general, that level should be low and focus upon a single aspect of interoperability, such as data interchange or conversion. Then define a set of system interfaces that support this base level of functionality; we recommend using ISO IDL. Most services have an additional interface to express finer-grained functional needs so the component interface should be small.

Having a base level of component services available to all clients in the domain encourages the development of thin clients that work well with existing and future services, without modification. By thin clients, we mean clients that do not require detailed knowledge of the services and architecture of the system; a framework may support and simplify their access to complex services. Having several plug-compatible implementations available increases the robustness of clients, as they potentially have many options in fulfilling their service request.

Applications will have clients that are written to more specialized (vertical) interfaces. Vertical clients should remain unaffected by the addition of the new component interfaces. Clients that require only the

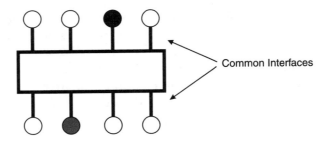

Order (N)

FIGURE 6.8 Component architectures model interoperability needs with common interfaces.

base level of functionality can be written to the horizontal interfaces, which should be more stable and easily supported by new or other existing applications. The horizontal interface should hide, via abstraction, all the lower-level details of a component and provide only the base-level functionality. The client should be written to handle whatever data types are indicated by the interface in order to support any future interchange of the horizontal component implementations. For example, if an "any" is returned, the client should be capable of handling all types that the "any" may contain. Admittedly, for CORBA implementations that don't support the transfer of new user-defined types at run time, type management may have to occur at the horizontal level; specifically, it may be necessary to convert vertical types into horizontal types that are known at compile time.

Incorporation of metadata into the component architecture is key to service discovery and service discrimination. A fundamental level of metadata support is through naming and trading services [Mowbray 97c]. Naming services enable the discovery of known objects; a trading service lists the available services and their properties for discovery by clients. Interoperable naming services are extended to incorporate some trading capabilities. More extensive use of metadata is usually required for enhanced decoupling of clients from services. For example, schema metadata for database services helps clients to adapt alternative schema and schema changes [Mowbray 95].

EXAMPLE

Figure 6.9 is a representation of a typical stovepipe system. There are three client subsystems and six service subsystems. Each subsystem has a unique software interface, and each subsystem instance is modeled as a class in the class diagram. When the system is constructed, unique interface software for each client corresponds to each of the integrated subsystems. If additional subsystems are added or substituted, the clients must be modified with additional code that integrates new unique interfaces.

The refactored solution to this example considers the common abstractions between the subsystems (Figure 6.10). Since there are two services of each type, it is possible for each model to have one or more service interface in common. Then each particular device or service can be wrapped to support the common interface abstraction. If additional devices are added to the system from these abstract subsystem categories,

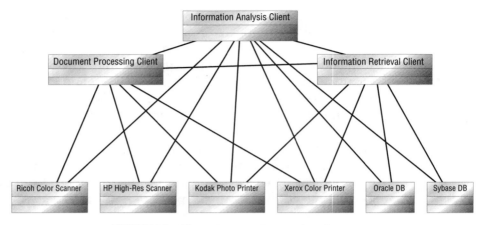

FIGURE 6.9 Client/server Stovepipe System.

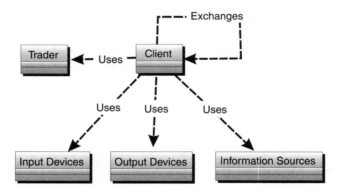

FIGURE 6.10 The refactored architecture abstracts subsystem differences.

they can be integrated transparently to the existing system software. The addition of a trader service adds the ability to discover and discriminate between the abstracted services.

RELATED SOLUTIONS

The Stovepipe Enterprise AntiPattern describes how stovepipe practices are promulgated on an enterprise scale. Note that Stovepipe Enterprise addresses a multisystem problem, which involves a larger scale of architecture than a single system.

APPLICABILITY TO OTHER VIEWPOINTS AND SCALES

The management consequences of Stovepipe Systems are: increased risk, bigger budget, and longer time to market. And because complexity increases throughout the life cycle of the system, the management problems magnify as development progresses. Eventually, the risks of system modification outweigh the potential benefits, and the Stovepipe System ceases to adapt to new business needs; the organization's business processes are frozen by the Stovepipe System. Since the architecture information is buried in the implementation, employee turnover in the software maintenance staff can lead to a total loss of capability to modify or maintain the system.

For developers, Stovepipe Systems mean they must spend more time on system discovery and testing. In early development, developers have a great deal of freedom to choose implementation strategies with minimal architectural guidance, but as the complexity of the stovepipe interfaces supercedes the documentation, the system becomes increasingly complex and brittle. Development in a stovepipe environment resembles walking through a mine field. Every decision involves guesswork, uncertainty, and experiments. Developer decisions have high-risk consequences for the business, and often lead to repeated crises.

Mini-AntiPattern: Cover Your Assets

AntiPattern Problem

Document-driven software processes often produce less-than-useful requirements and specifications because the authors evade making important decisions. In order to avoid making a mistake, the authors take a safer course and elaborate upon alternatives. The resulting documents are voluminous and become an enigma; there is no useful abstraction of the contents that convey the authors' intent. Unfortunate readers, who may have contractual obligations dependent upon the text, must pore through the mind-numbing details. When no decisions are made and no priorities are established, the documents have limited value. It is unreasonable to have hundreds of pages of requirements that are all equally important or mandatory. The developers are left without much useful guidance about what to implement in what priority.

Refactored Solution

Architecture blueprints are abstractions of information systems that facilitate communication of requirements and technical plans between the users and developers [Blueprint 97]. An architecture blueprint is a small set of diagrams and tables that communicate the operational, technical, and systems architecture of current and future information systems [C4ISR 96]. A typical blueprint comprises no more than a dozen diagrams and tables, and can be presented in an hour or less as a viewgraph presentation. Architecture blueprints are particularly useful in an enterprise with multiple information systems. Each system can establish its architecture blueprints, then the organization can compile enterprisewide blueprints based upon the system-specific details. Blueprints should characterize both existing systems and planned extensions. The extensions can be used to coordinate architecture planning across multiple systems. Because architecture blueprints allow multiple projects to portray their technologies, opportunities for interoperability and reuse are enhanced.

VENDOR LOCK-IN

AntiPattern Name: Vendor Lock-In

Also Known As: Product-Dependent Architecture, Bondage and Submission, Connector Conspiracy

Most Frequent Scale: System

Refactored Solution Name: Isolation Layer

Refactored Solution Type: Software

Root Causes: Sloth, Apathy, Pride/Ignorance (Gullibility)

Unbalanced Forces: Management of Technology Transfer, Management of Change

Anecdotal Evidence: We have often encountered software projects that claim their architecture is based upon a particular vendor or product line.

Other anecdotal evidence occurs around the time of product upgrades and new application installations: "When I try to read the new data files into the old version of the application, it crashes my system." "Once you read data into the new application, you can never get it out again." "The old software acts like it has a virus, but it's probably just the new application data." "Our architecture is . . . What's the name of our database again?"

> "Safe upon solid rock the ugly house stands: Come and see my
> shining palace built upon the sand!"
>
> —Edna St. Vincent Millay

BACKGROUND

A worst-case scenario of this AntiPattern would occur if your data and software licenses were completely allocated to online services, and one day, a modal dialog box popped up, as shown in Figure 6.11.

Interactive word processing became more popular than formatting language technologies (like SGML) because it allows the user to see the final format on the computer screen and print an exact copy of the on-screen appearance. This capability is called "What you see is what you get" (WYSIWIG). A pervasive variation of Vendor Lock-In is the phenomenon called "What you see is sort-of like what you get" (WYSISLWYG, pronounced "weasel wig"). Recently, given the desktop dominance of Microsoft, product misfeatures cause the printed versions of documents to vary significantly from their on-screen appearance. For example, symbols in drawings can change or disappear, and embedded objects are often printed as com-

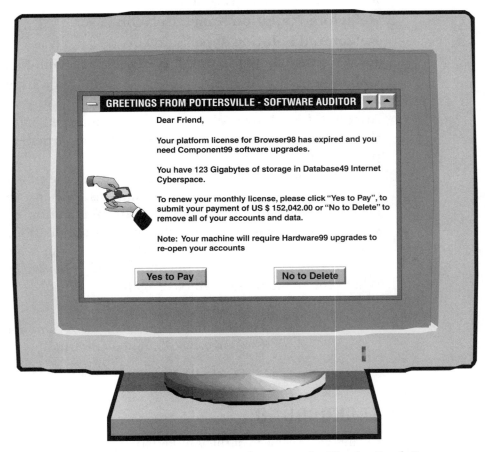

FIGURE 6.11 A situation in your future under Vendor Lock-In.

mand strings (like "{EMBEDDED POWERPOINT FIGURE}"). Documents from different versions of the same Microsoft product can cause support problems on corporate networks and system crashes. Many companies discourage or outlaw co-mingling of product versions. It is difficult to avoid this form of vendor lock-in and its product misfeatures because of organizational dependence on Microsoft's products for document interchange.

GENERAL FORM

A software project adopts a product technology and becomes completely dependent upon the vendor's implementation. When upgrades are done, software changes and interoperability problems occur, and continuous maintenance is required to keep the system running. In addition, expected new product features are often delayed, causing schedule slips and an inability to complete desired application software features.

SYMPTOMS AND CONSEQUENCES

- Commercial product upgrades drive the application software maintenance cycle.
- Promised product features are delayed or never delivered, subsequently, causing failure to deliver application updates.
- The product varies significantly from the advertised open systems standard.
- If a product upgrade is missed entirely, a product repurchase and reintegration is often necessary.

TYPICAL CAUSES

- The product varies from published open system standards because there is no effective conformance process for the standard.
- The product is selected based entirely upon marketing and sales information, and not upon more detailed technical inspection.
- There is no technical approach for isolating application software from direct dependency upon the product.

- Application programming requires in-depth product knowledge.
- The complexity and generality of the product technology greatly exceeds that of the application needs; direct dependence upon the product results in failure to manage the complexity of the application system architecture.

KNOWN EXCEPTIONS

The Vendor Lock-In AntiPattern is acceptable when a single vendor's code makes up the majority of code needed in an application.

REFACTORED SOLUTION

The refactioned solution to the Vendor Lock-In AntiPattern is called *isolation layer*. An isolation layer separates software packages and technology, as shown in Figure 6.12. It can be used to provide software portability from underlying middleware and platform-specific interfaces. This solution is applicable when one or more of the following conditions apply:

- *Isolation of application software from lower-level infrastructure.* This infrastructure may include middleware, operating systems, security mechanisms, or other low-level mechanisms.
- *Changes to the underlying infrastructure are anticipated within the life cycle of the affected software;* for example, new product releases or planned migration to new infrastructure.

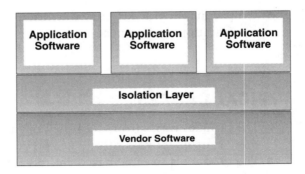

FIGURE 6.12 The isolation layer separates application software from product-dependent interfaces, which may change.

- *A more convenient programming interface is useful or necessary.* The level of abstraction provided by the infrastructure is either too primitive or too flexible for the intended applications and systems.
- *There a need for consistent handling of the infrastructure across many systems.* Some heavyweight conventions for default handling of infrastructure interfaces must be instituted.
- Multiple infrastructures must be supported, either during the life cycle or concurrently.

The solution entails creating a layer of software that abstracts the underlying infrastructure or product-dependent software interfaces. This layer provides an application interface that completely isolates the application software from the underlying interfaces. The application interface should implement a convenient language-specific interface to desired capabilities. The layering software should ensure default handling of some infrastructure calls and parameters, but expose other details when appropriate.

This isolation layer is used across multiple system development projects to assure interoperability, consistency, and isolation. To implement it, migrate the isolation to new infrastructures as necessary; also, update the isolation layer when the infrastructure is updated. In all cases, maintain the same application software interface, regardless of infrastructure changes.

It is also necessary to install gateways [Mowbray 97c] between multiple infrastructures that must be supported concurrently, and to install forward and reverse gateways during infrastructure migration [Brodie 95].

The benefits of this solution are:

- Mitigation of the risks and costs of infrastructure migration.
- Precluding obsolescence caused by to infrastructure changes.
- Reduction of the risk and cost of software upgrades required by infrastructure changes.
- Assurance of a less labor-intensive and more inexpensive programming interface to most application programmers.
- Support for the concurrent use of multiple infrastructures, transparently.
- Enforcement of coordinated default handling of flexible interfaces and parameters.
- Separation of infrastructure knowledge from application knowledge, thereby enabling a small team of infrastructure developers to maintain the isolation layer, while the majority of programmers have a customized interface to the layering software.

Other consequences of this solution are that:

- The isolation layer must be migrated and maintained, potentially on multiple platforms and infrastructures.
- The developers who define the initial isolation layer interfaces must be coordinated.
- Changes made to the application interfaces must be coordinated.

VARIATIONS

This solution is often used at the global level in commercial products and technologies. Typically, the isolation layer enables the vendor to provide a convenient language-specific interface to a lower-level technology. Some of this convenience comes in the form of default handling of lower-level interfaces that are more flexible than necessary for most applications. For example, the HP Object-Oriented Distributed Computing Environment (OO DCE) product comprises an isolation layer, and presents a C++ interface to application developers. Underlying this interface is an isolation layer of software that is built upon the C language DCE environment. Calls to the C++ APIs can invoke several underlying DCE procedure calls; in particular, just two calls are needed to initialize OO DCE security service interfaces. The underlying isolation layer, in turn, makes more than 50 calls to DCE APIs to achieve this initialization with the legacy DCE security service.

The isolation layer solution is most applicable at the enterprise level. However, individual systems have applied this solution to provide middleware isolation; for example, the Paragon Electronic Light Table (ELT) product uses an isolation layer above the Common Desktop Environment (CDE) middleware infrastructure, called ToolTalk. By isolating ToolTalk, Paragon can easily migrate its product to a CORBA infrastructure and support both CORBA and ToolTalk infrastructures.

EXAMPLE

The following examples are three known uses of the isolation layer solution:

1. The ORBlite framework, based on HP ORB plus, isolates application software from multiple language mappings and network protocols [Moore 97]. Thus, it was able to support multiple language

mappings for C++, given the evolution of the OMG mappings during the adoption and revision process [Moore 97].

2. Even though OpenDoc is no longer in the product strategy of its creator, some interesting technical approaches were used, including the isolation layer solution. The OpenDoc Parts Framework (OPF) institutes a higher-level C++ programming interface to the OpenDoc compound document interface, defined in ISO IDL. OPF includes interfaces to operating system functions (including display graphics), as well as OpenDoc functions. In doing so, OPF enables source code portability interfaces for middleware, windowing, and operating systems. Compound document parts written using OPF can be ported via recompilation and linking to OS/2, MacOS, and Windows95. A testing capability called LiveObjects, from the Component Integration Labs, the consortium responsible for OpenDoc, assures component portability and interoperability.

3. EOSDIS (Earth Observing System Data and Information System) is a large-scale information retrieval project funded by NASA. The EOSDIS middleware abstraction layer was used to isolate application software and evolving middleware. Initial prototypes used a beta-test CORBA product. These prototyping efforts proved unsuccessful, largely due to difficulties in using the beta-test product. Although program management acknowledged the need for future CORBA support, a proprietary object-oriented DCE extension was chosen for short-term implementations. Management also did not want to rely entirely on proprietary interfaces. The situation was resolved through the addition of a middleware abstraction layer that masked the choice of middleware from EOSDIS application software; it hid differences in object creation, object activation, and object invocation.

RELATED SOLUTIONS

This pattern is related to the Object Wrapper pattern [Mowbray 97c], which provides isolation to and from a single application to a single object infrastructure. The isolation layer pattern provides insulation of multiple applications from multiple infrastructures. This pattern is also related to the Profile pattern [Mowbray 97c], where an isolation layer can be viewed as a particular enterprise profile for the use of middleware.

The isolation layer can be thought of as one the levels in a layered architecture [Mowbray 97c]. In contrast to most layers, this is a very thin layer that does not contain application objects. Typically, an isolation layer serves only as a proxy for integrating clients and services with one or more infrastructures. The Proxy pattern is described in Buschmann (1996).

APPLICABILITY TO OTHER VIEWPOINTS AND SCALES

The impact of Vendor Lock-In on management is a loss of control of the technology, IT functionality, and O&M budgets to the dictates of vendor product releases. Vendor Lock-In also impacts risk management. The AntiPattern is often accepted with the understanding that future features will be implemented. Unfortunately, these feature often deliver later than expected or needed, if ever.

Vendor Lock-In affects developers by requiring they have in-depth product knowledge. But this knowledge is transient; it will be made obsolete by the next product release. Thus, developers are expected to be on a continuous learning-curve treadmill about product features, product bugs, and product futures.

Mini-AntiPattern: Wolf Ticket

AntiPattern Problem

There are many more information systems standards than there are mechanisms to assure conformance. Only 6 percent of information systems standards have test suites. Most of the testable standards are for programming language compilers—FORTRAN, COBOL, Ada, and so forth.

A Wolf Ticket is a product that claims openness and conformance to standards that have no enforceable meaning. The products are delivered with proprietary interfaces that may vary significantly from the published standard. A key problem is that technology consumers often assume that openness comes with some benefits. In reality, standards are more important to technology suppliers for brand recognition than for any benefits that the standards may offer users.

Standards do reduce technology migration costs and improve technology stability, but, differences in the implementation of the standards often negate their assumed benefits, such as multivendor interoperability and software portability. Furthermore, many standards specifications are too flexible to assure interoperability and portability; other standards are excessively complex, and these are implemented incompletely and inconsistently in products. Frequently, different subsets of the standard are implemented by various vendors.

Wolf Tickets are a significant problem for de facto standards (an informal standard established through popular usage or market exposure). Unfortunately, some de facto standards have no effective specification; for example, a nascent database technology that is commercially available with multiple proprietary interfaces, unique to each vendor, has become a de facto standard.

Refactored Solution

Technology gaps cause deficiencies in specifications, product availability, conformance, interoperability, robustness, and functionality. The closing of these gaps is necessary to enable the delivery of whole products, those comprising the infrastructure and services necessary for the realization of useful systems. In the 1960s, a sophisticated user group called **SHAPE** advised the industry to stabilize technology and create whole products for the computer mainframe market, required for the realization of successful nonstovepipe systems. As a result, the mainframe workset remains the only whole-product information technology market.

Technology gaps become political issues for end users, corporate developers, and systems integrators. Politics is the exercise of power, and consumers must demand the resolution of technology gaps before they will be effectively addressed. For example, consumers must demand guarantees of merchantability and "fitness for purpose" *before* products are offered by commercial suppliers.

The core strategy of grassroots politics is *heightening the contradiction*. By spreading awareness of the contradictions in a system (such as the technology market), the establishment (in this case, technology suppliers) will resolve the issues. Three elements constitute an effective political message. With these three elements, the message has a good chance of being reported by the media:

1. The message must be controversial.
2. The message must be repetitive.
3. The message must be entertaining.

Currently, we are working on an initiative in technology consumer politics.

What is needed are whole products supporting mission-critical system development. A whole product that enables the construction of any mission-critical system has five key services: naming, trading, database access, transactions, and system management. These services apply to mission-critical systems in any domain. *Naming* is a white-pages service that enables the retrieval of object references for known objects. *Trading* is a yellow-pages service that supports system extensibility through retrieval of candidate services based upon attributes. A standard *database access* service is necessary for retrieval and updating of information resources. *Transactions* assure robust access to state information and orderly cleanup in case of failures. *System management* is required for maintaining heterogeneous hardware and software environments.

Because today, developers cannot buy these whole products in a robust, interworking form, developers are forced to re-create these services or build stovepipe systems.

Variation

All computer technology consumers can participate in improving the technologies that they are currently using. To do so, simply call the vendor with your questions, complaints, and support problems. Keep in mind, for shrink-wrap products, the profit margin is less than the resources required to answer a phone call and address your questions. Most vendors track the support issues and incorporate relevant changes into their products in future releases. The priority for changes is usually based upon the frequency and urgency of the reported problems.

Background

The term Wolf Ticket originates from its slang use, where it is an unofficial pass sold to an event, such as a rock concert, by scalpers.

ARCHITECTURE BY IMPLICATION

AntiPattern Name: Architecture by Implication
Also Known As: Wherefore art thou architecture?
Most Frequent Scale: System
Refactored Solution Name: Goal Question Architecture
Refactored Solution Type: Documentation
Root Causes: Pride, Sloth
Unbalanced Forces: Management of Complexity, Change, and Risk
Anecdotal Evidence: "We've done systems like this before!" "There is no risk; we know what we're doing!"

BACKGROUND

Dwight Eisenhower said that planning is essential, but plans are inconsequential. Another soldier said that no plans survive first contact with the enemy. The planning culture in modern management owes some credit to Robert McNamara, founder of the RAND Corporation. In McNamara's approach, plans are generated for speculative purposes, to investigate the potential benefits and consequences of different courses of action. Given the large number of unknowns in systems development, planning for IT systems must be more pragmatic and iterative.

One professional planner said that 20 percent of an engineer's time should be devoted to planning. As we gain experience, our belief in this assertion increases. Productivity and efficiency can be greatly amplified when the work is well organized through planning. The unfortunate consequence is that many organizations attempt to formalize too much of the planning. Planning is most effective when it is personally motivated and utilized. Time management experts teach that a key element of stress reduction is planning to balance life's overall priorities. The form and use of time-management systems becomes increasingly personalized as the practice matures.

A group of CEOs from DoD Systems integration firms was formed to answer the question, "Wherefore art thou architecture?" The goal was to reflect on the changing nature of systems development, which has evolved into the reuse of existing legacy components and commercial software, and away from greenfield, custom code development (see the Reinvent the Wheel AntiPattern in this chapter).

 ## GENERAL FORM

This AntiPattern is characterized by the lack of architecture specifications for a system under development (see Figure 6.13). Usually, the architects responsible for the project have experience with previous system construction, and therefore assume that documentation is unnecessary. This over-confidence leads to exacerbated risks in key areas that affect system success. Architecture definitions are often missing from one or more of these areas:

FIGURE 6.13 Architecture by Implementation often involves coding without architecture planning.

- Software architecture and specifications that include language use, library use, coding standards, memory management, and so forth.
- Hardware architecture that includes client and service configurations.
- Communications architecture that includes networking protocols and devices.
- Persistence architecture that includes databases and file-handling mechanisms.
- Application security architecture that includes thread models and trusted system base.
- Systems management architecture.

SYMPTOMS AND CONSEQUENCES

- Lack of architecture planning and specification; insufficient definition of architecture for software, hardware, communications, persistence, security, and systems management.
- Hidden risks caused by scale, domain knowledge, technology, and complexity, all of which emerge as the project progresses.
- Impending project failure or unsuccessful system due to inadequate performance, excess complexity, misunderstood requirements, usability, and other system characteristics. For example, approximately 1 of 3 systems encounter serious performance problems during development and operations.
- Ignorance of new technologies.
- Absence of technical backup and contingency plans.

TYPICAL CAUSES

- No risk management.
- Overconfidence of managers, architects, and/or developers.
- Reliance on previous experience, which may differ in critical areas.
- Implicit and unresolved architecture issues caused by gaps in systems engineering.

KNOWN EXCEPTIONS

The Architecture by Implication AntiPattern is acceptable for a repeated solution, where there are minor differences in the code, such as installation scripts. This AntiPattern may also be useful in a new project domain as an exploratory effort to determine whether existing techniques are transferable into a new area.

REFACTORED SOLUTION

The refactored solution to the Architecture by Implication AntiPattern entails an organized approach to systems architecture definition, and relies on multiple views of the system. Each view models the system from the perspective of a system stakeholder, who may be real or imaginary, individual or aggregate. Each stakeholder is responsible for a high-priority set of questions and issues, and each view represents the entire information system and answers these key questions and issues. The views comprising a set of diagrams, tables, or specifications, are linked for consistency. Generally, a view is a lightweight specification. The purpose of the architecture documentation is to communicate architecture decisions and other issues resolutions. The documentation should be easy to understand and inexpensive to maintain.

That said, the only people who can define and implement a successful architecture are those who already fully understand it. Unfortunately, this is often not the case, as many projects adopt some new technology that is not well understood. Therefore, developing a good architecture from scratch is an iterative process and should be recognized as such. An initial reference architecture should have strong strategies that can be implemented within the time period of the first product development. Thereafter, it will have to be incrementally refined by future versions of the reference architecture, and driven by new versions of the first product or new products.

The steps to define a system architecture using viewpoints are as follows [Hilliard 96]:

1. *Define the architecture goals.* What must this architecture achieve? Which stakeholders, real and imaginary, must be satisfied with the design and implementation? What is the vision for the system? Where are we now and where are we going?
2. *Define the questions.* What are the specific questions that must be addressed to satisfy the stakeholder issues? Prioritize the questions to support view selection.
3. *Select the views.* Each view will represent a blueprint of the system architecture.

4. *Analyze each view.* Detail the architecture definition from each viewpoint. Create the system blueprints.

5. *Integrate the blueprints.* Verify that the views present a consistent architecture definition.

6. *Trace views to needs.* The views should address the known questions and issues to discover any gaps not addressed by the architecture specifications. Validate the architecture with respect to formal requirements. Prioritize the outstanding issues.

7. *Iterate the blueprints.* Refine the views until all questions, issues, and gaps are resolved. Utilize review processes to surface any remaining issues. If a significant number of unresolved issues remain, consider creating additional views.

8. *Promote the architecture.* Make an explicit effort to communicate the architecture to key stakeholders, particularly the system developers. Create lasting documents (such as a video tutorial) to provide valuable information throughout the development and maintenance life cycle.

9. *Validate the implementation.* The blueprints should represent an "as-built" design. Determine any deltas between the blueprints and the system implementation. Decide whether these differences should result in system modifications of updates to the blueprints. Upgrade the documentation for consistency.

We refer to this method as the goal-question architecture (GQA), analogous to the goal-question metric approach in software metrics [Kitchenham 96].

 ## VARIATIONS

A number of approaches consider the system architecture using viewpoints; in some, the viewpoints are predefined. Most of these approaches are open-ended, in that one can select additional viewpoints as described.

The Reference Model for Open Distributed Process (RM-ODP) is a popular, useful standard for distributed architectures. RM-ODP defines five standard viewpoints: enterprise, information, computational, engineering, and technology [ISO 96]. It also defines a useful set of transparency properties for distributed infrastructure through the engineering viewpoint.

Another approach, the Zachman Framework, analyzes system architectures from the perspectives of data, function, and network [Spewak 92].

Within each perspective are multiple levels of abstraction, corresponding to the planning needs of various groups of stakeholders. Enterprise Architecture Planning is an approach based upon the Zachman Framework for large-scale systems [Spewak 92]. Neither of these approaches is tailored to object-oriented systems development.

A third approach, the Command, Communication, Control, Computer, Intelligence, Surveillance, and Reconnaissance Architecture Framework (C4ISR-AF), is used to define various command and control system architectures. A version of C4ISR-AF is used for other types of civilian systems. This approach has been very beneficial in enabling communications between architects across disparate domains [Mowbray 97b].

A fourth, the 4 + 1 Model View, is a viewpoint-based architecture approach supported by software engineering tools, such as Rational Rose [Kruchten 95]. The viewpoints include logical, use-case, process, implementation, and deployment. Finally, GQA is a generalization of the underlying method used in several of these architecture approaches [Hilliard 96].

EXAMPLE

A common but bad practice is object-oriented modeling without defining the viewpoint. In most modeling approaches, there is a blurring of the viewpoints. Many of the modeling constructs contain implementation detail, and the default practice is to intermingle implementation and specification constructs.

Three fundamental viewpoints are: conceptual, specification, and implementation [Cook 94]. The *conceptual viewpoint* defines the system from the perspective of the user. This is typically referred to as an *analysis model*. The distinction between what is automated and what is not is usually not represented in the model; rather, the model is drawn so that a user can explain and defend it to his or her peers. The *specification viewpoint* concerns only interfaces. ISO IDL is one important notation that is strictly limited to defining interface information and excludes implementation specifics. The separation of interfaces from implementations enables the realization of many important object technology benefits, such as reuse, system extension, variation, substitutability, polymorphism, and distributed object computing. The final viewpoint, *implementation*, is best represented by the source code. Complex implementation structures are beneficially augmented with object-oriented design models to help current and future developers and maintainers understand the code.

Another example of the Architecture by Implication AntiPattern is the following, where the key stakeholders did not have collective experience in what was built. The project was intended to deliver a Microsoft Distributed Common Object Model (DCOM)-based solution to extract legacy mainframe data, filter it based on business rule, and display it on Web pages. However, the manager was a good software engineer with no distributed object technology (DOT) experience and the architect was a "dyed-in-the-wool" CORBA addict who helped the OMG derive its Object Management Architecture. To compound the problem, the project had few DCOM-aware staff; less than 10 percent.

In addition, the architecture and subsequent design were based on the OMA view of the DOT world, rather than DCOM. This led to an attempt to deliver CORBA services under a DCOM architecture. The resulting product suffered from a set of components that had no DOT consistency and were poor performers. Also, SIs found it very difficult to use, due to lack of a standardized approach. Finally, it failed in the marketplace.

RELATED SOLUTIONS

Architecture by Implication AntiPattern differs from the Stovepipe Systems AntiPattern in scope; the latter focuses on deficiencies in computational architecture. In particular, it identifies how improper abstraction of subsystem APIs leads to brittle architecture solutions. In contrast, the Architecture by Implication AntiPattern involves planning gaps constituted of multiple architecture viewpoints.

APPLICABILITY TO OTHER VIEWPOINTS AND SCALES

This AntiPattern significantly increases risk for managers, who defer important decisions until failures occur; often, it is too late to recover. Developers suffer from a lack of guidance for system implementation. They are given de facto responsibility for key architectural decisions for which they may not have the necessary architectural perspective. System-wide consequences of interface design decisions should be considered; in particular: system adaptability, consistent interface abstractions, metadata availability, and management of complexity.

Another important result of this AntiPattern is the deferment of resource allocation. The essential tools and technology components may not be available when needed due to lack of planning.

Mini-AntiPattern: Warm Bodies

Also Known As

Deadwood, Body Shop, Seat Warmers, Mythical Man-Month [Brooks 79]

Anecdotal Evidence

"One out of 20 programmers . . . produces 20 times the software compared to an average programmer."

There are approximately two million working software managers and developers in America. Currently, there are 200,000 additional job openings. These figures indicate a negative 10 percent unemployment rate.

AntiPattern Problem

Skilled programmers are essential to the success of a software project. So-called heroic programmers are exceptionally productive, but as few as 1 in 20 have this talent. They produce an order of magnitude of more working software than an average programmer.

Large-scale software projects are prevalent in many industries. These projects employ hundreds of programmers to build an enterprise system; a staff of 100 to 400 on a single project is not atypical. These large projects often involve outsourced development and contractual payments based upon labor-hours worked. Since profits are a percentage of the staff salaries, the more hours worked, the higher the profits. System requirements always change and increase during development; so there is little risk involved if the project is underbid initially; the contractor can grow the staff to meet inevitable problems and new requirements. The fallacy of adding more staff to an ongoing software project was described by Frederick Brooks in the *Mythical Man-Month* (1979).

Refactored Solution

The ideal project size is four programmers; the ideal project duration is four months [Edwards 97]. Software projects are subject to the same group dynamics as committee meetings (see the Design by Committee

AntiPattern, described next). Project teams that grow beyond five people generally experience escalating difficulties with group coordination. The members have trouble making efficient decisions and maintaining a common vision. Working toward a near-term deadline is essential to encourage the team to focus and begin producing a solution.

We submit that extremely large projects are futile efforts. Small project teams with individual accountability are much more likely to produce successful software.

Variations

Finding talented programmers is an important challenge for software-intensive companies. Some firms have resorted to incorporating testing as part of their hiring processes. These examinations resemble IQ tests. If the subject fails the test, he or she will probably end up on a large-scale project with hundreds of other programmers.

Working with independent contractors and consultants is an effective way to acquire programming talent quickly. In some areas of the United States, hundreds of contract programmers work out of their homes, and they can be engaged via a phone call or e-mail. These contract programmers can produce significant software products for reasonable rates, compared to the project failures and overruns that result from the Warm Bodies mini-AntiPattern.

DESIGN BY COMMITTEE

AntiPattern Name: Design by Committee

Also Known As: Gold Plating, Standards Disease, Make Everybody Happy, Political Party

Most Frequent Scale: Global

Refactored Solution Name: Meeting Facilitation

Refactored Solution Type: Process

Root Causes: Pride, Avarice

Unbalanced Forces: Management of Functionality, Complexity, and Resources

Anecdotal Evidence: "A camel is a horse designed by a committee." "Too many cooks spoil the broth."

 BACKGROUND

Object orientation is often described as a two-generation technology. Data-centric object analysis is characteristic of the first generation, and design patterns are characteristic of the second. The first generation espoused a philosophy that "objects are things you can touch." A consequence of this is that virtually all designs are uniquely vertical. In the first generation, people believed a number of assumptions that were unsubstantiated by practice. One of these was that project teams should be egalitarian; in other words, that everyone should have an equal say and that decisions are democratic. This leads to Design by Committee. Given that only a small number of object developers can define good abstractions, the majority rule invariably leads to a diffusion of abstraction and excess complexity.

GENERAL FORM

A complex software design is the product of a committee process. It has so many features and variations that it is infeasible for any group of developers to realize the specifications in a reasonable time frame. Even if the designs were possible, it would not be possible to test the full design due to excessive complexity, ambiguities, overconstraint, and other specification defects. The design would lack conceptual clarity because so many people contributed to it and extended it during its creation.

SYMPTOMS AND CONSEQUENCES

- The design documentation is overly complex, unreadable, incoherent, or is excessively defective.
- The design documentation is voluminous (hundreds or thousands of pages).
- Convergence and stability are missing from the requirements and the design.
- The committee meetings resemble bull sessions during which substantive issues are rarely discussed and progress is painstakingly slow. People talk and work serially; that is, there is a single thread of discussion, and most people are unproductive most of the time.
- The environment is politically changed, and few decisions and actions can be undertaken outside of the meeting; and the meeting process precludes reaching timely decisions.
- There is no prioritization of the design features, and no ready answer to the questions: Which features are essential? Which features will be implemented in the initial delivery?
- Architects and developers have conflicting interpretations of the design.
- Design development becomes significantly over-budget and overdue.
- It becomes necessary to employ specialists to interpret, develop, and manage the specifications. In other words, dealing with each specification that was designed by committee becomes a full-time job.

TYPICAL CAUSES

"The lunatics have taken charge of the asylum."

—Richard Rowland

- No designated project architect.
- A degenerate or ineffective software process.
- Bad meeting processes, marked by lack of facilitation or ineffective facilitation. The meetings are bull sessions; the loudest people win and the level of discourse is the lowest common denominator of sophistication.
- Gold plating—that is, features are added to the specification based on proprietary interests. This can happen for many reasons: marketability, the existence of proprietary technologies already containing these features, or speculative placement of features in the specification for potential future work.
- The attempt to make everybody happy, to satisfy all of the committee participants by incorporating their ideas. Unfortunately, it's impossible to accept every idea and still manage complexity.
- Design and editing is attempted during meetings with more than five people.
- Explicit priorities and a software-value system are undetermined [Mowbray 97c].
- Concerns are not separated, and reference models are not used.

KNOWN EXCEPTIONS

There are few exceptions to the Design by Committee AntiPattern, and they occur when the committee is small: approximately 6 to 10 people; more than that and consensus becomes unlikely; fewer than six people and the breadth of understanding and experience become insufficient. Also, committees should often be *tiger teams,* a small group of "experts" in a particular problem domain, organized for the duration of the solution for a specific problem or issue.

 ## REFACTORED SOLUTION

The essence of the solution to Design by Committee is to reform the meeting process. It's fair to say that most people are accustomed to enduring bad meetings, most of the time. Thus, even simple alterations in the meeting process can yield substantial productivity improvements. With improved productivity, there is an opportunity for enhanced quality and more sophisticated solutions. Typical gains for software optimizations are less than an order of magnitude (2 to 10 times). Meeting productivity gains are much more dramatic, with several orders of magnitude typical (100 times), and we have seen productivity gains over 100,000:1.

First, most meeting rooms do not have a clock on the wall, particularly in hotel facilities. Time awareness is essential to meeting progress. Participants should be coached to manage the time allotted efficiently; participants should start their comments with a "25-words-or-less" summary, and add details only if requested. Posting the meeting goals, an agenda, and a clock where they are visible to all participants can improve meetings dramatically.

Second, in all meetings it's important that group members answer two questions: "Why are we here?" and "What outcomes do we want?" When no meeting plan is prepared, it is particularly important that the group start with these two questions, and then work on generating the desired outcomes.

Another important reform is to assign explicit roles in the software process: owner, facilitator, architect, developers, testers, and domain experts. The owner is the manager responsible for the software development. He or she makes strategic decisions about the overall software process, and invites and organizes the participants. At the beginning of the meeting, the process owner sets the goals and establishes expectations regarding the handling of the outcomes. For example, the decisions made at the meeting may be regarded simply as advice or be implemented exactly as discussed.

The facilitator is in charge of running the meeting. He or she is responsible for the process; other participants are responsible for technical content. The facilitator turns to the process owner if there are any key decisions to be made regarding the process.

"My specialty is being right when other people are wrong."

—George Bernard Shaw

The architect is the senior technical lead for the software project. He or she controls the editing of the architecture documentation, and may be in charge of key, system-level boundaries, such as the subsystem application program interfaces. Each developer is typically responsible for a single subsystem and unit testing. Testers are responsible for monitoring specification quality and value-added testing such as integration, portability, and stress tests. The domain experts input key requirements to the process, but may not be involved in all aspects of development.

There are three categories of meeting processes: divergent, convergent, and information sharing. In a divergent process, ideas are generated for later utilization. In a convergent process, a selection or decision is made that represents a consensus. Information sharing can involve presentation, teaching, writing, and review.

The number of people involved in each meeting process is managed by the facilitator. Creative processes that require writing, highlighting, or drawing should be limited to breakout teams of five people or fewer. Groups larger than five are less effective at making progress in creative tasks, although they are successful at reviewing and integrating results after a creative process. Highly productive meetings involve many parallel processes, and frequent iterations of breakout and review groups. Encouraging people to make a paradigm shift between single-threaded discussion and parallel work is a key challenge for the facilitator.

The primary purpose of most meetings is problem solving. A general problem-solving approach begins with a convergent process: The problem is defined and scoped for the group to resolve. A divergent process is used to identify alternative solutions. Information sharing may be needed to explore the details and consequences of selected alternatives. Finally, a convergent process is used to select among the options.

One highly effective meeting process is called Spitwads [Herrington 91]. It's a general-purpose procedure that we have used on many occasions with excellent results.

1. *Ask the question.* The facilitator poses a question for the group to brainstorm. The question is written down on a viewgraph or flipchart) to avoid misunderstandings. The group is asked whether there are any suggested changes to the question before the brainstorming starts. Typical questions are: "What are ways that we can improve the performance of the system?" and "What is the most important requirement that has not been addressed?"

2. *Write silently.* The participants write responses on identical slips of paper. Each response is written on a separate piece of paper, and is limited to short phrases.

3. *Toss spitwads.* As the participants complete each idea, the facilitator instructs them to wad up the paper and toss it across the room into a receptacle—a cardboard box or a basket works best. This is done basketball style, and the facilitator encourages the participants to have fun with this exercise.

4. *Conduct spitwad roll call.* The "spitwads" are distributed randomly back to the participants, who one at a time read the ideas out loud to be recorded on a flipchart. Two flipchart recorders can be used simultaneously to speed up the process. The flipcharts are posted on the wall for all participants to see.

5. *Reach common understanding.* The ideas on the flipcharts are numbered. The facilitator then asks the group if there are any

ideas that they do not understand. If so, the members of the group are encouraged to offer definitions. If an idea cannot be defined, it is safe to eliminate it.

6. *Eliminate duplicates.* The facilitator asks the group to identify any ideas that are duplicates or that should be combined. Participants identify the ideas by number to suggest changes. If there is an objection, the changes are overruled. (This is a common facilitation approach for editing: If there are objections to a proposed change, then the change is not accepted.)

7. *Prioritize.* The group is directed to silently select the best ideas on the list by number. They can pick more than one. The facilitator walks through the list tabulating votes (raised hands, no discussion).

8. *Discuss.* The exercise is complete. The group discusses the highest-priority selections and suggests what the follow-up actions will be.

VARIATIONS

The Railroad (also known as Rubber Stamp) AntiPattern is a variation of Design by Committee, whereby a political coalition dominates the process and forces the adoption of designs with serious defects. The Railroad is often motivated by mutual business interests of many members of the committee. By adopting incomplete and defective specifications, details of the technology can be hidden effectively in the software. In this way, software from a coalition developer becomes the de facto standard, as opposed to the written specifications. Some developers outside the coalition will even attempt to implement the "misfeatures," resulting in wasted time and money.

EXAMPLE

Two classic examples of Design by Committee come from the domain of software standardization: the Structured Query Language (SQL) and Common Object Request Broker Architecture (CORBA).

SQL

The Structured Query Language (SQL) became an international standard in 1989. The original, SQL89, was a small document—115 pages—that represented an efficient, minimal design for the technology [Melton 93]. Virtually all relational database products implemented the full specification. In 1992, the second version of SQL was standardized with significant extensions that resulted in a 580-page document. The SQL92 specification was implemented with a unique dialect in every product; few products implemented the entire specification. The next version of SQL, called SQL3, may well be thousands of pages in length. The standards committee responsible for the design is adding a smorgasbord of new features that extend the concept well beyond the original intent. Some of the new features include object-orientation extensions, geospatial extensions, and temporal-logic extensions. It's unlikely that any product will ever fully implement SQL3, nor is it likely that any two products will implement the same subset in a portable manner. In this classic Design by Committee, the SQL standard has become a dumping ground for advanced database features.

An interesting solution to the problems of SQL convergence is presented by the technologies: Open Database Connectivity (ODBC) and Java Database Connectivity (JDBC). Each defined a standard application program interface for database access based on dynamic queries, query statements that are submitted and parsed at run time. Because ODBC and JDBC define the query interface and query language for the clients, they provide isolation from product-specific database features. Clients can access multiple database products transparently. ODBC became an industry standard through the SQL Access Group (SAG), a software industry consortium. Microsoft developed the ODBC specification independently of SAG, and then proposed it to the group. The specification was adopted rapidly by SAG and became a de facto industry standard. Vendors that promote proprietary solutions have had difficulty replacing this highly effective technology, which is universally supported by database vendors and database tool developers.

CORBA

The Common Object Request Broker Architecture (CORBA) standard was adopted by the industry in 1991. The original document—fewer than 200 pages—was easily readable by outsiders to the Object Management Group (OMG) process. In 1995, a revised CORBA2 specification released, with significant upgrades and extensions, including C++ and Smalltalk mappings, the Interface Repository, and the Internet Inter-ORB Protocol (IIOP). The C++ mapping in CORBA2, in particular, contained complex details that could not be implemented consistently by Object Request Broker (ORB) vendors, some of whom changed the APIs generated by their IDL/C++ compilers repeatedly. The Basic Object Adapter (BOA) had been substantially revised in CORBA2. A replacement of this part of CORBA, called the Portable Object Adapter (POA), was adopted in 1997. Since the POA duplicates BOA functionality already in working products, successful vendors may have little motivation to upgrade their products. And because of all this attention on the basic infrastructure, some of the more critical needs of users are allocated lower priority.

An alternative process used by OMG to identify and define technologies for adoption was used by the OMG to produce the CORBAfacilities Architecture. This process was reused by other task forces and end-user enterprises to define their architectures and road maps. The authors called this the "Lost Architecture Process" because it was undocumented (until now).

The Lost Architecture Process is a facilitated architecture-definition procedure that entails the following steps. It may be adapted to the needs of specific enterprises, by replacing OMG processes with organization-specific processes, such as internal surveys and off-site workshops.

1. *Release a request for information (RFI).* The purpose of the RFI is to survey interested parties both inside and outside OMG. Interested parties from any organization are asked to submit their requirements, architectural input, and descriptions of relevant technologies to assist in the planning process.

2. *Review the RFI responses.* Any responses received (typically a dozen or fewer) are reviewed by the task force. This completes the survey and data-collection phase of the process. Once the task force has reviewed this input, it becomes the responsibility of the people in the room to define the architecture. The RFI process is an important step psychologically, because it transforms an undefined set of stakeholders and implicit requirements into the responsibility of the meeting participants to define the architecture and draw the road map.

3. *Identify candidate services and facilities.* The candidate services are listed on flipcharts and posted in the meeting room for participants to review. This listing can begin during the RFI review process, and a brainstorming session can extend these lists with additional facilities. It is important to solicit all ideas, then to cull the list, watching for duplicates and overlapping services.

4. *Launch the initial RFP process.* Probably, at least one of the identified services will be an obvious candidate for an RFP release. It is highly likely that some team of vendors is attending the meeting with the goal of adopting a particular technology. This team can

break out to work on the initial RFP and start the task force adoption processes. The other services and facilities will be defined during the balance of the process.

5. *Diagram the architecture.* A small breakout group organizes the list of services into categories, in the form of a block diagram showing layers of services and horizontal delineations. Obviously, this group needs at least one person skilled in reference model diagramming techniques. This architecture reference diagram is a useful abstraction of the listed services, and will be an important illustration in the architecture document. All services and facilities are listed in the diagram.

6. *Define preliminary service.* The group parcels out services to be defined in terms of a number of viewgraph bullets. People meet in small groups or work individually to define the services in this form. The results are reviewed and discussed by the entire task force, during which additions and edits to the bulleted phrases are recommended and discussed.

7. *Write the service definitions.* Using the content portion of the RFP template, each of the identified services is written up. Writing assignments are worked on in between meetings. At this point, an architecture document editor (just one person is best) must be appointed to receive the inputs and create a draft document.

8. *Draft the document.* The document editor assembles the submitted service definitions and the architecture diagram into a draft document. The editor may add boilerplate descriptions of the overall architecture so that the document can stand on its own. A table of services and service categories is also included in the document to summarize and abstract the contents of the service definitions.

9. *Review the process.* An updated draft of the architecture document is reviewed at each meeting. Editorial changes are proposed and discussed for the next revision. Any missing sections or service write-ups are assigned to group members for independent work and incorporation by the editor.

10. *Define the road map.* The road map is a profile of the architecture that focuses on priority and schedule. Several key criteria establish the priorities and define the schedules. These include industry need for the technology, dependencies between technologies, broadness of technology applicability, and the workload of the task force. The road map definition is a critical part of the process

that allows member groups to organize resources and plan research relevant to the adoption processes.

11. *Conduct the approval process.* After several iterations of the review process, a motion is made to release the architecture and road map as version 1.0. Further revisions can occur after version 1.0 is released; however, the passage of this motion indicates that the task force has reached a consensus on the initial architecture.

Related Solutions, Patterns, and AntiPatterns

Kyle Brown posted a version of the Design by Committee AntiPattern on the Portland Patterns Repository site [Brown 95]. That pattern uses a different template, which focuses entirely on describing the problematic solution and not upon the refactored solution. In contrast, this book includes a refactored solution with each AntiPattern, noting that Socrates was put to death for exposing society's contradictions without offering any constructive suggestions.

 ## Applicability to Other Viewpoints and Scales

The impact of the Design by Committee AntiPattern on developers is that they are expected to implement a highly complex and ambiguous design, which is a stressful situation. They may find the need to quietly subvert the demands of the committee with more realistic design approaches.

Managers suffer from this AntiPattern through a dramatic increase in project risk caused by the excessive complexity. Correspondingly, the schedule and budget of the project are likely to increase dramatically as the consequences of the design are discovered in the laboratory.

At the system level, it might be reasonable to deliver a system based on a Design by Committee specification, if no variations (multiple configurations) are required and the proposed implementation schedule is extended by 30 percent or more. Most developers can manage only a few variations, in platforms, databases, and feature sets.

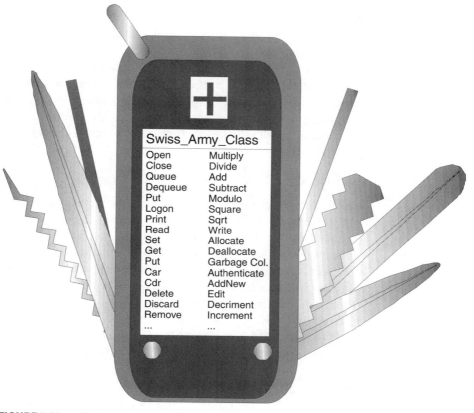

FIGURE 6.14 A Swiss Army Knife: The designers included everything they could think of but the kitchen sink!

Mini-AntiPattern: Swiss Army Knife

AntiPattern Problem

A Swiss Army Knife, also known as Kitchen Sink, is an excessively complex class interface (see Figure 6.14). The designer attempts to provide for all possible uses of the class. In the attempt, he or she adds a large number of interface signatures in a futile attempt to meet all possible needs. Real-world examples of Swiss Army Knife include from dozens to thousands of method signatures for a single class. The designer may not have a clear abstraction or purpose for the class, which is represented by the lack of focus in the interface. Swiss Army

Knives are prevalent in commercial software interfaces, where vendors are attempting to make their products applicable to all possible applications.

This AntiPattern is problematic because it ignores the force of managing complexity, that is, the complicated interface is difficult for other programmers to understand, and obscures how the class is intended to be used, even in simple cases. Other consequences of complexity include the difficulties of debugging, documentation, and maintenance.

Refactored Solution

Often, complex interfaces and standards are encountered that must be utilized in a software development project; therefore, it is important to define conventions for using these technologies so that management of the application's complex architecture is not compromised. This is called creating a *profile*. A profile is a documented convention explaining how to use a complex technology. Often, a profile is an implementation plan implementing the details of the technology. With profiles, two independent developers can use the same technology, with the likelihood of achieving interoperable software.

A profile of a software interface defines the subset of the signatures that are utilized, and should include conventions for the parameter values. In other words, the profile identifies the literal values that can be passed in each parameter. In addition, the profile may be required to define the dynamic behavior of the applications using the interfaces. This includes descriptions and specifications of sequences of execution, method calls, and exception handling.

Variations

A Swiss Army Knife differs from the Blob AntiPattern in that there may be several Swiss Army Knives in a single design. In addition, the intent of the Swiss Army Knife is that the designer is exposing complexity in a vain attempt to address all foreseeable needs for the class. The Blob is a singleton object that monopolizes the process or data in a system.

REINVENT THE WHEEL

AntiPattern Name: Reinvent the Wheel

Also Known As: Design in a Vacuum, Greenfield System

Most Frequent Scale: System

Refactored Solution Name: Architecture Mining

Refactored Solution Type: Process

Root Causes: Pride, Ignorance

Unbalanced Forces: Management of Change, Technology Transfer

Anecdotal Evidence: "Our problem is unique." Software developers generally have minimal knowledge of each other's code. Even widely used software packages available in source code rarely have more than one experienced developer for each program.

Virtually all systems development is done in isolation of projects and systems with overlapping functionality. Reuse is rare in most software organizations. In a recent study of more than 32 object-oriented software projects, the researchers found virtually no evidence of successful reuse [Goldberg 95].

BACKGROUND

Software and design reuse are significantly different paradigms. Software reuse involves the creation of a library of reusable components, the retrieval of those components, and the integration of the components with a software system. The typical result is a modest amount of reuse around the periphery of the system and additional software development to integrate the components. Design reuse involves the reuse of architecture and software interfaces in multiple application systems. It requires the identification of horizontal components with uses across multiple application systems. Design reuse also supports software reuse of the horizontal components without additional development for integration, thus it is a much more effective approach, in that a larger portion of the software system can be leveraged from reusable components.

The term *greenfield* (in Greenfield System, an alias of Reinvent the Wheel) originates from the construction industry. It refers to a new construction site where there are no legacy buildings to introduce constraints on the new building's architecture.

GENERAL FORM

Custom software systems are built from the ground up, even though several systems with overlapping functionality exist. The software process assumes "greenfield" (build from scratch) development of a single system. Because top-down analysis and design lead to new architectures and custom software, software reuse is limited and interoperability is accommodated after the fact.

Most current software methods assume that developers are building custom software from scratch, and that they are building a single system in isolation. These are called *greenfield system assumptions*. Greenfield systems inevitably become stovepipes that lack potential for interoperability, extension, and reuse. Greenfield assumptions are mismatched to most real-world software development problems, where legacy systems exist, and interoperation with them is an important requirement for many new systems. Greenfield assumptions also ignore significant reusable software assets in the form of Internet freeware and commercially available software.

SYMPTOMS AND CONSEQUENCES

- Closed system architectures—architectures and software—that are designed for one system at a time without provision for reuse and interoperability.
- Replication of commercial software functions.
- Immature and unstable architectures and requirements.
- Inadequate support for change management and interoperability.
- Extended development cycles involving failed and dead-end prototypes before the architecture is mature enough to support long-term system development and maintenance.
- Poor management of risks and costs, leading to schedule and budget overruns.

- Inability to deliver the desired features to the end user; extensive effort to replicate the functionality already operational in existing systems.

 ## TYPICAL CAUSES

- No communication and technology transfer between software development projects.
- Absence of an explicit architecture process that includes architecture mining and domain engineering.
- Assumption of greenfield development; in other words, the process assumes that the system will be built from scratch.
- Lack of enterprise management of the computational viewpoint, leading to unique software interfaces in each system.

KNOWN EXCEPTIONS

The Reinvent the Wheel AntiPattern is suitable for a research environment and in general software development to minimize coordination costs where developers with different skills work at logistically remote sites.

REFACTORED SOLUTION

Architecture mining is a way to quickly create successful object-oriented architectures that are robust, product-independent, reusable, and extensible. Most object-oriented design approaches assume that design information is invented as the process proceeds. In a top-down process, design information is generated from requirements, which may be represented as use cases and object-oriented analysis models. Requirements-driven architecture design is called *architecture farming.* In a spiral process, design information is invented during each iteration. As the spiral process proceeds, architects derive new design information as they learn more about the application problem. It's fair to say that these approaches *reinvent* much of their design information.

Precursor designs exist for most information systems applications and problems. These designs are in the form of legacy systems, commercial products, standards, prototypes, and design patterns. Experience proves it is not difficult to identify a half-dozen or more precursor designs for any given application problem. Valuable information is buried in pre-existing designs, information that enabled earlier architects to build useful systems. Extracting this information for use in object-oriented architectures is called *architecture mining.*

Mining may be applicable at the application level for certain complex design problems. In some cases, it may be less expensive and risky to exploit existing expertise than to create new code without exposure to pre-existing solutions. Mining is applicable at enterprise levels, but less so at global levels, given the reduced access to information resources.

Mining is a bottom-up design approach, incorporating design knowledge from working implementations. Mining can incorporate design input from top-down design processes, too, so that there can be both top-down traceability and bottom-up realism.

"Immature artists imitate. Mature artists steal."

—Lionel Trilling

Before mining starts, it is necessary to identify a set of representative technologies that are relevant to the design problem. Technology identification can be done by various means, such as searching literature, interviewing experts, attending technical conferences, and surfing the Net. All available resources should be pursued.

The first mining step is to model each representative technology, to produce specifications of relevant software interfaces. We recommend using OMG IDL as the interface notation because it is concise and free from implementation detail. OMG IDL is also a good design notation for the target architecture because it is language-independent, platform-neutral, and distribution-transparent. Modeling everything in the same notation creates a good basis for design comparison and trade-off.

While modeling, it is important to describe the as-built system, not the intended or desired design. Frequently, relevant design information is not documented as software interfaces. For example, some of the sought-after functionality may be accessible only through the user interface. Other key design lessons may be undocumented, and it is useful to capture this information, too.

In the second mining step, the designs are generalized to create a common interface specification. This step entails more art than science, as the goal is to create an initial "strawman" specification for the target architecture interfaces. It is usually not sufficient to generate a lowest-common denominator design from the representative technology. The generalized interfaces should resemble a best-of-breed solution that captures the common functionality, as well as some unique aspects inspired by particular systems. Unique aspects should be included when they create valuable features in the target architecture or represent areas of known system evolution. A robust assortment of representative technologies will contain indicators of likely areas of target system evolution.

At this point, it is appropriate to factor in the top-down design information as one of the inputs. Top-down information is usually at a much higher level of abstraction than bottom-up information. Reconciliation of these differences involves some important architecture trade-offs.

The final step in the mining process is to refine the design. Refinements can be driven by the architect's judgment, informal walkthroughs, review processes, new requirements, or additional mining studies.

VARIATIONS

Within an organization, software reuse is difficult to achieve. In a survey of several dozen object-oriented application projects, Goldberg and Rubin found no significant reuse [Goldberg 95]. Even if successful, the cost benefits of internal reuse are usually less than 15 percent [Griss 97]. Industry experience indicates that the primary role of internal reuse is as a investment in software for resale. Where large volumes make the potential savings significant, reuse can shorten time-to-market and support product customization.

On the other hand, we claim that reuse is prevalent, but in different forms: reuse of commercially available software and reuse of freeware. Because of larger user bases, commercial software and freeware often have significantly higher quality than custom-developed software. For infrastructure components upon which much application software depends, this enhanced quality can be critical to project success. Commercial software and freeware can reduce maintenance costs when the software is used without modification and can be readily replaced with upgraded versions.

EXAMPLE

Architecture mining requires the study of existing software architectures. Of particular interest are the software interfaces of extant systems. In our training courses on distributed object design patterns, we use the following example to illustrate the techniques and trade-offs required for architecture mining. The software interfaces for two existing systems that perform geospatial catalog queries are presented:

```
// ISO ODP IDL
module Legacy1 {
  struct GeoCoords {
    double lat, lon; // degrees
  };
  typedef string QueryId;
  typedef sequence<string> NameList;
  typedef sequence<string> QueryHitList;
  struct QueryResults {
    NameList     attribute_names;
    QueryHitList query_hits;
  };
  interface CA {
    // initiate query, get query results id, don't wait for query
    // completion
    QueryId boolean_query(
      in string boolean_query_expression); // Boolean Query
Syntax (BQS)
    // initiate query, get query results id, don't wait for query
    // completion
    QueryId point_query(
      in string    boolean_query_expression,
      in GeoCoords point_geo_location);
    // find out if query is finished
    boolean query_finished(in QueryId query_result_identifier);
    // get query results (after query is finished)
    void get_results(
      in QueryId        query_result_identifier,
      in unsigned long number_of_hits_to_return,
      out unsigned long number_of_hits_remaining,
      out QueryResults product_records);
  };
};
```

The second system has the following software interfaces:

```
module Legacy2 {
  struct GeoCoords {
    double lat, lon; // degrees
  };
  typedef sequence<GeoCoords> GeoCoordsList;
  typedef sequence<string> NameList;
  typedef sequence<string> QueryHitList;
  struct QueryResults {
    NameList     attribute_names;
    QueryHitList query_hits;
  };
  interface CA {
    // make query, get query results
    QueryResults boolean_query(
```

```
        in string boolean_query_expression); // Boolean Query
Syntax (BQS)
    // make query, get query results
    QueryResults polygonal_query(
      in string          boolean_query_expression,
      in GeoCoordsList polygon_vertices);
  };
};
```

The architect studies the interfaces in the preceding code sample with the aid of developers who maintain the corresponding systems. He pays particular attention to how the documented interfaces are utilized, as well as any differences between the documentation and the actual usage in the system. The architect needs to understand each of the operations and the parameters in detail. A resulting best-of-breed interface is shown next:

```
module BestOfBreed {
  struct GeoCoords {
    double lat, lon; // degrees
  };
  typedef sequence<GeoCoords> GeoCoordsList;
  typedef string QueryId;
  typedef sequence<string> NameList;
  typedef sequence<string> QueryHitList;
  struct QueryResults {
    NameList      attribute_names;
    QueryHitList query_hits;
  };
  interface CA {
    // initiate query, get query results id, don't wait for query
    // completion
    QueryId boolean_query(
      in string boolean_query_expression); // Boolean Query
Syntax (BQS)
    // initiate query, get query results id, don't wait for query
    // completion
    QueryId point_query(
      in string boolean_query_expression,
      in GeoCoords point_geo_location);
    // initiate query, get query results id, don't wait for query
    // completion
    QueryId polygonal_query(
      in string boolean_query_expression,
      in GeoCoordsList polygon_vertices);
    // find out if query is finished
    boolean query_finished(in QueryId query_result_identifier);
    // get query results (after query is finished)
    void get_results(
      in QueryId       query_result_identifier,
```

```
        in unsigned long number_of_hits_to_return,
        out unsigned long number_of_hits_remaining,
        out QueryResults product_records);
    };
};
```

Note that not every nuance of the original interfaces is incorporated into the best of breed. The design is not a simple, lowest-common denominator of the originals; neither is it a union of the two sets of interfaces and all of their features. The architect must generalize the features that are in common between the mined systems, then selectively incorporate the features that are unique to each system—some of which are predictive of future needs for the common interface. Other unique features will continue to be system-specific and will not belong in the common architecture definition.

RELATED SOLUTIONS

The impact upon management of complexity of architecture mining and the generalization to common interfaces is analyzed in Mowbray 95. Architecture mining is a recurring solution that addresses many of the problems caused by Stovepipe Systems. It is also one of the approaches for defining domain-specific component architectures.

APPLICABILITY TO OTHER VIEWPOINTS AND SCALES

The Reinvent the Wheel AntiPattern puts managers at higher risk, in the form of increased time-to-market and a lower degree of functionality than that expected of the end users. Potential savings from reuse range from 15 to 75 percent of development cost, reduction of 2 to 5 times in time-to-market, and reduction of defects from 5 to 10 times [Jacobson 97].

Mini-AntiPattern: The Grand Old Duke of York

Also Known As

Everyone Charges Up the Hill, Lack of Architecture Instinct, Abstractionists versus Implementationists

Anecdotal Evidence

Experts report that only 1 in 5 software developers is able to define good abstractions [Mowbray 95]. On hearing this, a practicing software architect retorted, "It's more like 1 out of 50."

Background

The term abstractionist originates from the fine arts community, where an abstractionist is an expressionist artist, who depicts his or her emotions and attitudes through nonrepresentational art. In our connotation, an abstractionist is an architect or software developer who has the architecture instinct.

AntiPattern Problem

Programming skill does not equate to skill in defining abstractions. There appear to be two distinct groups involved in software development: abstractionists and their counterparts (whom we call implementationists) [Riel 96]. Abstractionists are comfortable discussing software design concepts without delving into implementation details. As stated, they possess the architecture instinct, the ability to define and explain good software abstractions. Implementationists, on the other hand, often require source code examples before they can grasp abstract concepts; they are not particularly adept at defining new abstractions that can be readily understood by other developers.

Many object-oriented processes are egalitarian; design decisions made in meeting processes are approved by consensus (see the Design by Committee AntiPattern earlier in this chapter). According to experts, implementationists outnumber abstractionists approximately 4 to 1 [Mowbray 95]. Thus, unfortunately, abstractionists are often outvoted. Abstractionists know instinctively that management of complexity is a key design force. Good abstractions are often compromised because so few developers appreciate their significance. The primary consequence is software designs with excessive complexity, which make the system difficult to develop, modify, extend, document, and test. Software usability and system maintenance are impacted by a failure to use effective abstraction principles.

The egalitarian approach to object-oriented development has been rather ineffective in practice; it is reminiscent of a group of people charging up a hill simultaneously. Everyone must understand and concur on numerous decisions, and even though there may be sophisticated members, the overall sophistication of the group is diminished to the lowest common denominator and inhibited by the communication process.

Refactored Solution

A more effective approach involves several distinct roles in a software development organization. Architects are abstractionists with significant experience in the majority of key technologies. They facilitate communication between end users and developers; they are responsible for managing the complexity and ensuring the adaptability of systems. To do this, architects need to manage the computational architecture or system-level programming interfaces.

Component developers are highly skilled programmers. They work with systems programming languages such as C, C++, and Java; they create the software infrastructure and reusable software components.

Application developers are other programmers who integrate these components to create working systems. They primarily use scripting languages such as Visual Basic, JavaScript, Python, Tcl, and Perl. The higher-level nature of the scripting languages enables a wider range of programming skills to be productive.

Variations

The specialization of software development roles indicates that there are multiple disciplines required to build safe and effective software systems. Certification is a potential mechanism for establishing and validating professional capabilities. Certification is required for many professionals, for example, cosmetologists, chauffeurs, lawyers, and certified public accountants. Why not for software architects?

7

Software Project Management AntiPatterns

In the modern engineering profession, more than half of the job involves human communication and resolving people issues. The management AntiPatterns identify some of the key scenarios in which these issues are destructive to software processes.

Changing Role of Management

The role of the technical manager is changing. Before ubiquitous electronic mail and intranets, managers were primarily organizational communicators. Management chains conveyed information across organizational boundaries, whereas in the electronic organization, communication can occur seamlessly across space, time, and boundaries.

Traditionally, a key role of management has been to authorize exceptions to rules and procedures. But business-process reengineering (BPR) of organizational structures has changed that role significantly. Before reengineering, organizational boundaries enforced legacy business rules that were often counterproductive. In reengineered organizations, unpro-

DILBERT reprinted by permission of United Feature Syndicate, Inc.

ductive boundaries are eliminated, and people are empowered to solve problems without management intervention.

In software development, however, managers still play several important roles, in the areas of:

- Software process management.
- Resource management (human & IT infrastructure).
- External relationship management (e.g., customers, development partners).

Death March Projects

We are not the first to write about the contradictions and pitfalls in software projects [Webster 95, 97]. Yourdon has described the *death march project* as one with unreasonable commitments [Yourdon 97]. He defines any project with goals or resources that are scoped 50 percent outside of reasonable norms as a death march project. This means one or more of the following:

- The schedule is 50 percent too short.
- The size of the staff is only half as large as necessary.
- The budget is 50 percent too small.
- The number of features is 50 percent greater than comparable successful projects. Some cynics contend that all software projects are death march projects.

We agree with many of Yourdon's points with one significant exception. Using a quote from Scott Adams (Dilbert Cartoonist), Yourdon asserts that the root cause of death march projects is that "people are idiots." Our view is that because people are human, they share all human failings. We need to recognize our failings in the light of product development in order to overcome them. The more people involved in a product development, the more complexity this adds to the tasks of error identification (process, role, software defects, etc.) and error rectification.

The purpose of management AntiPatterns is to build new awareness that enables you to enhance your success. Management AntiPatterns describe how software projects are impaired by people issues, processes, resources, and external relationships. The patterns also describe some of the most effective solutions to these problems.

We have compassion for developers who suffer through stressful software projects. We have even greater compassion for software managers, the people who suffer the dire consequences of project failure [Yourdon 97]. Good managers help moderate the stress levels of the entire software organization. As a consequence, many of them take on much of this stress personally. In addition to the AntiPattern solutions discussed here, we recommend time-management training as an effective way for software professionals to learn how to manage stress.

Management AntiPattern Summaries

The following summaries are an overview of the management AntiPatterns. They also include descriptions of management mini-AntiPatterns that are discussed in conjunction with the main AntiPatterns.

Blowhard Jamboree: The opinions of so-called industry experts often influence technology decisions. Controversial reports that criticize particular technologies frequently appear in popular media and private publications. In addition to technical responsibilities, developers spend too much time answering the concerns of managers and decision makers arising from these reports.

Analysis Paralysis: Striving for perfection and completeness in the analysis phase often leads to project gridlock and excessive thrashing of requirements/models. The refactored solution includes a description of incremental, iterative development processes that defer detailed analysis until the knowledge is needed.

Viewgraph Engineering: On some projects, developers become stuck preparing viewgraphs and documents instead of developing software. Management never obtains the proper development tools, and engineers have no alternative but to use office automation software to produce psuedo-technical diagrams and papers.

Death by Planning: Excessive planning for software projects leads to complex schedules that cause downstream problems. We explain how to plan a reasonable software development process that includes incorporating known facts and incremental replanning.

Fear of Success: An interesting phenomenon often occurs when people and projects are on the brink of success. Some people begin to worry obsessively about the kinds of things that *can* go wrong. Insecurities about professional competence come to the surface.

Corncob: Difficult people frequently obstruct and divert the software development process. Corncobs can be dealt with by addressing their agendas through various tactical, operational, and strategic organizational actions.

Intellectual Violence: Intellectual violence occurs when someone who understands a theory, technology, or buzzword uses this knowledge to intimidate others in a meeting situation.

Irrational Management: Habitual indecisiveness and other bad management habits lead to de facto decisions and chronic development crises. We explain how to utilize rational management decision-making techniques to improve project resolution and for keeping managers on track.

Smoke and Mirrors: Demonstration systems are important sales tools, as they are often interpreted by end users as representational of production-quality capabilities. A management team, eager for new business, sometimes (inadvertently) encourages these misperceptions and makes commitments beyond the capabilities of the organization to deliver operational technology.

Project Mismanagement: Inattention to the management of software development processes can cause directionlessness and other symptoms. Proper monitoring and control of software projects is necessary to successful development activities. Running a product development is as complex an activity as creating the project plan, and developing software is as complex as building skyscrapers, involving as many steps and processes, including checks and balances. Often, key activities are overlooked or minimized.

Throw It over the Wall: Object-oriented methods, design patterns, and implementation plans intended as flexible guidelines are too often taken literally by the downstream managers and object-oriented developers. As guidelines progress through approval and publication processes, they often are attributed with unfulfilled qualities of completeness, prescriptiveness, and mandated implementation.

Fire Drill: Airline pilots describe flying as "hours of boredom followed by 15 seconds of sheer terror." Many software projects resemble this situation: "Months of boredom followed by demands for immediate delivery." The months of boredom may include protracted requirements analysis, replanning, waiting for funding, waiting for approval, or any number of technopolitical reasons.

The Feud: Personality conflicts between managers can dramatically affect the work environment. The employees reporting to these managers often suffer the consequences of their supervisors' disagreements. Animosity between managers is reflected in the attitudes and actions of their employees.

E-mail Is Dangerous: E-mail is an important communication medium for software managers. Unfortunately, it is an inappropriate medium for many topics and sensitive communications.

Mini-AntiPattern: Blowhard Jamboree

AntiPattern Problem

The opinions of so-called industry experts often influence technology decisions. Controversial reports that criticize particular technologies frequently appear in popular media and private publications. In addition to technical responsibilities, developers spend too much time answering the concerns of managers and decision makers arising from such reports. Many of these so-called experts are misinformed; occasionally, they represent biased viewpoints. Often, the information they are reporting is second-hand. Rarely is there any hands-on research and experience backing up their conclusions.

Refactored Solution

An in-house expert on each key technology is an invaluable asset to every organization. He or she can discriminate between facts, misinformation, and opinions in popular media and other reports. If your organization does not have in-house experts, appoint staff to follow particular technologies and develop their expertise through reading, training courses, standards activities, and hands-on experiments, such as prototyping.

Electronic mailing lists often contribute to the spread of misinformation. Therefore, avoid forwarding press releases to such lists. Press releases are properly called propaganda; they circulate selected information that benefits a particular organization. As an alternative, direct an in-house expert to disseminate a factual summary of important announcements.

ANALYSIS PARALYSIS

AntiPattern Name: Analysis Paralysis

Also Known As: Waterfall, Process Mismatch

Most Frequent Scale: System

Refactored Solution Name: Iterative-Incremental Development

Refactored Solution Type: Software

Root Causes: Pride, Narrow-Mindedness

Unbalanced Forces: Management of Complexity

Anecdotal Evidence: "We need to redo this analysis to make it more object-oriented, and use much more inheritance to get lots of reuse." "We need to complete object-oriented analysis, and design before we can begin any coding." "Well, what if the user wants to create the employee list based on the fourth and fifth letters of their first name combined with the project they charged the most hours to between Thanksgiving and Memorial Day of the preceding four years?" "If you treat each object attribute as an object, you can reuse field formatting between unrelated classes."

BACKGROUND

Analysis Paralysis is one of the classic AntiPatterns in object-oriented software development. Object-oriented analysis is focused on decomposing a problem into its constituent parts, but there is no obvious method for identifying the exact level of detail necessary for system design [Webster 95]. Frequently, the focus is shifted from decomposing to a level where the problem can be easily understood by the designers to applying the techniques to achieve the mythical "completeness." Also, system developers often willingly fall prey to Analysis Paralysis, as "designs never fail, only implementations." By prolonging the analysis and design phases, they avoid risking accountability for results. Of course, this is a losing strategy, because usually there is some point after which a working implementation is expected.

GENERAL FORM

Analysis Paralysis occurs when the goal is to achieve perfection and completeness of the analysis phase. This AntiPattern is characterized by turnover, revision of the models, and the generation of detailed models that are less than useful to downstream processes.

Many developers new to object-oriented methods do too much up-front analysis and design. Sometimes, they use analysis modeling as an exercise to feel comfortable in the problem domain. One of the benefits of object-oriented methods is developing analysis models with the participation of domain experts. Otherwise, it's easy to get bogged down in the analysis process when the goal is to create a comprehensive model.

Analysis Paralysis usually involves waterfall assumptions:

- Detailed analysis can be successfully completed prior to coding.
- Everything about the problem is known a priori.
- The analysis models will not be extended nor revisited during development. Object-oriented development is poorly matched to waterfall analysis, design, and implementation processes. Effective object-oriented development is an incremental process during which incremental and iterative results of analysis are validated through design and implementation and used as feedback into later system analysis.

> "Ah! What is man? Wherefore does he why? Whence did he whence? Whither is he withering?"
>
> —Dan Leno (George Galvin)

A key indicator of Analysis Paralysis is that the analysis documents no longer make sense to the domain experts. As Analysis Paralysis progresses, the analysis models more frequently cover details that are of no interest to the domain experts. For example, the domain model of a health care system for a hospital should be understandable by the administrators and staff of the hospital. If the domain model defines unexpected software concepts, categories, and specializations, the analysis modeling has probably gone too far. If the meaning of these new classes has to be explained in detail to the people intimately familiar with the current system, it is likely that the problem has been overanalyzed.

SYMPTOMS AND CONSEQUENCES

- There are multiple project restarts and much model rework, due to personnel changes or changes in project direction.
- Design and implementation issues are continually reintroduced in the analysis phase.
- Cost of analysis exceeds expectation without a predictable end point.
- The analysis phase no longer involves user interaction. Much of the analysis performed is speculative.
- The complexity of the analysis models results in intricate implementations, making the system difficult to develop, document, and test.
- Design and implementation decisions such as those used in the Gang of Four design patterns are made in the analysis phase.

TYPICAL CAUSES

- The management process assumes a waterfall progression of phases. In reality, virtually all systems are built incrementally even if not acknowledged in the formal process.
- Management has more confidence in their ability to analyze and decompose the problem than to design and implement.
- Management insists on completing all analysis before the design phase begins.
- Goals in the analysis phase are not well defined.
- Planning or leadership lapses when moving past the analysis phase.
- Management is unwilling to make firm decisions about when parts of the domain are sufficiently described.
- The project vision and focus on the goal/deliverable to customer is diffused. Analysis goes beyond providing meaningful value.

KNOWN EXCEPTIONS

There should never be any exceptions to the Analysis Paralysis AntiPattern.

 **REFACTORED SOLUTION**

Key to the success of object-oriented development is incremental development. Whereas a waterfall process assumes a priori knowledge of the problem, incremental development processes assume that details of the problem and its solution will be learned in the course of the development process. In incremental development, all phases of the object-oriented process occur with each iteration—analysis, design, coding, test, and validation. Initial analysis comprises a high-level review of the system so that the goals and general functionality of the system can be validated with the users. Each increment fully details a part of the system.

There are two kinds of increments: internal and external. An *internal increment* builds software that is essential to the infrastructure of the implementation. For example, a third-tier database and data-access layer would comprise an internal increment. Internal increments build a common infrastructure that is utilized by multiple use cases. In general, internal increments minimize rework. An *external increment* comprises user-visible functionality. External increments are essential to winning political consensus for the project by showing progress. External increments are also essential for user validation. They usually involve some throwaway coding to simulate missing parts of the infrastructure and back-end tiers. It's the prerogative of the project manager to select the increments that balance the forces of project survival, user validation, and minimal cost. See the Project Mismanagement AntiPattern later in this chapter regarding scheduling of increments with regard to risk.

Frequently, when performing object-oriented analysis, it's easier to continue the analysis than to end it and move on to the design of the software. Since many of the analysis techniques are also applied at some level to the design, it's easy to use the analysis phase to direct the specifics of the overall design. Sometimes, this also results from thinking that minimal analysis is needed concurrently with design, and that design can be started then gone back to. Typically, this results in a product that neither resembles a domain model a user can understand nor a desirable design for an implemented system.

Analysis Paralysis is also applicable at the architectural level and takes on a similar form to the AntiPattern at the developmental level. An architecture can certainly be specified far beyond what is necessary for the developers to adhere to the architectural principles and constructs. For example, specifying the known and allowable subclasses used by an architectural construct designed to operate solely on the object's base class interface is overkill. Rather, it is preferable to specify the necessary constraints in the base class on which the architectural component operates and trust (and perhaps also verify) the developers to maintain the constraints in their subclasses.

At the managerial level, Analysis Paralysis is known as micromanagement and occurs when managers overspecify assignments and oversupervise delegated assignments.

Mini-AntiPattern: Viewgraph Engineering

AntiPattern Problem

On some projects, developers become stuck preparing viewgraphs and documents instead of developing software. Management never obtains the proper development tools, and engineers have no alternative but to use office automation software to produce psuedo-technical diagrams and papers. This situation is frustrating to the engineers, it does not use their real talents, and allows their skills to obsolesce.

Refactored Solution

Many of the developers caught in viewgraph engineering roles should be redirected to construct prototypes. Prototyping, underutilized by many organizations, has many roles in a project beyond the creation of a sales tool. It is a key element of iterative, incremental development processes. Prototypes can answer technical questions that cannot be deduced through paper analyses, and can be used to reduce many types of risks, including those related to technology and user acceptance. Prototyping helps to shorten learning curves for new technologies.

Two principal kinds of prototypes are: mockups and engineering prototypes. A mockup is a prototype that simulates user-interface appearance and behavior. When mockups are coupled with system usability experiments (with actual end users), requirements issues and user acceptance can be assessed. Engineering prototypes include some operational functionality, such as application services, databases, and integration with legacy systems. Prototyping a system in an alternative language (such as Smalltalk) prior to production system development is a useful exercise. This prototype can help to validate an architecture prior to implementation in a more efficient, but more costly and less flexible technology.

DEATH BY PLANNING

AntiPattern Name: Death by Planning

Also Known As: Glass Case Plan, Detailitis Plan

Most Frequent Scale: Enterprise

Refactored Solution Name: Rational Planning

Refactored Solution Type: Process

Root Causes: Avarice, Ignorance, Haste

Unbalanced Forces: Management of Complexity

Anecdotal Evidence: "We can't get started until we have a complete program plan." "The plan is the only thing that will ensure our success." "As long as we follow the plan and don't diverge from it, we will be successful." "We have a plan; we just need to follow it!"

 ## BACKGROUND

In many organizational cultures, detailed planning is an assumed activity for any project. This assumption is appropriate for manufacturing activities and many other types of projects, but not necessarily for many software projects, which contain many unknowns and chaotic activities by their very nature. Death by Planning occurs when detailed plans for software projects are taken too seriously.

GENERAL FORM

Many projects fail from *over* planning. Over planning often occurs as a result of cost tracking and staff utilization monitoring. The two types of over planning are known as the Glass Case Plan and Detailitis Plan. The Glass Case Plan is a subset of the Detailitis Plan in that (over) planning ceases once the project starts. In the Detailitis Plan, over planning continues until the project ceases to exist, for a variety of unfulfilling reasons.

GLASS CASE PLAN

Often, a plan produced at the start of a project is always referenced as if it's an accurate, current view of the project even if it's never updated. This practice gives management a "comfortable view" of delivery before the project starts. However, when the plan is never tracked against, nor updated, it becomes increasingly inaccurate as the project progresses. This false view is often compounded by the absence of concrete information on progress, which often is known only after a critical deliverable slips its schedule.

Figure 7.1 shows a project plan created prior to project launch. Management assumes that the plan guarantees delivery automatically— exactly as specified with no intervention (or management) necessary.

DETAILITIS PLAN

Sometimes the solution to effective delivery is regarded as a high degree of control via a continuous planning exercise that involves most of the senior developers, as well as the managers. This approach often evolves into a

FIGURE 7.1 Glass Case Plan.

hierarchical sequence of plans, which show additional (and unecessary) levels of detail. The ability to define such a high level of detail gives the perception that the project is fully under control (see Figure 7.2).

SYMPTOMS AND CONSEQUENCES

The Glass Case Plan symptoms are the first noticed in both it and the Detailitis Plan.

GLASS CASE PLAN

The symptoms usually include at least one of the following:

- Inability to plan at a pragmatic level.
- Focus on costs rather than delivery.
- Enough greed to commit to any detail as long as the project is funded.

The consequences are incremental:

- Ignorance of the status of the project's development. The plan has no meaning, and control of delivery lessens as time goes on. The project may be well ahead or behind the intended deliverable state and no one would know.
- Failure to deliver a critical deliverable (the final consequence).

Consequences grow incrementally until finally the project overruns, with the usual options of:

- Further investment.
- Crisis project management.
- Cancellation.
- Possible loss of key staff.

> "Art for Art's Sake."
>
> —Howard Dietz

DETAILITIS PLAN

The symptoms are a superset of the Glass Case Plan:

- Inability to plan at a pragmatic level.
- Focus on costs rather than delivery.

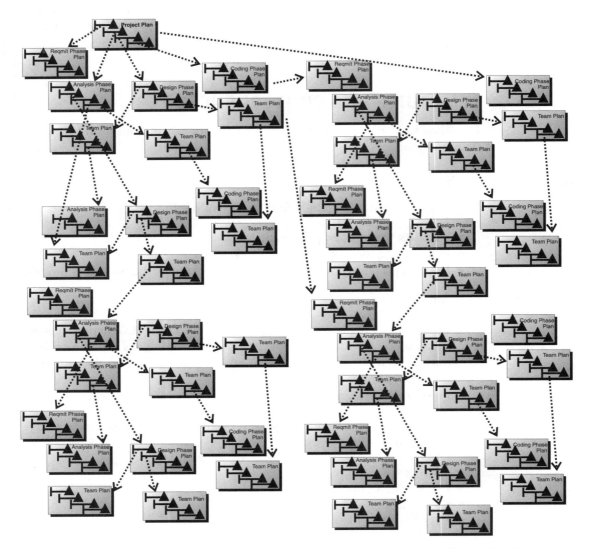

FIGURE 7.2 Death by Planning involves thorough preplanning, regardless of unknowns.

- Spending more time planning, detailing progress, and replanning than on delivering software:
  - Project manager plans the project's activities.
  - Team leaders plan the team's activities and the developers' activities.
- Project developers break down their activities into tasks.

The consequences are intertwined and feed off each other:

- Each planner has to monitor and capture progress at the level shown by his or her plan, and reestimate.
- Endless planning and replanning causes further planning and replanning.
- The objective shifts from delivery of software to delivery of a set of plans. Management assumes that because effort and cost are tracked, progress must be equivalent. In fact, there is no direct correlation.
- Continual delays to software delivery and eventual project failure.

TYPICAL CAUSES

In both cases, Glass Case Plan and Detailitis Plan the primary cause is lack of a pragmatic, common-sense approach to planning, schedules, and capture of progress.

GLASS CASE PLAN

- No up-to-date project plan that shows the software component deliverables and their dates.
- Ignorance of basic project-management principles.
- Overzealous initial planning to attempt to enforce absolute control of development.
- A sales aid for contract acquisition.

DETAILITIS PLAN

- Overzealous continual planning to attempt to enforce absolute control of development.
- Planning as the primary project activity.
- Forced customer compliance.
- Forced executive management compliance.

KNOWN EXCEPTIONS

There should never be any exceptions to the Death by Planning AntiPattern.

REFACTORED SOLUTION

The solution is the same for both the Glass Case and Detailitis Plans. A project plan should show primarily deliverables (regardless of how many teams are working on the project). Deliverables should be identified at two levels:

1. *Product(s).* Those artifacts sold to a customer, which include the internal corporate lines of business that use them.
2. *Components (within products).* Basic technology artifacts required to support a business service.

Deliverables include such things as:

Business requirements statement

Technical description

Measurable acceptance criteria

Product usage scenarios

Component use cases

The plan should be supplemented with validation milestones for each component, as well as the overall product, such as:

Conceptual design approval

Specification design approval

Implementation design approval

Test plan approval

The deliverable plans should be updated weekly to ensure appropriate planning and controls that reduce project risks. This allows issues, risks, slippages, and early deliveries of defined deliverables to be dealt with by appropriate, timely responses.

Tracking is done on the estimated level of completeness, as shown in Figure 7.3. This sometimes means regressing the completeness that was input to the plan in a previous time period. Completeness should be gross measurements rather than fine measurements, for example, tracking in 25 percent steps rather than 5 percent steps.

A Gantt chart can be used effectively to visually illustrate deliverables, associated dates, and interdependencies. By tracking against a

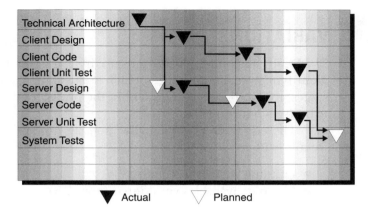

FIGURE 7.3 Proper planning involves tracking of actuals and replanning.

baseline plan, the following states of deliverables will be immediately obvious:

- On schedule.
- Delivered.
- Early (with estimated new delivery date).
- Late (with estimated new delivery date).

It is essential to baseline early and rarely. Otherwise the ability to track changes is lost. Furthermore activities/tasks/deliverables should have dependencies set between them where they exist.

When estimating it is advisable to allow a contingency period for all those inevitable "unknowns," such as:

- Requirements increase (creep).
- Design dead ends.
- Third-party software workarounds.
- Defect identification (finding the problem in a set of integrated components).
- Defect correction (bug fixing).

It is also important to establish a minimum time frame in which to accomplish any activity. This prevents such constraints as two days to code and test a "simple" program.

VARIATIONS

The Death by Planning variations are in levels of detail, and can go from identifying major milestones, which are usually tied to funding/approval stages, to micro-deliverables within the project delivery stages for each team (see Figure 7.4).

These variations are equally applicable to both the Glass Case and Detailitis Plans:

- Funding variations (Figure 7.4)
- Micro-deliverables variation (Figure 7.5)

The Glass Case version of the micro-deliverables plan only varies from the Detailitis Plan in that it is never updated. It shows very minor deliverables that cannot be fully understood prior to starting the project. Therefore, any estimates must by definition be incorrect based upon the lack of any real understanding of the software to be built. This type of plan is usually produced by technically gifted amateurs. Although the tasks need to be clearly understood, putting them in a plan results only in unnecessary planning and tracking (in the case of the Detailitis Plan), as opposed to doing.

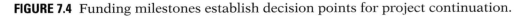

FIGURE 7.4 Funding milestones establish decision points for project continuation.

Requirements			
	Draft Requirements		
		Client GUI	
			Scope
			Functions
			Constraints
			Usage Scenarios
			Performance Criteria
		Client Application	
			Scope
			Functions
			Constraints
			Usage Scenarios
			Performance Criteria
		Application Server	
			Scope
			Functions
			Constraints
			Usage Scenarios
			Performance Criteria
		Security Server	
			Scope
			Functions
			Constraints
			Usage Scenarios
			Performance Criteria
	Final Requirements		
		Client GUI	
			Scope
			Functions
			Constraints
			Usage Scenarios
			Performance Criteria

FIGURE 7.5 Micro-deliverables plan.

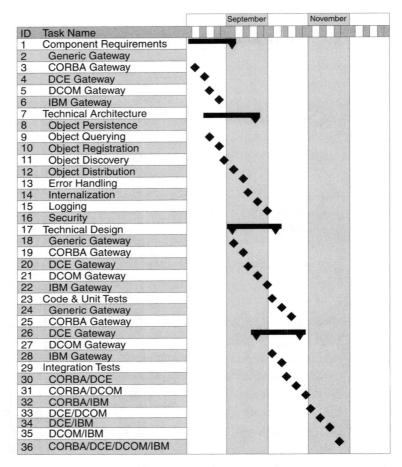

FIGURE 7.6 Glass Case Plan example.

 EXAMPLE

The examples are based on our own experiences in learning "the hard way."

GLASS CASE PLAN

For this example, we'll say a systems integrator decides to build a middleware component not yet available from any of the major vendors, in spite of international standards issued over a year ago. The systems integrator agrees to a detailed delivery plan in advance of starting any project work in order to obtain a funding source. The plan is based upon estimates from staff who have not yet delivered software "in anger." The plan is highly specific technically, and the estimates are very optimistic; and it is continually referenced by the project manager, but never updated to reflect any actual effort. This leads to missed delivery dates. There is a general lack of knowledge as to the real progress of the project; the systems integrator is apprised of delivery date failure only *after* the dates have passed. The plan shown in Figure 7.6 is an extract from such a development project.

DETAILITIS PLAN

In an attempt to control development to ensure that full control is established, an end-user company produces a plan that has three levels:

1. phases of development.
2. team tasks and effort.
3. team member tasks and effort.

The plan in Figure 7.7 indicates the complexity.

Detailitis causes an inability to track against the plan without taking considerable focus away from delivering the system. This results in significantly reduced staff productivity. Plan management quickly becomes unrealistic due to complexity.

The solution is to replace the detailed plan with one that shows key deliverables against dates, with dependencies and constraints. If the deliverable is missed, then something important has occurred. The previous plan attempted to track progress by effort that was unrealistic: Effort = staff × days elapsed. So what? $E = MC^2$, but the formula does not create nuclear power!

RELATED SOLUTIONS

The Analysis Paralysis AntiPattern can exacerbate the consequences of Death by Planning. If the analysis phase runs over its allotted schedule, either a schedule must slip or inadequate analysis models are applied to downstream phases.

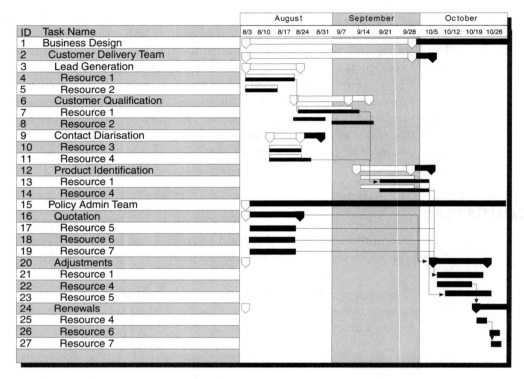

ID	Task Name	August					September				October			
		8/3	8/10	8/17	8/24	8/31	9/7	9/14	9/21	9/28	10/5	10/12	10/19	10/26
1	Business Design													
2	Customer Delivery Team													
3	Lead Generation													
4	Resource 1													
5	Resource 2													
6	Customer Qualification													
7	Resource 1													
8	Resource 2													
9	Contact Diarisation													
10	Resource 3													
11	Resource 4													
12	Product Identification													
13	Resource 1													
14	Resource 4													
15	Policy Admin Team													
16	Quotation													
17	Resource 5													
18	Resource 6													
19	Resource 7													
20	Adjustments													
21	Resource 1													
22	Resource 4													
23	Resource 5													
24	Renewals													
25	Resource 4													
26	Resource 6													
27	Resource 7													

FIGURE 7.7 Detailitis Plan example.

APPLICABILITY TO OTHER VIEWPOINTS AND SCALES

Death by Planning cannot match the chaotic (white-water) nature of software development, because it creates a significant disparity between the management's planning models and actual development activities. Architects and developers often have to live double lives: On one hand, they must visibly cooperate with management's plan for the project; at the same time, they have to confront the actual status of the software, which may not resemble the management model. For example, the plan may be used to pressure developers into declaring software modules complete before they are mature. This causes downstream problems in integration and testing.

Mini-AntiPattern: Fear of Success

Anecdotal Evidence

Wayne & Garth: "We are not worthy!"
The Crazies: "It's fear of success mate!"

AntiPattern Problem

An interesting phenomenon often occurs when people and projects are on the brink of success. Some people begin to worry obsessively about the kinds of things that *can* go wrong. Insecurities about professional competence come to the surface. When discussed openly, these worries and insecurities can occupy the minds of the project team members. Irrational decisions may be made and inappropriate actions may be taken to address these concerns. For example, these discussions may generate negative publicity outside the project team that affects how the deliverable is perceived, and may ultimately have a destructive effect on the project outcome.

Fear of Success is related to *termination* issues. In general, group dynamics progress through a number of phases, discernable for both one-week projects and efforts of lengthier duration. The first phase addresses group acceptance issues. In the second phase, as relationships are formed, individuals assume various roles in the group, including both formal roles in the organization and informal self-determined roles. This is an important factor in team building. After the roles are established, the work is accomplished (third phase). Many personality issues may arise during this phase. Because project completion may result in dissolution of the group, these issues often emerge as project termination approaches (fourth phase). In the termination phase, concerns about the outcome of the project, its future life cycle, and the group's subsequent activities are often expressed in indirect ways. In other words, people do crazy things.

Refactored Solution

One important action that management can take near the end of a project is to *declare success*. Statements by management that support the successful outcome of the project are needed, even if the actual outcome is ambiguous. It is important to help the project team to accept the significance of their achievements and lessons learned. Declaring success also helps to mitigate termination issues, maintain the team's commitment to the organization, and pave the way for future project activities. An award ceremony, complete with the issuance of certificates or plaques, is an appropriate gesture for this purpose. Professional recognition is inexpensive and highly valued by recipients.

Variations

Personal consultation and mentoring is an effective way to cope with the concerns of individuals. Senior staff who have experience on several projects can help others to cope with the stresses of termination issues. Exhibiting patience during the transition to success is important behavior to demonstrate and emulate.

CORNCOB

AntiPattern Name: Corncob

Also Known As: Corporate Shark, Loose Cannon, Third-World Information Systems Troubles (TWIT)

Most Frequent Scale: Enterprise

Refactored Solution Name: Corncob Removal Service

Refactored Solution Type: Role

Root Causes: Avarice, Pride, Narrow-Mindedness

Unbalanced Forces: Management of Resources, Technology Transfer

Anecdotal Evidence: "Why is Bill so difficult to work with?" "Management always listens to whomever shouts longest and loudest." "I own development and I have made a decision that you will follow." "We need to change the build process and accept that we will delay delivery a month or two."

 BACKGROUND

Corncobs are difficult people who can be prevalent in the software development business. This attitude can be due to aspects of individual personality, but often, difficulties arise from personal motivations for recognition or monetary incentives.

Due to rigorous schedules and budget pressure, software development can become stressful. Corncobs exacerbate these problems and create unnecessary, additional stress, in what may be an already overstressed environment.

"Corncob" is a slang term frequently used at Object Management Group, a software consortium, to describe difficult people.

GENERAL FORM

A difficult person (the Corncob) causes problems through destructive behaviors for a software development team or, even worse, throughout an enterprise. This person may be a member of the team or a member of external senior staff (such as a technical architect or development manager) who adversely impacts the team through various means: technical, political, and personal. When dealing with Corncobs, it's important to remember that politics is the exercise of power, and Corncobs focus much more on politics than technology. They are usually experts at manipulating politics at personal and/or organizational levels. Technology-focused people can become unwilling easy victims of the Corncob's tactics.

SYMPTOMS AND CONSEQUENCES

- A development team or project is unable to make progress because someone disagrees with their key objectives or essential processes and continually tries to change them.
- One person continually raises objections, under the guise of concern, which are intractable: performance, reliability, technology market share, and so on.
- The destructive behavior is well known to many people in the enterprise, but it's tolerated and supported (in some way) by management because they are unaware of, or unwilling to address, the damage it causes.
- Political forces create an environment where it's difficult to keep technical discussions on track.
- Political forces result in frequent changes to the scope or requirements of the system. The project becomes much more reactive than proactive, because everyone is responding to the "endless improvements" from the Corncob.
- Often, the destructive person is a manager who is not under the direct authority of a senior software development manager or project manager.

- The company has no defined decision-making process that enables it to resolve issues and move on. This allows a manager to inappropriately interfere beyond his or her area of accountability.

TYPICAL CAUSES

- Management supports the Corncob's destructive behavior, by virtue of not acknowledging the impact of the Corncob's actions. Management's view of the situation is often supplied from the Corncob.
- The Corncob has a hidden agenda, which conflicts with the team's goals.
- There is a fundamental disagreement between team members that no amount of communication can resolve.
- Management doesn't isolate the group from internal and external forces, and has inappropriately allocated roles to staff, who abuse them for their own ends; even worse, management has failed to allocate accountability at all.

KNOWN EXCEPTIONS

The Corncob AntiPattern is acceptable when a company or product development manager is willing to live with the actions of the Corncob. This is a subjective judgment of benefits and disadvantages.

In projects that involve multiple organizations, it's sometimes useful to have a designated Corncob, whose role is to defend an existing architecture from inappropriate changes. When there are many conflicting technical viewpoints, a dominant personality is often required to enforce the reference architecture.

REFACTORED SOLUTION

Solutions to the Corncob AntiPattern are applied at several levels of authority, including strategic, operational, and tactical. In all cases, the key action lever is management support for the destructive behaviors. By eliminating management support at the aforementioned levels, the Corncob loses support, and the best interests of the software development team can dominate.

TACTICAL SOLUTIONS

Tactical solutions are actions employed on the fly, such as in a meeting. They include the following:

- *Transfer the responsibility.* Give the naysayer full responsibility for solving the problems they identify within an agreed-on time period. In other words, turn the responsibility for planning and resolution over to the person who raises the concerns.
- *Isolate the issue.* Often, the Corncob's is an isolated opinion. Appealing to the group's interests is an effective way to defend against an individual's behavior or isolated concerns. If the Corncob is confrontational, remember to never take anything personally; doing so is always a mistake. Facilitate the group to discuss and frame the key objections, then try to gain consensus to overrule the objector. A straw poll is an effective technique for revealing group feeling.
- *Question the question.* When the Corncob uses ambiguous or "loaded" words or phrases, ask him or her to clarify their meaning. When he or she uses hearsay evidence to make an assertion, ask him or her to substantiate the claims and to identify his or her personal position.

OPERATIONAL SOLUTIONS

Operational actions are taken offline, within a limited organizational scope. These include:

- *Corrective interview.* Management meets individually with the person causing the problems, and explains the impact of his or her behavior. The purpose of the corrective interview is to raise awareness and reach agreement on how to change the behavior.
- *Friendly outplacement.* Recommend a Corncob to employment headhunters to help him or her to exit gracefully a difficult situation in an organization.

STRATEGIC SOLUTIONS

Strategic actions are long term and have a wider enterprise scope, such as:

- *Corncob support group.* If there are several Corncobs in an organization, management can transfer them into the same group. In this way, they have to contend with each other's personalities and behaviors. Often, each will approach management and ask why he or she has to work with such difficult people, giving the manager the opening to explain that the person is him- or herself described as difficult by others. This can result in self-awareness, and perhaps, improvement.

- *Empty department.* Managers who are themselves difficult can be transferred to departments in which they are the only employee. These managers usually "get the message" and retire or pursue careers in other companies.
- *Reduction in force.* Sometimes there is no other recourse than to eliminate difficult people from the project team or environment.

 VARIATIONS

Variations on the preceding solutions include:

- *Sidelining.* Sidelining entails reassigning the Corncob to minimal duties. That said, we have found sidelining to be an ineffective practice, as it gives the Corncob more time to think and lobby his or her (often hidden) agenda.
- *Third-World Information System Troubles (TWIT).* This term was introduced by Randall Oakes, MD, to refer to naysayers who resist IT change, even though the majority of people are experiencing negative consequences under current conditions. The TWIT benefits in some way from the status quo. As Dr. Oakes points out, helping the person manage his or her stress levels can lead to trust, friendship, and more open-mindedness.
- *Corporate Shark.* A Corporate Shark is an experienced manager whose career consists of managing relationships rather than his or her technical expertise, which may, as a result, be long neglected. Sharks survive by who they know not what they know. The Corporate Shark knows how to "work the system," and can easily create difficult political situations for those focused on technical issues. In the working world, everybody needs a friend. The best friend is the influential person in the company who defends you to the hilt when confronted by attacks from Corporate Sharks. The best way to manage a relationship with Corporate Sharks is to avoid them altogether, because the only likely outcomes are negative.
- *Bonus Monster.* Someone stands to reap a short-term gain (such as an executive bonus) by cutting corners in the software development process. Bonus monsters are particularly destructive by encouraging internal competition between different departments within an enterprise.

The problem is remedied by restructuring or eliminating the bonus system. A Bonus Monster is usually also a Corporate Shark, but a shark with strong motivation to push for bonus-generating outcomes.

- *Firebrand.* A Firebrand is a person who deliberately creates a political emergency. For example, the Firebrand might be responsible for the late delivery of a critical piece of software by generating various misdirections and obstructions. His or her purpose is to create an emergency so that later he or she can be recognized as a hero for saving the organization. In order to achieve success, the firebrand extinguishes the fire; that is, he or she removes all the obstructions and readjusts the focus of the developers, as needed, to allow them to succeed.

- *Egomaniac.* An Egomaniac is obsessed with his or her image as a key influencer or dominant figure. Egomaniacs are also called Prima Donnas. A remedy for senior managers who are Egomaniacs is to transfer them to an empty department. In meetings, Egomaniacs can be managed by publicly recognizing their expertise and importance. However, this sometimes backfires by encouraging their narcissist tendencies.

- *Loose Cannon.* Certain people are consistently difficult to deal with due to their extrovert behavior. Their actions can have destructive effects on the project's image and morale; for example, indiscrete disclosures of information and insensitivity to important organizational relationships. Loose Cannons are easy to detect; during group situations, they quickly make their presence known. The most effective way to deal with Loose Cannons is to alert management, who should conduct a corrective interview.

- *Technology Bigot.* A Technology Bigot is a Loose Cannon who promulgates marketing hype and refuses to consider other viewpoints; for example, people who insist that all information technology will become Microsoft-based, or that CORBA is the only true way to implement distributed objects.

> "It's not enough to succeed. Others must fail."
>
> —Gore Vidal

- *Territorial Corncob.* Individuals who attempt to protect organizational or technical turf often exhibit defensive behaviors. They need to defend their territory as a way of quieting underlying insecurities about their competence. Territorial Corncobs often can be placated with flattery and sensitivity to their weaknesses. Avoid appealing to their greed; Territorial Corncobs are particularly difficult to discourage once they sense the potential for new opportunities or power within the scope of their territory.

- *Corncobs out of the Woodwork.* When a particularly difficult or stressful situation arises such as serious project problems or impending layoffs, some Corncobs amplify their behavior. In the case of layoffs, if you are a competent person who can obtain another job, consider volunteering for layoff so that others can retain their jobs and salaries that they may desperately need.
- *Saboteur.* A Saboteur is someone about to exit the group who begins to manipulate the work environment in favor of their next assignment. For example, Saboteurs often try to make colleagues leave the project through active recruiting, rumors, and negative behaviors. This is a particularly difficult situation to detect and remedy because the Saboteur often conceals his or her intention to depart. One large computer manufacturer gave frequent after-hours parties—complete with large quantities of liquor—at which it encouraged its employees to discuss outside career plans. The Saboteur usually has one or more confidants who know of their plans. Once a Saboteur is discovered, he or she should be precluded from impacting the work environment.
- *Careerist.* This is a variation of the Saboteur, a person who influences a technical choice that widens his or her personal expertise and job marketability. For example, a technical architect may choose to use an object database for object persistence, even though an RDBMS with an object API is a more appropriate technical solution.
- *Anachronist.* This is a Corncob who resists innovation simply because he or she doesn't understand it. The Anachronist may be quite knowledgeable about legacy technologies, and resists new technologies arbitrarily. Education of the anachronist is often an effective solution.

 **EXAMPLES**

One of the Corporate Sharks that we encountered years ago was recently transferred to a one-person department and then laid off because the consequences of his personality traits outweighed his benefits to the corporation. In our experience, Corncobs eventually self-destruct and leave the organization. The downside to this is that they sometimes come back.

A friend of ours underwent a dramatic personality change (for the better) when he withdrew from participation in a corporate bonus system.

242 of CHAPTER SEVEN

While under the bonus system, our friend engaged in a number of confrontational interventions in various software processes due to his desire for short-term outcomes (executive bonuses).

Territorial Corncobs can be the most abrasive variation. In particular, if a person or group of people believe they "own" a particular buzzword, such as "architecture," they may attempt to vigorously suppress anyone who uses it. E-mail is a particularly effective weapon of the Territorial Corncob because it produces tangible evidence. E-mail is also an easily manipulated medium for engaging in emotional confrontations and flaming.

RELATED SOLUTIONS

The technology bigot variation of this AntiPattern is also a form of the Golden Hammer AntiPattern. See the Golden Hammer AntiPattern for a related solution.

APPLICABILITY TO OTHER VIEWPOINTS AND SCALES

The impact of Corncobs on architecture and development is usually to slow down progress. Confrontational issues raised by Corncobs tend to decrease the sophistication of the discussion and to instead focus on specific forces. In some sense, Corncob behaviors reverse the intended benefits of design patterns. Instead of making the software process more sophisticated and efficient, Corncobs make it less sophisticated and less efficient. Instead of making the process more balanced, by taking into consideration all of the significant forces, the Corncob tends to bias the discussion and decision making toward selected forces, which may not be the most significant.

Mini-AntiPattern: Intellectual Violence

Background

The Lambda Calculus is a relatively straightforward theory about the mathematics of functions and variable substitutions. It is one of the important theories underlying the Lisp programming language and is taught at selected universities in undergraduate computer science courses. People with this training often assume that everybody knows about Lambda Calculus. This leads to misunderstandings that may be instances of Intellectual Violence. A short chalk-talk (informal tutorial) could clear up any misunderstandings.

AntiPattern Problem

Intellectual Violence occurs when someone who understands a theory, technology, or buzzword uses this knowledge to intimidate others in a meeting situation. This may happen inadvertently due to the normal reticence of technical people to expose their ignorance. In short, Intellectual Violence is a breakdown of communication. When some or most people on a project do not understand a new concept, progress may be stalled indefinitely as they work through their feelings of inferiority or avoid the topic altogether. When Intellectual Violence is pervasive, a defensive culture arises, which inhibits productivity. People control and conceal information instead of sharing it.

Refactored Solution

An alternative organizational culture is based upon mentoring, where people cross-train constantly. It is recognized that everybody has unique talents and knowledge, regardless of their position in the organizational hierarchy. In a mentoring culture, people are encouraged to share their knowledge to promote the overall success of the organization. A mentoring culture is best facilitated through leadership by example. If the principals in the organization actively engage in mentoring, it becomes more socially acceptable at all levels to do so. Encouraging people to share information is an effective way to utilize knowledge resources and limit reinvention.

IRRATIONAL MANAGEMENT

Antipattern Name: Irrational Management

Also Known As: Pathological Supervisor, Short-Term Thinking, Managing by Reaction, Decision Phobia, Managers Playing with Technical Toys

Most Frequent Scale: Enterprise

Refactored Solution Name: Rational Decision Making

Refactored Solution Type: Role and Process

Root Causes: Responsibility (the universal cause)

Unbalanced Forces: Management of Resources

Anecdotal Evidence: "Who's running this project?" "I wish he'd make up his bloody mind!" "What do we do now?" "We better clear this with management before we get started." "Don't bother asking; they'll just say no."

BACKGROUND

Irrational Management covers a range of commonly occurring software project problems that can be traced back to the personalities of the person(s) running the project. For example, the manager may have obsessive interests in some aspect of the technology or personality limitations that cause them to become ineffective or irrational managers. Irrational management can be viewed as a skewed set of priorities where the manager's personal priorities, no matter how nonsensible, guide the software project in irrational directions.

GENERAL FORM

The manager (or management team) of one or more development projects cannot make decisions. This may a personality defect or the result of an obsession with details. The details may be personal interests or behaviors of the manager, such as technical "toys" or micromanagement. When faced with a crisis, the manager's decisions are knee-jerk reactions rather than carefully thought-out strategies or tactical actions. These reactions often cause further problems. The cycle of indecision and reaction can escalate in frequency and severity of consequences.

The Irrational Management AntiPattern is significantly compounded by a manager's inability to direct development staff. This is also called a lack of good people-management skills, characterized by the inability to:

- Recognize staff capabilities, both strengths and weaknesses.
- Provide clear objectives that are appropriate to staff skills.
- Communicate effectively with staff.

SYMPTOMS AND CONSEQUENCES

The primary symptom of the Irrational Management AntiPattern is *project thrashing*, an ongoing debate on a critical topic. A decision must be made to allow development staff to progress. Thrashing has several consequences.

- Increased staff frustration.
- Incremental delays to delivery.
- Exploitation by Corncobs.

TYPICAL CAUSES

The manager lacks the ability to manage:

- Development staff.
- Other managers.
- Development processes.

He or she also has no clear vision and strategy, and therefore:

- Cannot make decisions.
- Fears success (see the associated Mini-AntiPattern).
- Is ignorant of the true state of project activities and deliverables.

KNOWN EXCEPTIONS

There should never be any exceptions to the Irrational Management AntiPattern. However, a "golden child" who possesses guru-level skills that are completely unique in some manner and provides a major technical advantage should be tolerated, while a better and longer-term solution is planned.

REFACTORED SOLUTION

Follow these guidelines to resolve the Irrational Management AntiPattern:

1. *Admit you have a problem and get help.* When managers suffer from one or more of the typical causes, they must first recognize that they have a problem. Assuming that they are unaware of their situation, the first step is to identify key indicators, the most common of which is that of "finding out the hard way." For example, rather than technical staff addressing a growing problem and asking for help in dealing with it, the irrational manager finds out only after a problem has reached crisis stage; no one is willing to discuss problems, because doing so never helps. Managers must surround themselves with talented staff (or consultants) who share the complex job of managing and are willing to listen to them.

2. *Understand the development staff.* Managers need to understand both the technical skills and the personality traits of their staff members. Awareness of technical skills helps a manager delegate work; awareness of personalities helps a manager designate working relationships.

3. *Provide clear, short-term goals.* Easily achievable objectives should be specified for the project. Long-term objectives are necessary, but do not as successfully motivate staff on a daily basis. A manager must ensure that short-term, highly specific objectives are set and that staff understands how they can be achieved.

4. *Share a focus.* Project staff must share the purpose of their project to ensure they are all working toward the same goals. The manager must initiate and grow the focus.

5. *Look for process improvement.* Recognizing that every project is slightly different from the previous one, a manager must monitor the development processes and improve them where and when necessary. Although these are often small tweaks to make a spe-

cific process more pragmatic, they can significantly improve productivity.

6. *Facilitate communication.* Whenever a "hot" topic fuels debate, deciding on the way to move forward is best achieved in a facilitated session. To do so:

   - Identify the key players.
   - Collect evidence on the debate.
   - Get clear agreement on the problem(s).
   - Make sure everyone's voice is heard.
   - Confirm that the solution options are understood by all.
   - Agree to the preferred option.
   - Involve the concerned staff in implementing the solution where possible.

7. *Manage communication mechanisms.* E-mail and newsgroups in general are useful communication mechanisms, but both can set people on a winding path of destruction. E-mails can quickly get out of hand, and newsgroups can generate arrogant and aggressive debates. The solution is to track e-mails and newsgroup postings daily and identify any miscommunications. Talk directly to the involved parties and tell them to stop the electronic debate. If it's important to find a solution, then a facilitated meeting is usually faster and far more effective.

8. *Manage by exception.* Extremes are always dangerous, and over-management is no exception. Daily meetings and weekly reviews that require a manager's involvement in all threads of a project are examples of over- or micromanagement. Instead, manage by exception; watch, but don't interfere. Allow problems some time to be resolved by others. Step in only when necessary.

9. *Apply effective decision-making techniques.* Two rational management techniques from Kepner-Tregoe are particularly effective in software decision making. The first is called *situation analysis* [Kepner 81]. This technique assists in the organization and management of unstructured and chaotic environments. It can be used on an individual or group basis. The second is called *decision analysis* [Kepner 81]. This technique is essential for making decisions objectively. Subjective biases in decision-making processes can have devastating consequences in software projects. We have often seen these kind of biases result in software disasters. Biases can be

generated by friendships, the timing of the sales call, unnecessary platform constraints, and invisible infrastructure constraints.

These two techniques are explained in some depth in the following subsections.

SITUATION ANALYSIS

The purpose of situation analysis is to identify the highest-priority concerns in a complex situation. A tailored version of this technique contains the following steps:

1. *List all of the concerns.* These may include known issues, action items, commitments, technology gaps, and other items. In other words, the list may contain virtually anything that affects the project at hand.
2. *Rate the concerns with respect to three criteria: seriousness, urgency, and growth potential.* Use three levels: high, medium, and low. For example, if the concern is critical to project success, it is highly serious. If the concern must be resolved immediately for the resolution to be effective, it is rated highly urgent. If the seriousness is expected to increase dramatically in time, it is rated as having high growth potential.
3. *Tabulate scores for each item based upon the ratings.* Assign numbers to the rating levels: high = 2, medium = 1, and low = 0. For example, a rating of high/medium/low would score 3 points (2 + 1 + 0).
4. *Prioritize the items in terms of the scores.* For all of the concerns that score 6, choose the most important, second important, and so forth. Continue the priority assignment with the items scoring 5 and lower, until the entire list of concerns is assigned a priority number.
5. *Assign the items that can be resolved to the appropriate staff.* Some items on the list will be controlled by external forces, and it would be unreasonable to expend energy resolving them until the situation changes. Other items must be resolved before others due to dependencies. For the properly qualified staff, the resolution of most items will be straightforward: Program a necessary object, create an analysis model, reduce risk through testing, and so forth. The manager must make the best match of staff resources to the concerns that must be resolved.

6. *Work on the top-priority items on the list.* The situation analysis technique works on the principle of addressing first things first and second things never. Using situation analysis, the manager can effectively address the most important issues from among the confusing list of concerns confronting software projects.

DECISION ANALYSIS

A tailored process for decision analysis contains these steps:

1. *Define the scope of the decision to be addressed.* In other words, the process must begin with a written question to resolve.
2. *Identify alternative solutions for resolving the decision.* These can include specific concrete alternatives, such as specific software products or categories of solutions that can be evaluated.
3. *Define the decision criteria.* Situation analysis can be used to create this list.
4. *Divide the criteria between the essentials and desirables.* The essential criteria are characteristics that must be part of the solution in order for it to be acceptable. If any essential criteria are missing from an alternative, the alternative is disqualified. For this reason, the essential criteria should be a carefully chosen, short list. All other criteria are called desirables, and they must be prioritized. Use the priority assignment process from situation analysis for this purpose, then assign the desirable alternatives a weight. For example, if there are seven criteria, the most important has a weight of 7; the next most important has a weight of 6, and so forth.
5. *Determine whether the alternatives satisfy all the essential criteria.* If not, eliminate the unsatisfactory alternatives.
6. *Perform any fact finding.* Research to assess the satisfaction of the criteria by each of the alternatives.
7. *Set up a table that displays the alternatives in columns and the criteria in rows.* In the table, rank the alternatives for desirable criteria. For example, if there are five alternatives, the best alternative gets a rank of 5; next best gets a rank of 4, and so forth.
8. *Multiply the weights by the ranks to calculate a score for each position in the matrix.* Add up the scores in each column to calculate the score for each alternative. The highest scoring alternative is the rational (or best) choice.
9. *Be aware that the rational choice may not be the choice that managers or customers will accept.* An important bias or criteria that

was not properly reflected in the decision analysis may cause this, in which case, it is important to evaluate the decision criteria. Experiment with the weights on the desirable criteria, and add new criteria until the decision analysis selects the acceptable alternative. Confirm that the resulting criteria and weights match the subjective decision criteria that drive this solution. Perhaps the decision-making authorities will change their criteria to more realistic assumptions when confronted with the actual influence that their biases have on the decision.

VARIATIONS

Consultants can be an invaluable resource. They can bring missing knowledge and skills to an organization, and can give advice that is independent of internal politics and detailitis; that is, they can be objective in a charged situation. Consultants can play three key roles in a software project. These categories are based on Block's model for general consulting practice [Block 81]:

1. Pair of Hands.
2. Technical Expert.
3. Management Peer.

Filling the Pair-of-Hands role, the consultant becomes another software developer, similar to that of an ordinary employee. As a Technical-Expert, the consultant resolves problems in a specific domain. As a Management-Peer, the consultant is an advisor to management, providing a mentoring knowledge transfer from his or her related experience. Although it's professionally rewarding for the consultant to be in the latter two roles, we have seen outstanding results from the Pair-of-Hands role, particularly in rapid prototyping situations with new technologies.

EXAMPLES

A manager we worked with came into a project at the halfway point. He did not have an understanding of the staff's skills, nor a good background on the project to date. When problems occurred, he reallocated staff. This created more serious problems. Staff members were moved onto projects to which they had no previous exposure. This resulted in diminished effectiveness. The situation was partially resolved when the manager left the company. The new manager was a very strong "people-person" who made sure that employees' skills matched the necessary activities. Unfortunately, the delays already experienced could not be made up for.

In another situation, a project architect (a Corncob) voiced his opinions on C++ coding standards via e-mail to all project staff. The project had several guru-level C++ developers who took exception to some of the architect's statements. This resulted in a two-month e-mail and newsgroup "war." The eventual solution was that the project manager appointed a "tiger team" to resolve the issue. This was a facilitated solution based upon the run-ahead principle. Unfortunately, no precautions were taken to eliminate similar destructive communications on a variety of other topics. The instance was dealt with rather than the overriding problem.

In a third example, a system's integrator project had an irrational management team. The individual managers were owners of their part of the process. This created stovepipe processes with neither coherence nor contiguity, as shown in Figure 7.8. This resulted in various ownership wars. One war was based on the entrance criteria to move from one phase of the development to the next. This caused a month of thrashing and disagreement, which then diffused focus on emerging development problems. Corporate management had to step in. And because the resolution was enforced from above, it was not sustainable.

The final solution, after several wars between the owners, was the appointment of a process facilitator whose job was to ensure that:

- A coherent and contiguous process was produced.
- The entrance criteria were agreed on for each phase of the development, which supported iterative delivery.
- Process improvements were implemented across the relevant processes.

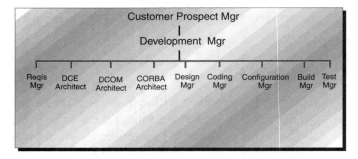

FIGURE 7.8 Irrational management team.

Mini-AntiPattern: Smoke and Mirrors

AntiPattern Problem

Demonstration systems are important sales tools, as they are often interpreted by end users as representional of production-quality capabilities. A management team, eager for new business, sometimes (inadvertently) encourage these misperceptions and makes commitments beyond the capabilities of the organization to deliver operational technology. This puts developers in a tough situation because they are then pressured to deliver the capabilities promised. The ultimate loser is the end user, who does not receive the expected capability at the promised cost and time; or when the system is delivered, the end user often receives a hastily crafted Stovepipe System that resembles the demonstration environment, but lacks maintainability.

A principal cause of this AntiPattern, also called Vaporware, concerns the management of expections. The end user is led to believe that capabilities can be delivered when in fact they cannot, at least not within the predetermined functionality, budget, and schedule. When the development project fails to deliver, the project is considered unsuccessful, and the development organization loses credibility.

Refactored Solution

The management of end-user expectations is important both for ethical reasons and for continued credibility. A typical rule of software engineering is that a deliverable system costs three times as much as an engineering prototype. A set of reusable software costs up to three times as much as software for a deliverable system. Another rule, supported by survey evidence, is that any software development will take about twice as long and cost twice as much as expected [Johnson 95].

Managing expectations often means it is better to let people expect *less* than can be delivered. When the expectations are exceeded, the recipients are pleasantly surprised, and are likely to become repeat customers.

Variations

When the Smoke and Mirrors AntiPattern is a demonstration of a commercial product, effective additional precautions can be taken. One strategy is to have competent engineers attend the vendor's training course. Usually, training courses are not part of the marketing communications program, and convey unfiltered information about the products. But competent engineers can determine the product's true capabilities and report back to the development team. A less costly solution is to request a copy of the product's technical documentation, and conduct a review of these materials by one or more competent engineers. Also, carefully review the installation requirements and software license agreement. The installation requirements may call for operating system versions and product releases that are incompatible with the target environment. Few software licenses guarantee merchantability. In other words, there may be no legal assurance that the product will perform a useful function. Such a guarantee can be added to the purchase agreement, along with extended product support. Such guarantees are commonplace in industries such as telecommunications, where product support is provided for up to 80 years (the full system life cycle).

PROJECT MISMANAGEMENT

Antipattern Name: Project Mismanagement
Also Known As: Humpty Dumpty
Most Frequent Scale: Enterprise
Refactored Solution Name: Risk Management
Refactored Solution Type: Process and Role
Root Causes: Responsibility (the universal cause)
Unbalanced Forces: Management of Risk (the universal force)
Anecdotal Evidence: "What went wrong? Everything was fine and then suddenly . . . KABOOM!"

BACKGROUND

This AntiPattern concerns the monitoring and controlling of software projects. The timeframe for this occurs after planning activities, and during the actual analysis, design, construction, and testing of the software system. Project mismanagement involves mistakes made in the day to day running of a project, assuming planning errors (such as Death By Planning) have not been made.

GENERAL FORM

Running a project is as complex an activity as creating the project plan, and developing software is as complex as building skyscrapers, involving as many steps and processes, including checks and balances. Often, key activities are overlooked or minimized. These include technical planning (architecture) and quality-control activities (inspection and test). In particular, basic mistakes include: inadequate architecture definition, insufficient code review (software inspection), and inadequate test coverage. Under the test umbrella, several phases are needed, but often minimized:

unit, integration, and system testing. Simple integration testing comprises basic checking of unit-tested components for interoperability. Full integration testing checks all known success paths and error states.

> "All you need in this life is ignorance and confidence; then success is sure."
>
> —Mark Twain

Architecture establishes the detailed technology plan for the project, including the criteria for inspection and testing. When an inadequate architecture is defined, there is insufficient basis for checking the design during the inspection and testing phases. When testing is performed, the software modules may be integrated according the architecture, but are not able to interoperate according to the application's needs.

SYMPTOMS AND CONSEQUENCES

- The design is difficult to implement due to lack of an architectural strategy.
- Code reviews and inspections happen infrequently and add minimal value.
- The test design requires extra effort and guesswork because the behavioral guidelines for the system are inadequately defined.
- In the integration and system testing phases, there is much project "thrashing" due to a large number of defects that should have been eliminated in earlier phases such as architecture, design, inspection, and unit testing.
- Defect reports escalate toward the end of the development and delivery/acceptance phases.

TYPICAL CAUSES

- An inadequate architecture does not define the technical criteria for inspection, testing, integration, and interoperability.
- Code reviews and software inspections do not evaluate design defects, which then must be addressed in more expensive phases such as acceptance testing.
- Insufficient test suites check basic integration needs, but do not address full interoperability needs for the application.

- All of the preceding factors indicate ineffective risk management, which can be traced to the professional practices of the architect, designers, and management.

KNOWN EXCEPTIONS

There should never be any exceptions to the Project Mismanagement AntiPattern.

REFACTORED SOLUTION

Proper risk management is an effective means of resolving predictable symptoms and consequences of the Project Mismanagement AntiPattern. Risks are categorized in several useful ways: managerial, common project failure points [Moynihan 89], and quality. It's necessary to understand these categories in order to better qualify the risks.

MANAGERIAL

These risks are primarily caused and resolved by corporate management:

- *Processes.* An end-to-end definition of product development.
- *Roles.* The specific responsibilities for implementation of the processes.

COMMON PROJECT FAILURE POINTS

These key project risks are based upon twenty-three risk drivers:

- Cost overruns.
- Premature termination of project.
- Development of the wrong product.
- Technical failure.

QUALITY

- *Program and project management.* The effectiveness of the planning and control process.
- *Product identification.* The accuracy of the problem definition.
- *Architecture definition.* The specification of a design and coding strategy.

- *Solution design.* The ability to deliver a consistent and optimized code specification that fully supports the solution.
- *Solution implementation (coding).* The ability to produce an accurate code implementation of the design, which functions in the expected manner.
- *Solution validation (testing).* The proof that the implemented solution fully meets the problem requirements.
- *Product support.* The ongoing ability to maintain and enhance a released product.

COMMON UNDERSTANDING

Often, a theme of risk management is the absence of a common understanding, resulting in an inconsistent view of development, which leads to the risk of the solution not meeting the scope of the problem requirements. A company must understand its software developments across all sites and all projects. Every project must share common knowledge about its development.

Ideally, all (or most) development staff on a project will have a reasonable, overall comprehension of the problem requirements and the intended solution. Unfortunately, often this is not the case, leading to one or more of these failings:

- *Missed functionality.* One or more component services were never built because there was no shared view of how all of the components would interact on the delivery platform.
- *Incorrect functionality.* Some component does not perform the full functionality required because its use was never shared by developers with users (other developers).
- *Overfunctionality.* The requirements were never clearly understood and "the devil in the details" was never extricated. This leads to software development under "good intentions," without any requirement or need ever being clearly established.
- *Code modules will interface but not fully interoperate.* There was no definition of the threads of control across system and module boundaries.

The refactored solution entails activities at the architectural and design stages of development. At the architecture level, the dependencies between modules must be defined. This includes the assignment of responsibilities that define the interdependence between modules and the partitioning of the system's functionality. At the design level, the threads of control (use cases) across modules must be defined. This includes all of the successful use cases as well as defined error states.

VARIATIONS

A formal risk management activity is one way to document and plan for risk mitigation. Formal risk management entails the identification and documentation of project risks, usually in a tabular format, which includes columns for risk severity, risk description, and risk mitigation. Risk management plans are often produced with the formal documentation of projects, but are rarely translated into funded project activities. It is important to prioritize the project risks and budget research in risk-mitigation activities that represent critical points of failure.

Another variation, a run-ahead team, is often employed to investigate the capabilities of new products and the compatibility of technologies. The run-ahead team creates prototypes that resemble the target architecture of the system, using the primary technologies or technical backups. The run-ahead team also identifies any technology shortcomings and investigates workaround strategies. The team then educates the rest of the project staff on the new technology, thereby shortening learning curves. Finally, the run-ahead team must precede the main development activity by one to three months. Otherwise, the main project may be delayed waiting for the results of the run-ahead research.

EXAMPLE

A software development does not manage it's code delivery. The development teams are left to their own devices as to how to get from design to delivery. This means that they each have to deal with quality and process issues via self-derived mechanisms and manage their own activities. The risk becomes unacceptable code through lack of adherence to:

- Coding standards (including traceability to the design)
- Code reviews
- Test planning
- Unit testing
- API testing
- Integration testing

- Feature testing
- Program documentation

The risk manifests itself as poorly documented code that has been largely untested and does not integrate, nor fully meet the requirements.

The appointment of a new project manager results in quality/process improvements. The improvements are incremental and are actively owned by the teams through a series of facilitated "lookback" sessions to identify problems and issues, and then the creation of emissary groups to address them via incremental process improvements.

Each emissary group consists of a facilitator from product support and a development team owner (for each team) for that part of the process:

- Design
- Coding
- Testing
- Documentation

Each emissary group team member is responsible for:

- Refining the specific process.
- Educating their team.
- Providing subjective assessment of the team's implementation of the specific process and the quality of it's deliverables.
- Liaising with other emissaries to maintain a consistent standard of process implementation and problem resolution.

Within six months each process had been incrementally refined several times and each team had implemented each process at least once. The improvements were major reductions (over 50%) in:

- Code defects
- Documentation defects
- Untested code

RELATED SOLUTIONS

A variation of the Smoke and Mirrors mini-AntiPattern describes the incorporation of technical backups into the project plan and activities.

This is an important complement to risk management, and mitigates key strategic errors introduced by Project Mismanagement.

Brad Appleton presents an excellent design pattern language for improving software development processes in his paper on process improvement [Appleton 97]. Implementing process improvement is a key element in resolving project mismanagement.

Mini-AntiPattern: Throw It over the Wall

Anecdotal Evidence

The Code is finished (no testing, no documentation).

Background

Rarely is documentation entirely self-explanatory, yet understanding the vision and insight of the authors is an essential part of understanding the documentation. This is especially true of guideline documents, where there is an implicit assumption of independent decision making. This assumption also implies an in-depth knowledge of the authors' intent.

By its nature, all human knowledge is personal. Even the most eminent scientists possess a personal insight that drives their discovery and articulation of new information. Understanding this personal insight is essential to understanding their work.

AntiPattern Problem

Object-oriented methods, design patterns, and implementation plans intended as flexible guidelines are too often taken literally by down-stream managers and OO developers. As guidelines progress through approval and publication processes, they may be attributed with unful-filled qualities of completeness, prescriptiveness, and mandated implementation.

Such literal interpretation of flexible guidelines can lead to unintended results. Decisions may be made based upon guidelines that were intended only to inspire careful analysis and locally optimized decision making. For example, effort may be wasted on useless analyses and documentation because it appears mandated, although nobody on the development team understands its purpose. This phenomenon happens in both large and small organizations and may be due to miscommunication between development phases. Another important cause is the desire to satisfy the apparent expectations of management instead of the needs of the system's end users.

Refactored Solution

In order for technical documentation to be interpreted and implemented as intended, the material must be communicated through several important techniques. One is to deliver the knowledge through a tutorial. Whenever new policies and guidelines are established, there should be a corresponding transfer of information to promulgate the information and communicate the motivations.

We have found that a one-day training session is usually sufficient for development specifications of up to 100 pages. It may, however, be useful to conduct the session in two parts: a management introduction and a technical briefing for developers, as these two different audiences have substantially different needs. If you combine these groups, the management discussion often extends into the time needed to cover the technical details. Follow-up support, including telephone and electronic mail contacts, is useful to ensure successful technology transfer.

Mini-AntiPattern: Fire Drill

AntiPattern Problem

A Fire Drill is a recurring scenario in many software development organizations. A project is initiated, but the staff delays design and development activities for several months while various technopolitical issues are resolved at a management level. (One software developer described strategies for on-the-job software delivery as: "Wait until management is desperate, and they will accept anything you give them.") Management prevents the development staff from making progress either by telling them to wait or by giving uncertain and conflicting directions. Perhaps most destructive are the externally generated changes in project direction that lead to rework and inhibit progress.

A few months into the project schedule, it becomes clear to management that development must progress immediately. Impending project cancellation is the usual motivator. This situation is announced at an "all hands" Fire Drill launch meeting for development staff, during which management makes ambitious (or unrealistic) demands for software delivery. A typical example is a project that spends six months performing requirements analysis and planning, and then endeavors to design, implement, and demonstrate the software in less than four weeks.

Because the entire project is pressed for time, compromises are willingly made in software quality and testing. In a perverse way, the emergency situation makes the job easier for some software developers, as management will accept almost any software (or documentation) product with few questions if it is behind schedule. However, conscientious developers who deliver products before their deadlines are often compelled by management to rework their solutions.

Refactored Solution

An effective solution that project management can implement is called *sheltering*. Project management is responsible for delivering a software product, regardless of the unresolved management-level issues. The work environment required for quality software development differs significantly from the Fire Drill environment. In particular, architecture-driven development requires lengthy time frames and long-term commitments. Architecture-driven development is the most effective approach for software success according to Booch (1996) and other authorities. In contrast, Fire Drill environments preclude staff retention, an important issue for software managers today.

In the sheltering solution, management creates and maintains two alternative project environments: internal and external. The majority of the software development staff operate in the internal environment, where the focus is long term and encourages continual progress toward software delivery. As much as 80 percent of software in systems is not application-specific—the so-called internal model [Mowbray 97c]. The internal project environment can proceed to construct the internal model independent of changes in external technopolitical issues. Building internal increments is also the most efficient use of software development resources in iterative-incremental projects [Korson 97].

The external environment is also called the project's "public image." Its purpose is to maintain relationships with outside entities: upper management, customers, and peer projects (with which resource competition and reuse opportunities exist). The external environment staff may need to generate repeated project crises to obtain essential resources. In a Fire Drill culture, emergency scenarios may be seen as the equivalent of assertiveness, when projects compete for management attention and resources. A small number of managers and development staff can maintain the external environment. Their job is to address the changes in the external environment so that the majority of the project staff are sheltered. Some examples of external environment activities include: progress reports, status reviews, procurement, staffing, customer presentations, and marketing demonstrations. Sheltering effectively isolates most staff members from these activities.

Occasionally, however, emergencies are real, and heroic commitments of development time and effort may be needed. Nevertheless, it is important to limit the frequency of Fire Drills so that development staff members are available to handle the demands of real emergencies.

Related Solutions

The Fire Drill mini-AntiPattern is related to several other key AntiPatterns, including: Analysis Paralysis, Viewgraph Engineering, and Mushroom Management. In Analysis Paralysis, the quest for perfection in analysis modeling leads to a protracted analysis phase, which compresses the development schedule, thus creating a Fire Drill. In Viewgraph Engineering, an organization never makes the transition from paper-based analysis to software development; the work environment is very similar to the situation preceding the Fire Drill launch-meeting. In Mushroom Management, the developers are isolated unnecessarily from the real end users (not the end-user management). Developers are unable to obtain clear requirements or feedback on user-interface capabilities. The Mushroom Management solution favors constructive interchanges between operational end users and developers, whereas the Fire Drill solution favors destructive interchanges between developers and end-user management, when changes in direction and uncertainties can derail the software process.

Mini-AntiPattern: The Feud

AntiPattern Problem

Also known as Dueling Corncobs, Territorial Managers, and Turf Wars, the Feud is marked by personality conflicts between managers that can dramatically affect the work environment. The employees reporting to these managers often suffer the consequences of their disagreements, because animosity between managers is generally reflected in the attitudes and actions of their employees, which always become negative.

Consequently, software developers suffer from a lack of productive communications, and a general lack of cooperation inhibits any form of useful technology transfer. Thereafter, the corporate productivity and image can be negatively impacted.

When the conflict erupts into ballistic verbal exchanges, verbal assassinations are carried out against staff to senior management. Such behavior can engage entire corporate management organizations, wasting time and energy. E-mail confrontations can greatly exacerbate the conflict (see the E-mail Is Dangerous mini-AntiPattern sidebar). Management feuds can drag on for years, with chronic recurrences of open hostilities, if not addressed promptly.

Refactored Solution

Dr. Randall Oakes, veteran of many information technology migrations, has said that "there is no problem that a pizza party cannot solve" [Oakes 95]. He means that organizational problems can often be resolved during a friendly office gathering.

We have used the pizza party technique on several occasions with positive outcomes. These events are also useful as icebreakers to encourage team building, to facilitate formation of friendships, and to foster cross-organizational communications.

A pizza party may have the most benefits for the financial sponsor. Following a pizza party, coworkers may perceive this person in a new light: "He or she is not such an ogre after all; he or she bought us pizza, and we had a good time." Pizza party sponsors can thus reform their image.

Variations

A corporate intervention is a technique for resolving organizational differences. Professional meeting facilitators and various psychologists practice these techniques [GDSS 94]. Using electronic meeting tools, a two-day off-site intervention can achieve significant results. These meetings help organizations to "reinvent the corporation" by using the off-site group's creativity to resolve their differences. The meeting facilitates intransigent managers to communicate and form new relationships. Participants generate innovative solutions to problems once thought to be intractable.

Mini-AntiPattern: E-mail Is Dangerous

Also Known As

Blame-Storming

AntiPattern Problem

E-mail is an important communication medium for software developers. Unfortunately, it is an inappropriate medium for many topics and sensitive communications. For example, e-mail is inappropriate for most confrontational discussions. Tempers flair and feelings get hurt easily in e-mail debates. Worse, e-mail makes a public event out of the disagreement. Productivity and morale of a software project can quickly degenerate when other staff members get caught up in lengthy e-mail confrontations.

Also known as E-mail Flaming, this mini-AntiPattern can cause a variety of negative outcomes, some of which are listed here, followed by recommended preventive measures:

- A "confidential" message is likely to end up in the inbox of the person you least want to read it. The best advice is to treat every e-mail as if it were going directly to your worst enemies and toughest competitors.

- E-mail can be distributed to large numbers of people instantaneously; for example, to entire departments, companies, customer mailing lists, and public Internet forums. Treat every e-mail as if it will be printed on the front page of *The Washington Post*.
- An e-mail message can become a permanent written record. Treat every e-mail as if it could be used as evidence in a court of law.

E-mail is an inefficient mode of communication for complex topics. Due to the technology and other key characteristics of the medium, e-mail is subject to misinterpretation, because often large e-mail exchanges reduce the discussion to the lowest common denominator. Furthermore, e-mail discussion groups send dozens of postings on all kinds of topics, including the trivial and nonessential. These lengthy discussions are time-consuming and labor-intensive.

Refactored Solution

Use e-mail cautiously, as suggested. Avoid using e-mail for the following types of messages: confrontations, criticisms, sensitive information, politically incorrect topics, and legally actionable statements. Use other media if there is any doubt about the appropriateness of e-mail. Although telephone conversations, fax transmissions, and face-to-face discussions are also vulnerable to disclosure, their potential for damage is much less imminent.

A P P E N D I X

AntiPatterns Synopsis

The AntiPatterns are summarized in Table A.1. The mini-AntiPatterns are summarized in Table A.2.

The chapter column (far right) indicates the chapter in which the AntiPattern was described. The chapters each represent a different viewpoint, as follows:

- Chapter 5: software developer viewpoint
- Chapter 6: architecture viewpoint
- Chapter 7: manager viewpoint

TABLE A.1 AntiPatterns Summary

Name	*AntiPattern Solution*	*Refactored Solution*	*Ch.*
Analysis Paralysis	Striving for perfection and completeness in the analysis phase leads to project gridlock.	Incremental, iterative development processes defer the detailed analysis until the knowledge is available.	7
Architecture by Implication	System developed without a documented architecture, often due to overconfidence based on recent success.	Define architecture in terms of multiple viewpoints corresponding to system stakeholders.	6

TABLE A.1 *(Continued).*

Name	AntiPattern Solution	Refactored Solution	Ch.
The Blob	Procedural-style design results in one object with numerous responsibilities and most other objects holding only data.	Refactor the design to distribute responsibilities more uniformly and isolate the effect of changes.	5
Corncob	Difficult people obstruct and divert the software development process.	Address agendas of the individual through various tactical, operational, and strategic organizational actions.	7
Cut-and-Paste Programming	Code reused by copying source statements causes significant maintenance problems.	Institute black-box reuse to reduce maintenance issues by having a common source code, testing, and documentation for multiple reuses.	5
Death by Planning	Excessive preplanning of software projects leads to postponement of development work and useless plans.	Pursue iterative software development process, which includes modest planning with known facts and incremental replanning.	7
Design by Committee	Committee designs are overly complex and lack a common architectural vision.	Assign proper facilitation and software development roles for more effective committee-based processes.	6
Functional Decomposition	Non-OO design (possibly from legacy) is coded in OO language and notation.	Redesign using OO principles; there is no straightforward way to refactor.	5
Golden Hammer	A familiar technology or concept is applied obsessively to many problems.	Expand the knowledge of developers through education, training, and book study groups to expose developers to new solutions.	5
Irrational Management	Habitual indecisiveness and other habits result in de facto decisions and development emergencies.	Utilize rational decision-making management techniques.	7
Lava Flow	Dead code and forgotten design information are frozen in an ever-changing design.	Install configuration control processes to eliminate dead code, and evolve/refactor design toward increasing quality.	5
Poltergeists	Classes have very limited roles and life cycles, often starting processes for other objects.	Allocate the responsibility to longer-lived objects, and eliminate the poltergeists.	5
Project Mismanagement	Inattention to the management of software development process can cause indirection and other symptoms.	Monitor and control software projects to conduct successful development activities.	7

TABLE A.1 *(Continued).*

Name	AntiPattern Solution	Refactored Solution	Ch.
Reinvent the Wheel	Legacy systems with overlapping functionality don't interoperate. Every system is built in isolation.	Use architecture mining and "best of breed" generalization to define a common interface; then use object wrapping to integrate.	6
Spaghetti Code	An ad hoc software structure makes it difficult to extend and optimize code.	Refactor code frequently to improve software structure; support software maintenance and iterative development.	5
Stovepipe Enterprise	Uncoordinated software architectures lead to lack of adaptability, reuse, and interoperability.	Use enterprise architecture planning to coordinate system conventions, reuse, and interoperability.	6
Stovepipe System	Ad hoc integration solutions and absence of abstraction result in brittle, unmaintainable architectures.	Use of abstraction, subsystem facades, and metadata to generate adaptable systems.	6
Vendor Lock-In	Proprietary, product-dependent architectures do not manage complexity and lead to out-of-control architecture and maintenance costs.	Install an isolation layer between product-dependent interfaces and the majority of application software to enable management of complexity and architecture.	6

TABLE A.2 Mini-AntiPatterns Synopsis

Name	AntiPattern Solution	Refactored Solution	Ch.
Ambiguous Viewpoint	Unclear modeling viewpoint causes problematic ambiguities in object models.	Clarify which of the three essential viewpoints is modeled: business, specification, or implementation.	5
Autogenerated Stovepipe	Automatic generation of interfaces for distributed, large-scale systems from fine-grain header files.	Separate the architecture-level framework design from the subsystem-specific design to manage complexity.	6
Blowhard Jamboree	Industry pundits disseminate marketing information that concerns consumers.	Assign in-house expertise to separate the facts from the hype.	7
Boat Anchor	A costly technology is purchased by a systems development project, but goes unused.	Send competent engineers to evaluate the product before buying it.	5

TABLE A.2 (Continued).

Name	AntiPattern Solution	Refactored Solution	Ch.
Continuous Obsolescence	Internet-time technology releases surpass the ability to keep up and synchronize other technologies.	Depend upon stable technologies and interfaces that you control. Open systems standards provide stability.	5
Cover Your Assets	Document-driven software processes often employ authors who list alternatives instead of making decisions.	Establish clear purposes and guidelines for documentation tasks; inspect the results for the value of documented decisions.	6
Dead End	Direct modification of commercial software or reusable software creates significant maintenance burdens for a software system.	Avoid modification of supported software. Choose mainstream, supported products and platforms whenever possible.	5
E-mail Is Dangerous	E-mail is a useful, but volatile, way to communicate.	Avoid using e-mail for sensitive, controversial, or confrontational messages.	7
Fear of Success	People (software developers included) do crazy things when a project is near successful completion.	When project completion is imminent, make a clear declaration of success.	7
The Feud	Managers who engage in protracted conflicts with peers have serious negative impacts on their staffs.	Use professional facilitation or informal gatherings to resolve differences.	7
Fire Drill	Management waits until the last possible moment to allow developers to proceed with design and implementation; then they want results almost immediately.	Engage in proactive design and prototyping, even if customers and management staff are not completely on-board.	7
The Grand Old Duke of York	Four out of five developers cannot define good abstractions; this leads to excess complexity.	Designate project team architects who are abstractionists—that is, who possess the architecture instinct.	6
Input Kludge	Custom-programmed input algorithms contain many bugs that are apparent to users and testers.	Utilize production-quality input processing techniques, including lexical analysis, parser generators, and features matrices.	5
Intellectual Violence	People use obscure references to esoteric papers, theories, and standards for intimidation or short-term gain.	Encourage education and practice mentoring throughout the organization.	7

TABLE A.2 *(Continued).*

Name	AntiPattern Solution	Refactored Solution	Ch.
Jumble	Interface designs are an unfactored mixture of horizontal and vertical elements, which necessitates frequent interface changes and an inability to reuse.	Partition architectural designs with respect to horizontal, vertical, and metadata elements.	6
Mushroom Management	Developers are kept in the dark and fed fertilizer. End-user interaction is prohibited.	Solicit frequent user interaction to maximize usability and acceptance.	5
Smoke and Mirrors	End users mistakenly assume that a brittle demonstration is a capability ready for operational use.	Practice proper ethics to manage expectations, risk, liabilities, and consequences in computing sales and marketing situations.	7
Swiss Army Knife	Overdesign of interfaces results in objects with numerous methods that attempt to anticipate every possible need. This leads to designs that are difficult to comprehend, utilize, and debug, as well as implementation dependencies.	Define a clear purpose for the component and properly abstract the interface to manage complexity.	6
Throw It over the Wall	Documents are produced and disseminated without any provision for technology transfer. Flexible guidelines are mistakenly interpreted as de facto policies or formal processes.	Ensure the delivery and dissemination of information to the planned implementation of any new processes or guidelines. Include instructional development, training delivery, and technology transfer kits.	7
Viewgraph Engineering	Organizations with limited technical capabilities for system development are taken at face value because they produce substantive documents and polished briefings.	Verify the development capabilities of the organization and key project staff. Utilize prototyping and mock-ups as part of any system development process.	7
Walking through a Mine Field	Software technology is much less robust than people imagine; bugs are pervasive and potentially catastrophic.	Invest in software testing and inspection to reduce the frequency and density of software defects.	5
Warm Bodies	Large software project teams make for ineffective organizations and overruns. Heroic programmers are essential.	Plan small projects (four people in four months); they are much more likely to produce software success.	6

TABLE A.2 *(Continued).*

Name	AntiPattern Solution	Refactored Solution	Ch.
Wolf Ticket	A technology is assumed to have positive qualities due to its open systems packaging or claimed standards compliance. Few standards have test suites (less than 6 percent), and few products are actually tested for conformance.	Discover the truth behind the claims; question authority; assume nothing. Shift the burden of proof to the marketing organization. Talk directly to the technical product experts and developers.	6

B

AntiPatterns Terminology

Action Lever   The most effective mechanism for effecting change or problem solving. For example, in performance optimization, an action lever is a small code segment causing a performance bottleneck, discovered through measurement.

Also Known As   An AntiPattern template section, which includes additional common names and phrases that are popularly used or descriptive of the AntiPattern.

Anecdotal Evidence   An AntiPattern template section. Any cliche phrases or comedic material describing the AntiPattern appear here.

AntiPattern   A commonly occuring pattern or solution that generates decidedly negative consequences. An AntiPattern may be a pattern in the wrong context. When properly documented, an AntiPattern comprises a paired AntiPattern solution with a refactored solution.

Applicability to Other Viewpoints and Scales   An AntiPattern template section that defines how the AntiPattern impacts other viewpoints: managerial, architectural, or developer. Optionally, this section includes interesting implications of the AntiPattern to other scales of development.

Architectural Benefits   The positive outcomes that result from the design and utilization of good architecture and associated software interfaces. Typical benefits include adaptability, cost and risk reduction, and so forth.

Architectural Characteristics   Characteristics associated with a design artifact that affect its usage and placement within architectural partitions; for example, maturity, domain specificity, flexibility, constraint, implementation dependence, complexity, stability, and so forth.

Architectural Partition   Architecture defines boundaries between categories of design artifacts. These partitions separate categories of entities with different characteristics. Partitions help to delineate concerns, reducing the number of conflicting forces, and make problem solving easier. Partitions also isolate entities that are likely to change independently, for example, between a generic reusable object and one that is domain-specific.

Architectural Placement Criteria   Design patterns reside at a level where the problem statement is most applicable and the boundaries of the solution are within the scope of the level. This definition has two criteria, so problem applicability takes precedence over solution scope. Certain design patterns could potentially be placed at more than one level. The scalability section of the pattern template addresses the use of the pattern at alternative levels.

Architecture   Multiple views of a whole system. An architecture comprises various views from each of the potential stakeholders in the system, such as end users, developers, software architects, specialists, and managers.

Background   An AntiPattern template section. Any additional comments about the AntiPattern, divergent from the purpose of the other sections, appear here.

Bytecode   An intermediate representation between a high-level programming language, such as Java, and machine code.

Component, or Software Component   A small-scale software module, at application-level or smaller scales. In a component architecture, a component shares a common interface and metadata with other components to support interoperability, component substitution, and system extension.

Design Artifact   A particular instance of a design choice.

Design Pattern   A problem statement and solution that explains a predefined common-sense approach to solving a design problem. Properly documented patterns are described using a consistent template, which guarantees conciseness and comprehensive coverage of the details, issues, and trade-offs.

Design Point   A specific trade-off within an allowable range of options within a design pattern. The full range of design options for a given problem forms a continuum of alternative choices. A design point is one of these choices, which resolves the forces and achieves the right balance of benefits and consequences; for example, choosing a string data type as opposed to an enumeration in an IDL parameter specification. Whereas the enumeration has a fixed set of alternatives that is not extensible without change to the IDL, a string type could support a wide range of uses and extensions.

Example   An AntiPattern template section, giving an example of the AntiPattern and its refactored solution.

Forces   The contextual motivating factors that influence design choices. Forces are identified in the applicability section of the design pattern template, and are resolved in the solution section of the template. *See also* Horizontal Forces, Vertical Forces, and Primal Forces.

General Form   An AntiPattern template section identifying the generic characteristics of the AntiPattern. The refactored solution resolves the general AntiPattern posed by this section.

Horizontal Forces   Forces applicable across multiple domains or problems and that influence design choices across several software modules or components. With horizontal forces, design choices made elsewhere may have a direct or indirect impact on design choices made locally.

Implementation   The code (or software) comprising the mechanism that provides services conforming to an interface. Also called an *object implementation.*

Interface   A software boundary between the consumers of a service (the clients) and the providers of a service (an implementation).

Java Virtual Machine   A run-time system used by the Java language to dynamically interpret Java bytecode. It is also responsible for the management of other Java capabilities such as garbage collection and object creation.

Mining   The study of preexisting solutions and legacy systems in order to rapidly gain a robust understanding of the purposes of solving a new problem. Mining leads to potential reuse of previous solutions, horizontal generalization of multiple solutions, or an understanding of the wrappering requirements for legacy systems.

Module, or Software Module   A generic term for a piece of software. Module is used to refer to software at various scales. An application-level module is a subsystem; a system-level module is an entire software system, and so forth. A module is separable from other modules at the same scale.

Most Frequent Scale   An AntiPattern template section. From the Software Design-Level Model (SDLM), the scale of software development at which the AntiPattern usually occurs. The options include: Idiom, Micro-Architecture, Framework, Application, System, Enterprise, or Global/Industry. The scale contrains the scope of the solution.

Name   An AntiPattern template section; a unique noun or noun phrase, intended to be pejorative. Alternative names, if any, are identified in the Also Known As section.

PLoP   Pattern Languages of Programs. An annual conference on the creation and documentation of patterns and pattern languages.

Primal Forces   A class of horizontal forces that are pervasive in software architecture and development. Primal forces are present in most design situations, and should be considered part of the contextual forces driving most solutions.

Refactored Solution   An AntiPattern template section, where the solution for the AntiPattern is described. This section corresponds to the General Form section. The solution is described without variations, and can be structured in step form.

Related Solutions   An AntiPattern template section identifying any citations or cross-references that are appropriate to explain differences between the AntiPattern and others.

Root Causes   An AntiPattern template section listing the general causes for the AntiPattern. Derived from the architecture column, "Deadly Sins of Object-Oriented Architecture" [Mowbray 97a], with Biblical relevance, the options include: Haste, Avarice, Pride, Ignorance, Apathy, Narrow-Mindedness, and Sloth. Neglected responsibility is the universal cause.

Solution Type   An AntiPattern template section based on the Software Design-Level Model (SDLM) that identifies the type of action that results from the AntiPattern solution. Choices are: Software, Technology, Process, or Role. The choice "Software" indicates that new software is created by the solution. The choice "Technology" indicates that the solution entails acquisition of a technology or product. The choice "Process" indicates that the solution entails pursuing a process. The choice "Role" indicates that the solution entails assigning responsibility to an individual or group.

Symptoms and Consequences   An AntiPattern template section listing symptoms and consequences resulting from the AntiPattern.

Template   The outline used to define the explanatory sections of a design pattern or AntiPattern. Each template section answers important questions about the pattern or AntiPattern.

Typical Causes   An AntiPattern template section where the unique causes of the AntiPattern are identified, along with its root causes.

Unbalanced Forces   An AntiPattern template section based on the Software Design-Level Model (SDLM) that lists the general forces ignored, misused, or overused in the AntiPattern. Choices are: Management of Functionality, Performance, Complexity, Change, IT Resources, Technology Transfer. Management of Risk is the universal force.

Variations   An AntiPattern template section listing any known major variations of the AntiPattern. Well-known alternative solutions are described here as well.

Vertical Forces   Situation-specific forces that exist within some particular domain or problem context. Domain-specific forces are unique to a particular situation. Because vertical forces are unique (or local) to one software situation, resolution of vertical forces usually results in unique solutions for each software problem. Interfaces generated that are based solely upon vertical forces are called *vertical interfaces*.

Acronyms Used in AntiPatterns

ACID	Atomic, Consistent, Isolated, Durable
ANSI	American National Standards Institute
API	Application Program Interface
CASE	Computer-Aided Software Engineering
CD-ROM	Compact Disc Read-Only Memory
CIO	Chief Information Officer
CMU	Carnegie Mellon University
COM	Microsoft Component Object Model
CORBA	Common Object Request Broker Architecture
COSE	Common Open Software Environment
COTS	Commercial off-the-shelf
DIN	German National Standards Organization
ECMA	European Computer Manufacturers Association
E-R	Entity-Relationship Modeling
FIPS	Federal Information Processing Standard

FGDC	Federal Geographic Data Committee
FTP	File Transfer Protocol
GOTS	Government off-the-shelf
GPL	Gamma Pattern Language
HVM	Horizontal-Vertical-Metadata
IBM	International Business Machines
ICD	Interface Control Document
IDL	ISO/CORBA Interface Definition Language
IEEE	Institute of Electrical and Electronics Engineers
ISO	International Standards Organization
IT	Information Technology
MVC	Model-View-Controller
O&M	Operations and Maintenance
ODMG	Object Database Management Group
ODP	Open Distributed Processing
OLE	Microsoft Object Linking and Embedding
OLTP	Online Transaction Processing
OMG	Object Management Group
ONC	Open Network Computing
OO	Object Oriented
OOA	Object-Oriented Analysis
OOA&D	Object-Oriented Analysis and Design
OOD	Object-Oriented Design
OODBMS	Object-Oriented Database Management System
OQL	ODMG Object Query Language
OSE	Open Systems Environment
OSF	Open Software Foundation
OMA	Object Management Architecture
PLoP	Pattern Languages of Programs Conference
RFC	Request for Comment
RFP	Request for Proposal
SEI	Software Engineering Institute
SGML	Standard General Markup Language
SPC	Software Productivity Consortium
SQL	Structured Query Language

SYSMAN	X/Open Systems Management
TCP/IP	Transmission Control Protocol/Internet Protocol
TWIT	Third-World Information Systems Troubles
URL	Universal Resource Locator
WAIS	Wide Area Information Search

APPENDIX D

Bibliography

The following sources are cited in the text using the name-date notation, for example [Katz 93]. Note that this is not Year 2000-compliant. The Year 2000 problem is a complex set of software development AntiPatterns for which there is no single AntiPattern solution.

[Adams 96a] Adams, Scott, "The Dilbert Principle: A Cubicle's Eye View of Bosses, Meetings, Management Fads, and Other Workplace Afflictions," New York: HarperBusiness, 1996.

[Adams 96b] Adams, Scott, "Dogbert's Top Secret Management Handbook," New York: HarperBusiness, 1996.

[Adams 97] Adams, Scott, "Dilbert Future: Thriving on Stupidity in the 21st Century," New York: HarperBusiness, 1997.

[Akroyd 96] Akroyd, Michael, "AntiPatterns Session Notes," Object World West, San Francisco, 1996.

[Alexander 77] Alexander, Christopher, *A Pattern Language,* Oxford: Oxford University Press, 1977.

[Alexander 79] Alexander, Christopher, *The Timeless Way of Building,* Oxford: Oxford University Press, 1979.

[Appleton 97] Appleton, Brad, "Patterns for Conducting Process Improvement," PLoP, 1997.

[Augarde 91] Augarde, Tony, *The Oxford Dictionary of Modern Quotations,* Oxford: Oxford University Press, 1991.

[Bates 96] Bates, M.E., *The Online Deskbook,* New York: Pemberton Press, 1996.

[Beck 96] Beck, Kent, "Guest Editor's Introduction to Special Issue on Design Patterns," *OBJECT Magazine,* SIGS Publications, January 1996, pp 23–63.

[Beizer 97a] Bezier, Boris, "Introduction to Software Testing," International Conference on Computer Aided Testing, McLean, VA, 1997.

[Beizer 97b] Beizer, Boris, "Foundations of Testing Computer Software," Workshop, 14th International Conference and Exposition on Testing Computer Software, Vienna, VA, July 1997.

[Blueprint 97] Blueprint Technologies, "Software Silhouettes," McLean, Virginia, 1997.

[Block 81] Block, Peter, *Flawless Consulting: A Guide to Getting Your Expertise Used,* San Diego: Pfeiffer & Company, 1981.

[Booch 96] Booch, Grady, *Object Solutions,* Reading, MA: Addison-Wesley-Longman, 1996.

[Bowen 97] Bowen, Jonathan P., and Hinchey, Michael G., "The Use of Industrial-Strength Formal Methods," Proceedings of the Twenty-First Annual Computer Software and Applications Conference (COMPSAC 97), IEEE, August 1997.

[Brodie 95] Brodie, Michael, and Stonebraker, Michael, *Migrating Legacy Systems: Gateways, Interfaces, and the Incremental Approach,* Menlo Park, CA: Morgan Kaufmann Publishers, 1995.

[Brooks 79] Brooks, Frederick P., *The Mythical Man-Month,* Reading, MA: Addison-Wesley, 1979.

[Brown 95] Brown, Kyle, "Design by Committee," on the Portland Patterns Repository Web site, http://c2.com/ppr/index.html.

[Brown 96] Brown, William J., "Leading a Successful Migration," *Object Magazine,* October 1996, pp. 38–43.

[Buschmann 96] Buschmann, Frank; Meunier, Regine; Rohnert, Hans; Sommerlad, Peter; Stal, Michael, *Pattern-Oriented Software Architecture: A System of Patterns,* New York: John Wiley & Sons, Inc., 1996.

[C4ISR 96] C4I Integration Support Activity, "C4ISR Architecture Framework," version 1.0, Integrated Architectures Panel, U.S. Government Document CISA-0000-104-96, Washington, DC, June 1996.

[Cargill 89] Cargill, Carl F., *Information Technology Standardization: Theory, Process, and Organizations*, Bedford, MA: Digital Press, 1989.

[Connell 87] Connell, John, *Rapid Structured Prototyping*, Reading, MA: Addison-Wesley, 1987.

[Constantine 95] Constantine, Larry, *Constantine on Peopleware*, Englewood Cliffs, NJ: Prentice-Hall, 1995.

[Cook 94] Cook, Steve, and Daniels, John, *Designing Object Systems*, Englewood Cliffs, NJ: Prentice-Hall, 1994.

[Coplien 94] Coplien, James O., "A Development Process Generative Pattern Language," PLoP, 1994.

[Coplien 94] Coplien, James O., Object World briefing on design patterns, AT&T Bell Labs Conference Tutorial, San Francisco, 1994.

[Cusumano 95] Cusumano, M.A., and Selby, R.W., *Microsoft Secrets*, New York: Free Press, 1995.

[Davis 93] Davis, Alan M., *Objects, Functions, and States*, Englewood Cliffs, NJ: Prentice-Hall, 1993.

[Dikel 97] Dikel, David; Hermansen, Christy; Kane, David; and Malveau, Raphael; "Organizational Patterns for Software Architecture," PLoP, 1997.

[Dolberg 92] Dolberg, S.H., "Integrating Applications in the Real World," *Open Information Systems: Guide to UNIX and Other Open Systems*, Boston: Patricia Seybold Group, July 1992.

[Duell 97] Duell, M., "Resign Patterns: Ailments of Unsuitable Project-Disoriented Software," *The Software Practioner*, vol. 7, No. 3, May–June 1997, p. 14.

[Edwards 97] Edwards, Jeri, and Devoe, D., "10 Tips for Three-Tier Success," *D.O.C. Magazine*, July 1997, pp. 39–42.

[Foote 97] Foote, Brian and Yoder, Joseph, "Big Ball of Mud," *Proceedings of Pattern Languages of Programming*, PLoP, 1997.

[Fowler 97] Fowler, Martin, *Analysis Patterns: Reusable Object Models*, Reading, MA: Addison-Wesley 1997.

[Gamma 94] Gamma, Erich; Helm, Richard; Johnson, Ralph; and Vlissides, John; *Design Patterns*, Reading, MA: Addison-Wesley, 1994.

[Gaskin 79] Gaskin, Stephen, *Mind at Play*, Summerville, TN: The Book Publishing Company, 1979.

[GDSS 94] Group Decision Support Systems, "Group Faciltation Using Groupsystems V," Training Course, Georgetown, Washington DC, 1994.

[Gilb 93] Gilb, Tom, and Graham, Dorothy, *Software Inspection*, Workingham, UK: Addison-Wesley, 1993.

[Goldberg 95] Goldberg, Adele, and Rubin, Kenny S., *Succeeding with Objects: Decision Frameworks for Project Management*, New York: Addison-Wesley, 1995.

[Griss 97] Griss, Martin, "Software Reuse: Architecture, Process, and Organization for Business Success," Object World, San Francisco, 1997.

[Halliwell 93] Halliwell, Chris, "Camp Development and the Art of Building a Market through Standards," *IEEE Micro*, vol. 13, no. 6, December 1993, pp. 10–18.

[Herrington 91] Herrington, Dean, and Herrington, Selina, "Meeting Power," The Herrington Group, Inc., Houston, TX, 1991.

[Hilliard 96] Hilliard, Richard; Emery, Dale; and Rice, Tom, "Experiences Applying a Practical Architectural Method." In *Reliable Software Technologies: Ada Europe '96*, A. Strohmeier (ed.), New York: Springer-Verlag, *Lecture Notes in Computer Science*, vol. 1088, 1996.

[Horowitz, 93] Horowitz, Barry M., *Strategic Buying for the Future*, Washington DC: Libey Publishing, 1993.

[Hutt 94] Hutt, Andrew (ed.), *Object Oriented Analysis and Design*, New York: John Wiley & Sons, Inc., 1994.

[ISO 1996] International Standards Organization, "Reference Model for Open Distributed Processing," International Standard 10746-1, ITU Recommendation X.901, 1996.

[Jacobson 92] Jacobson, Ivar, *Object-Oriented Software Engineering*, Reading, MA: Addison-Wesley, 1992.

[Jacobson 97] Jacobson, Ivar; Griss, Martin; and Jonsson, Patrick; *Software Reuse: Architecture Process and Organization for Business Success*, Reading, MA: Addison-Wesley, 1997.

[Jacobson 91] Jacobson, Ivar and Lindstrom, F., "Reengineering of Old Systems to an Object-Oriented Architecture," *OOPSLA Conference Proceedings*, 1991.

[Johnson 95] Johnson, Johnny, "Creating Chaos," *American Programmer*, July 1995.

[Johnson 93] Johnson, Ralph, "Tutorial on Object-Oriented Frameworks," *OOPSLA93 Tutorial Notes,* Association for Computing Machinery, 1993.

[Kane 97] Kane, David; Opdyke, William; and Dykel, David; "Managing Change to Reusable Software," PLoP, 1997.

[Katz 93] Katz, Melony; Cornwell, Donna; and Mowbray, Thomas J; "System Integration with Minimal Object Wrappers," *Proceedings of TOOLS '93,* August 1993.

[Kepner 81] Kepner, C.H., and Tregoe, B.B., *The New Rational Manager,* Princeton, NJ: Kepner-Tregoe, Inc., 1981.

[Kitchenham 96] Kitchenham, Barbara, *Software Metrics,* Cambridge, MA: Blackwell Publishers, 1996.

[Korson 97] Korson, Timothy, "Process for the Development of Object-Oriented Systems," Tutorial Notes, Object World West Conference, July 1997.

[Kreindler 95] Kreindler, R. Jordan, and Vlissides, John, *Object-Oriented Patterns and Frameworks,* IBM International Conference on Object Technology, San Francisco, CA, 1995.

[Kruchten 95] Kruchten, Phillipe B., "The 4+1 View Model of Architecture," *IEEE Software,* November 1995, pp. 42–50.

[McCarthy 95] McCarthy, J., "Dynamics of Software Development," Redmond, WA: Microsoft Press, 1995.

[McConnell 96] McConnell, Steve, *Rapid Development,* Redmond, WA: Microsoft Press, 1996.

[Melton 93] Melton J., and Simon, A.R., *Understanding the New SQL,* Menlo Park, CA: Morgan Kaufmann Publishers, 1993.

[Moore 97] Moore, K.E., and Kirschenbaum, E.R., "Building Evolvable Systems: The ORBlite Project," *Hewlett-Packard Journal,* February 1997.

[Mowbray 95] Mowbray, Thomas J., and Zahavi, Ron, *The Essential CORBA,* New York: John Wiley & Sons, Inc., 1995.

[Mowbray 97a] Mowbray, Thomas J., "The Seven Deadly Sins of Object-Oriented Architecture," *OBJECT Magazine,* March 1997, pp. 22–24.

[Mowbray 97b] Mowbray, Thomas J., "What Is Architecture?" *OBJECT Magazine,* Architecture column, September 1997.

[Mowbray 97c] Mowbray, Thomas J., and Malveau, Raphael C., *CORBA Design Patterns,* New York: John Wiley & Sons, Inc., 1997.

[Moynihan 89] Moynihan, T.; McCluskey, G.; and Verbruggen, R.; "Riskman1: A Prototype Tool for Risk Analysis for Computer Software," Third International Conference on Computer-Aided Software Engineering, London, 1989.

[Oakes 95] Oakes, R., Presentation at Healthcare Software Development Conference, Medical Records Institute, Boston, 1995.

[Opdyke 92] Opdyke, W.F., "Refactoring Object-Oriented Frameworks," Ph.D. thesis, University of Illinois, Urbana, IL, 1992.

[PLoP 94] *Proceedings of the First Conference on Pattern Languages of Programs*, August 1994.

[PLoP 95] *Proceedings of the Second Conference on Pattern Languages of Programs*, August 1995.

[PLoP 96] *Proceedings of the Third Conference on Pattern Languages of Programs*, August 1996.

[PLoP 97] *Proceedings of the Fourth Conference on Pattern Languages of Programs*, September 1997.

[Pree 95] Pree, Wolfgang, *Design Patterns for Object-Oriented Software Development*, Reading, MA: Addison-Wesley, 1995.

[RDA 96] RDA Consultants, "Experiences Using CASE Tools on ROOP Projects," Tinomium, MD, 1996.

[Riel 96] Riel, A.J., *Object-Oriented Design Heuristics*, Reading, MA: Addison-Wesley, 1996.

[Roetzheim 91] Roetzheim, W.H., *Developing Software to Government Standards*, Englewood Cliffs, NJ: Prentice-Hall, 1991.

[Rogers 97] Rogers, Gregory F., *Framework-Based Software Development in C++*, Short Hillzs, NJ: Prentice-Hall, 1997.

[Ruh 97] Ruh, William A., and Mowbray, Thomas J., *Inside CORBA*, Reading, MA: Addison-Wesley, 1997.

[Schmidt 95] Schmidt, Douglas, "Using Design Patterns to Develop Reusable Object-Oriented Communication Software," *Communications of the ACM*, October 1995, pp 65–74.

[Schmidt 95] Schmidt, Douglas C., and Coplien, James O., *Pattern Languages of Program Design*, Reading, MA: Addison-Wesley, 1995.

[Shaw 93] Shaw, M. "Software Architecture for Shared Information Systems," Carnegie Mellon University, Software Engineering Institute, Technical Report No. CMU/SEI-93-TR-3, ESC-TR-93-180, March 1993.

[Shaw 96] Shaw, Mary, and Garlan, David, *Software Architecture: Perspectives on an Emerging Discipline,* Englewood Cliffs, NJ: Prentice-Hall, 1996.

[Spewak 92] Spewak, S.H., and Hill, S.C., *Enterprise Architecture Planning,* New York: John Wiley & Sons, Inc., 1992.

[Strikeleather 96] J. Strikeleather, "The Importance of Architecture," *OBJECT* 6(2), April 1996.

[Taylor 92] Taylor, D.A., *Object-Oriented Information Systems,* New York: John Wiley & Sons, Inc., 1992.

[Vlissides 96] Vlissides, John M.; Coplien, James O.; and Kerth, Norman L., *Pattern Languages of Program Design,* Reading, MA: Addison-Wesley, 1996.

[Walden 95] Walden, Kim, and Nerson, Jean-Marc, *Seamless Object-Oriented Software Architecture,* Englewood Cliffs, NJ: Prentice-Hall, 1995.

[Webster 95] Webster, Bruce F., *Pitfalls of Object-Oriented Development,* New York: M&T Books, 1995.

[Webster 97] Webster, Bruce F., "Everything You Know Is Wrong," Object World West '97, SOFTBANK-COMDEX, 1997.

[Yourdon 93] Yourdon, Edward, Software Reusability: *The Decline and Fall of the American Programmer,* Englewood Cliffs, NJ: Prentice-Hall, 1993.

[Yourdon 97] Yourdon, Edward, *Death March,* Short Hills, NJ: Prentice-Hall, 1997.

I N D E X

293